Cormac's Corner

Cormac MacConnell

A Collection of His Classic Stories from the West of Ireland

Illustrations by Caty Bartholomew

The GreenBranch Company L.L.C.

The GreenBranch Company L.L.C.
8 South Michigan Avenue, Ste. 2310
Chicago, Illinois 60603

Copyright (c) 2000 The GreenBranch Company L.L.C.
Copyright (c) 2000 Cormac MacConnell.
Illustrations, copyright 2000 by Caty Bartholomew. All rights reserved.

All rights reserved. No part of this book may be reproduced or transmitted in any form or by any means, electronic or mechanical, including photocopying, recording, or by an information storage and retrieval system—except by a reviewer who may quote brief passages in a review to be printed in a magazine or newspaper—without permission in writing from the publisher. For information, please contact The GreenBranch Company L.L.C.

Editor: Meg Quigley.

Library of Congress Cataloging-in-Publication Data
Cormac's Corner/Cormac MacConnell
ISBN 0-9705877-0-8
Library of Congress Card Number: 00-110166

Design, layout and cover art by:

Trungale, Egan & Associates L.L.C.
8 South Michigan Avenue, Ste. 2310
Chicago, Illinois 60603
www.trungaleegan.com

Printed in the United States of America

To the Dutch Nation!

Book I

Book II

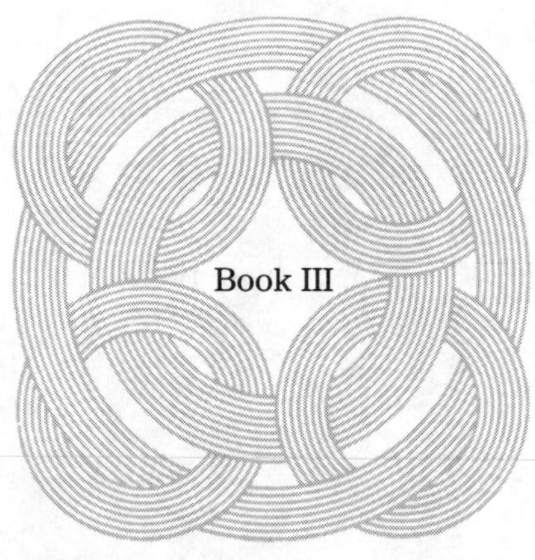
Book III

Book IV

Foreword

Irish Americans are a special breed. They combine the best of the Irish and American experiences, and they understand the failures and triumphs of the Irish because they and their forefathers have lived them. They are also devoted to good writing, and the phenomenal success of many Irish American books such as *Angela's Ashes* in the past few years is a clear indication of their buying power.

They love a good writer, and they adore a great one, which is why Cormac MacConnell has consistently been the most popular columnist in our newspaper, the *Irish Voice*. He has a knowledge and insight into Ireland which cannot be found anywhere else, in publications either here or in Ireland. It is the knowledge of the insider, the man who knows the rhythms of life and the countless small towns and villages on Ireland's western seaboard better than anyone alive.

There is always a tendency to sentimentalize Ireland and to go over the top, as movies like *The Quiet Man* did, in portraying the native Irish. Cormac never makes that mistake. He is sentimental but shrewd, he is of them but not one of them.

His perception of Irish country life is a complex portrait. We meet the ordinary people who do extraordinary things, but we also meet the desperate ones, the sons left on the land too long, the loveless marriages, and the continuing fate of the emigrant Irish.

One of his greatest columns, *Paddy (London) at the Funeral*, dealt with the emigrant son returning home for his father's funeral, and the one line he merited in the death notices — "Also regretted by Paddy (London)."

Cormac writes like a poet. His imagery is drawn from the native soil and is magnificent in its vividness. He has no parallel in Ireland today as a chronicler of rural life, and for providing insight into a lifestyle that is passing all too quickly into history. But in case we ever feel maudlin about such passages, there is always Cormac's humor. The extraordinary quick wit, honed on the shores of Lough Erne in his native Fermanagh, and brought to bear on the kind of everyday occurrences that fill his columns. There was most memorably *The Cat Who Died for Ireland*, a hilarious escapade involving the Troubles and a certain cat who has gone down in local folklore.

Often times in speaking with our readers, they refer to him as "Cormac." Simply that, as if they know him as well as their own neighbor. Over the years he has brought us so close to his own life that he was even able to sell his house through his *Irish Voice* column. Many a reader has written to us about their pilgrimages to meet with this great bard of the West, who has now been writing for us for more than 15 years.

The sad part, for me, is that he is far more acknowledged in America than he is in Ireland. In the land of the Celtic Tiger, a man who can cast a cold eye on developments there and pound such an unfashionable beat as rural Ireland hasn't got a proper place in the scheme of things. In their headlong rush to be Europeanized, Americanized or whatever identity they wish to assume, Cormac does not fit with the rush to bury many traces of Irish identity.

But read about his wedding in his recent columns for the *Irish Voice* — the songs, laughter, gaiety and mischief that went on for days, the characters who showed up, the puzzlement of his Dutch in-laws as they sought to make sense of this bearded little man more than 20 years older than their daughter — and you understand something. Cormac is a guide to a new land. It is one we are familiar with on the outside, but only he can take us on that journey through the heart and soul of old Ireland and many aspects of it that still survive.

In the old rebel song *The Wearing of the Green*, Napper Tandy is asked, "How is old Ireland and how does she stand?" These days Cormac MacConnell would be the best person to answer that question. That would be the greatest tribute we can pay him.

Niall O'Dowd
Founding Publisher
The Irish Voice
October, 2000

Introduction

It is difficult to categorize Cormac MacConnell. The sheer variety of his works, the use of language, the humor, pathos, descriptive power and characterization are of consistently high level and often extraordinary. His tales have an underset current about them that stirs beneath the surface and tugs at the reader aswim in the currents of the main story line.

One uses the word *obvious* gingerly with MacConnell. After a few stories, the obvious becomes less obvious. The reader gets the uneasy feeling that the story line runs counter to other themes, which can only be elucidated by indirection, by the collision of contrariness: the ptarmigan faking a broken wing to draw off pursuers of her chicks; the fox that doubles back or leads the hounds onto a railway bridge as a train is approaching, the stone that is rejected only to become the corner stone. The surface winds and tidal flow of incident and character and circumstance, time and place shift imperceptibly as if to warn us that things are not always as they seem.

Throughout, the stories present a "fourth wall" of geography both real and imagined, but always at a bit of a remove from the main setting. MacConnell shows us a tension in the dislocations of the characters, the jar of accents indicative of a native or a stranger, in the clash of actions, deft, awkward, subtle, with ramifications that cross genders and generations. What political opinions MacConnell may support, he holds as closely to the vest as a discreet detail pointed up in a description of a character's carriage, gait, demeanor and deportment, inflection, or in a throat clearing, a cough or the taking of a deep breath. The slightest halt in mid-sentence is the harbinger of something significant, as another character enters, or the end of the life of the story looms.

MacConnell's characters have such vividness in them, they are more alive than some people, and one senses that they themselves at times realize with delight or dismay when the page must be turned, and they rage or cooperate to round out their little lives as their personalities dictate. I would go as far as to say some of the characters don't mind dying off because they are confident of the life to come in the very next story, and wink at our sadness as they pass into the wings of their little printed stage.

In *Man-Eating Plant Takes Revenge on British Empire*, an Irishman who always longed to travel dies and is cremated, and his ashes cross the ocean in death like a ship in a bottle. *Watch Out for Church Spiders* tells of a tiny creature that gathers size and strength over the years by creeping down and suppling of the holy oil, until it becomes a prepossessing outsized arachnid. *Shaftie O'Neill's Cuppa* juggles the themes of the shy, unassertive Irishman in a foreign land, seizing fortune by the handle of a teacup. *This*

Judge Didn't Know What Hit Him is a multi-layered virtuoso work of symbolism even as it tells an engaging tale of mischief. And *Paddy (London) at the Funeral* digs into the well of emotion as a desensitized shambling laborer returns from exile to disclose the deepest wellspring of emotion amid the bloodless refinement of his educated family.

MacConnell's language, neologism and portmanteau words are ravishing to the ear and form an ever burgeoning lexicon of his imagined Ireland, so much truer and more accurate than the real. Reading these stories reminds one of standing on the railing of a ship as it draws away from land — the words and images glisten and move, stir with a life of their own, with a light beneath the light, and one is never sure if it's a wave, a trick of the eye or some great animal lolling just beneath the surface of a full sea.

If anything can improve MacConnell's works, it is the pen and ink drawings of artist Caty Bartholomew, his long-time illustrator. Over the years, she has perfectly captured the tone, the moods, the twists and turns, humor and tragedy, ebb and flow of the stories. Her illustrations complement and comment upon MacConnell's stories with beauty, wit and delicacy.

Ronan Geraty
October, 2000

Book I

The Last Of The Little People

he May morning is so fantastically beautiful as to suspend reality. There is a gallant young sun striding out like a spailpin - a lad for hiring - across the acres of a wondrous sky. There is not a blade of grass, nor a wild flower of this morning, that isn't drunk with the rich jewels of the risenfall of the morning dew.

There is not a blackbird that doesn't believe he is Caruso or Count McCormack, not a lark but knows, from under the striding spailpin sun, that she and she alone is Callas. There is a breeze that is wearing warm velvet gloves. All the harsh stabby whitethorns of winter are clad in the delicate white chamise of May Blossom. Each little white flower of the trillionzillions of flowers on the thorns is so delicately made that even the fingers of a Carrickmacross lacemaker, reaching gently, would break the integrity of 10 little flowers.

Yet the breeze with the velvet gloves is so subtly gentle that it doesn't let even a single petal fall. And the robins walk on tippitoes on the bared topmost twigs so that they do not harm either. And I walk on my road between the hiding thorns and almost hold my breath.

And, where the mossed stone wall begins, just at the curve toward the boglands, on this fantastic morning, silently in my rubber soles, don't I catch

Now, as ye well know, I would be the kind of man that would claim in my head that leprechauns never existed while, at the same time, hoping in my heart that they did.

Ireland's very last leprechaun unawares! With his back to me, for Heaven's sake, in his waistcoat and shirt-sleeves, the rooster's pinfeathers in the small peaked cap on top of his head, whistling through his teeth, cutting himself a smoke with a very sharp knife from the weeniest plug of tobacco you ever saw in your life. And there he is!

Now, as ye well know, I would be the kind of man that would claim in my head that leprechauns never existed while, at the same time, hoping in my heart that they did. And I never saw one before, not in all my life, nor met a really genuine sound man or woman that had. So this is magic. And I react with almost magical speed, even though I say so myself. Three steps, the last one a bound, and I have him clasped around the waist in my two hands. My fingers met at the front, they can span the small size of him with ease.

I apologize to ye at this point for being unable to print the precise rectangular oath which I emitted as I seized him but ye can put two and two together yourselves and make up the proper four.

And then I said, "I have you. Fair and square." And I had. It was a strange feeling to have the wiry feel of a real live leprechaun in your hands. (They have a hardy feel, like a tinker's child, or a good fox terrier; not the feline feel of a cat.) This lad had a little pot belly on him, under my fingers I could feel it, and I'd say, because the curls under the cap were silvery, that he was about 70, maybe, in manyear terms.

"Do you think?" says he, as calm as the gloved breeze, the first words he spoke. "Do you think that you could catch me if I didn't let you? Will you for God's sake stop strangling me and sit up on the wall beside me and let me smoke my pipe? Will you have a bit of sense, man?" And I could feel his little elbows working away all the time, without a break, cutting the scraps of tobacco for the pipe.

"You're MacConnell," says he, as I hesitated, still grasping him firmly.

"You write about things like this, and lads like me. And I'm Sebastian De La Toursalle, the very last of the Irish leprechauns, the only one left. Don't you think we should have a more civilized encounter than this, the pair of us, and I only doing you a favor?"

I said, instantly, being a wise enough human, that I would expect the legendary leprechaun to say something like him, to escape unscathed with his pot of gold. I did not release him. I said, however, that I was surprised at his Spanish kind of name.

"The Armada," he responded instantly. "One of my great-grandfathers came across from Cadiz inside a cannonball. The galleon went down off the Mayo coast. My great-grandmother was attracted to strange foreign spirits and she found the cannonball one morning near Ballina."

He clearly didn't feel any further explanation was necessary. He looked at me, over his shoulder, and though he had the classic leprechaun face he was a bit swarthier alright, than I expected. He also looked quite old and tired. He had very blue eyes. I made a lightning decision and let him go. I sat up on the wall beside him. I deliberately looked away from him, which you are not supposed to do, and when I looked back he was still there, with the pipe lit. It was a crooked pipe, black briar, with what looked like gold band around the stem.

"Sensible man," he said. "Thanks a lot. How is life treating yourself these days?"

So we had a chat, sitting there in the May magic of a morning. I told him my troubles-and-joys and he told me his. And they were troubles. He is the very last of his breed, he says, because, in a way, the Irish killed the rest. With disinterest and scorn.

"How so?" says I.

When times were bad in Ireland says Sebastian, the Irish were mad about leprechauns. The attracted thousands of tourists. They represented a folksy, non-violent, puckish little image.

Leprechauns thrived on it and, says he, showed themselves at least twice a year though, of course, they never yielded up any pots of gold. "We never had much anyway, just two or three pots between us. We were never well off." Then, he says, times got better, the Irish rose above themselves, decided they did not like the leprechaun image and stopped talking about leprechauns, writing about them, making statues of them for tourists, using them on Irish products like calendars and tea towels and things like that. "We weren't good enough for ye anymore," says Sebastian, shaking his little head sadly, "and ye turned your back on us and we died as a race."

And it happened quickly, he said, because the Small People can only live and breathe, in some strange magic way, as long as there are grown-up humans, in some numbers in every parish, who believe in leprechauns. It was the magical power of our belief, in generations gone, that actually filled up the great iron pots with real gold. But when the belief faltered, in the '70s and '80s, the Small People died in the saddest way. First they lost the power of speech, to talk to each other. And finally they became deaf.

"Listen to that breeze," said old Sebastian. "Listen to those blackbirds and robins and larks. All the leprechauns that used to dwell around here and that are gone, can only whisper to me nowadays, the little scraps and scrippets, through the throat of a May zephyr, or a wren maybe, or a wild small bird. They're all gone now but myself."

He said I would never know how much energy he had to expend in order to materialize himself to me. "I almost didn't make it either," he said. And he didn't know if the renewed energy he would get from our conversation and communion would be enough to enable him to do it again. I might be the last human that would ever see him, he said. And he was sad.

If a couple of young bright strong humans could see him as well as myself, he said, it would be a great help. No aspersions on myself but my spirit level wasn't as high as it used to be. If he drew out all the energy he needed, he said, I would never see home again. So I looked out across the fields from us and I saw two of the Connolly boys, about 17 and 18 years of age, walking down from the bog. I hailed them. Sebastian sat silently beside me, smoking his little pipe.

"Hello Mr. MacConnell," they said to me, the Connolly boys, when they came up to me. "How are you doing today?"

"I'm fine lads," I said. "I'm fine. I was just wondering if either of ye had a box of matches."

They had a box. They gave me a light for my cigarette. The older boy, Mark, said I looked very relaxed, sitting there all alone on the stone wall...

A Fire Went Out Of The Island

They had a lovely tradition on the island, a tradition as old as time. When any of the islanders were emigrating, and they emigrated often on a seasonal basis, they brought a few smoking sods of turf from their fire to the home of the nearest neighbor and asked that man to "look after the fire" for them when they were gone, as they always put it, "out to The Country."

We have great turf, they would say, hefting a sod of it in their hands before throwing it on to the fire.

There was a strong and vibrant community on that island at the beginning of this century, and, by the same token, a vibrant tradition of migration in the winter. The fires were carried on shovels from the homes of those migrating to the homes of those staying behind, and when the year was bad, poor fishing or poor harvest, the islanders would always say to each other that there would be a lot of hot shovels when winter came. Usually there were, too.

The man who received the fire for safe-keeping from his neighbor would put the sods deep into the red heart of his own fire... which was banked up at night and never went out... and, in the spring, when his neighbor came back home, he would bring his fire back to him. It was a lovely tradition, a ritual, a celebration both of the sense of continuing life and the closely knit nature of the community on that island that I know well.

One of the riches they had was the big black bog in the belly of the island. It is not many islands that are blessed with bogs where you could cut the finest of turf for winter fuel, but this island was wealthy in its fine bog, thick and blackly slick over the granite, producing a turf that was the envy of the mainlanders a half-mile out across stormy water.

That turf was as good as coal, and the islanders were proud of it. We have great turf, they would say, hefting a sod of it in their hands before throwing it on to the fire. Many's the time it warmed me when I called, and usually, in the winter, the fire you sat before might have sods from two departed neighbors' fires, or the symbols of them, burning in there as well. But the men who owned them always came back in the spring to reclaim their own and burn the fire of their lives again on their own home hearthstones.

But then, in the '50s, the young ones seemed to begin to sprout wings that would only fly one way.

And then, with the passage of the generations, the worst thing of all happened in the mid-'70s, and that was that the fine bog became exhausted. All the turf was at last cut away. The granite skull of the island, exposed to the air at last, began to be blanched as white as the bones of dead men. The islanders cut inferior turf from around the fringes of the original bog for a few seasons after that, but eventually, they had to go cap in hand to the mainland and buy their turf.

Families began following in the wild, airy tracks of the young ones, and, increasingly often, they never came back either. Ten years ago, the school was closed down finally, and, by then, there were only four currachs at the slip, and there were far more tombstones tilting in the sandy cemetery than there were walking islanders. And there were five or six fires burning in every hearth that was burning still.

Seven years ago the tragedy came. Three men were lost in the currachs bringing the turf home when the tides ripped into them at the wrong time and in the wrong place. When I arrived on the mainland strand, you could see the turf they died for, floating in the writhing water. It was a bad day, and it finally killed off the island. All of them, except John, decided that they would leave and go to the "The Country." "There is too much hardship," they said. Like more of my trade, I witnessed the ritual of their leaving. The faces were as if carved from oak, and no man or woman looked back. Only John stayed.

And in the last enactment of the ritual of the fires, the four islander families who were leaving, for the last time, brought coals from their dying fires to John's house, on shovels, and no word at all was spoken as he put them into the red heart of his own fire, the last fire on the island.

He died ten days ago. An islander settled on the mainland now came out to see his cattle, grazing near the dead houses with their backsides to the gales, and he looked through the window as he passed, and John was dead.

It had happened only a little earlier for his hands were still warm, and his fire, that had seven fires in it, was still burning. But it's not burning now, I passed along the mainland road yesterday. I looked across the cruel strip of water, and the last chimney was cold. The spray flew, the seagulls screamed, you could see the white skull of the dead island, and I shivered.

An Ill Wind Of Destiny

It was a windy hank of destiny, surely, which drove the Gilligan Traveling Show into the remote and airy beauty of Glangowla in the early autumn of 1960. The first gale of the season had ruined their flimsy tent on the Fairgreen in the town the previous night, ripped it apart to the four winds during the last act of The Red Barn, and old John Gilligan, maybe the last of the traveling Irish Showmen, knew that drastic action had to be taken or else the family show would perish in its tracks.

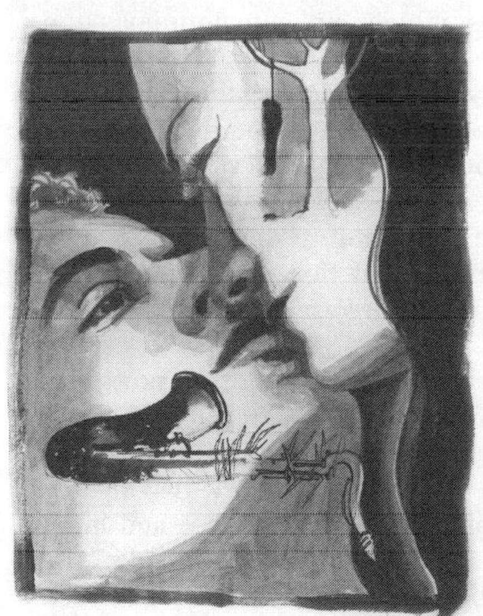

And, because there was a little-used parish hall in remote Glangowla, another in Mantua 15 miles away across the mountain, another in Tooreen down the road, it was the shrewd thinking of Gilligan that he could rent the halls for three weeks and thereby build up enough money to properly repair the old tent. And so the old blue Ford van with its bright theatrical logos and legends, truly, was driven by the winds of destiny to Glangowla, and groaningly in first gear around the great sycamore tree at the top of the hill and then down in front of the tiny parish hall.

Inside four hours the hall had been rented for a week, the bright posters erected all across the parish and hinterland, and the flimsy set for the great melodramas like *The Red Barn* and *The Colleen Bawn* and *Double Dutch* were bringing exotic

But it is a hard truth in the Glangowlas of this Ireland, even now, that traveling showmen, in the eyes of small farmers, are no better than beggars.

challenging life to the still musty bowels of Glangowla parish hall. And the news that the traveling show was in town was spreading like wildfire.

And it was destiny, certainly, that had Mary O'Malley in Glangowla that week from America, home to see her aging parents, and destiny that sent her walking, on the first evening of the traveling show, on the path past the sycamore tree, and destiny that had young John Gilligan sitting there, under the tree, repairing his saxophone for the night's performance.

And one look led to another, and one word led to another, and her red hair was fire to his black locks... and the O'Malleys were always wild anyway... and so the saxophone was not repaired until just before the show that evening and, in the glade just behind the sycamore tree, the grass was sweetly bruised by the kind of passions which make melodramas the popular stuff of traveling shows.

And it was the black face of destiny beyond doubt, the bleak and scowling visage of the bad ones that are always also in melodrama, that had the two O'Malley brothers of Mary, great bears of men with slow heads but sharp eyes, come also down the path towards the sycamore tree at just the wrong time in the velvet evening, the sun beginning to dip its sharp edge towards the misting earth. And they saw all, all that was happening... because the sun glinted on the false gold of the forgotten saxophone... and they said nothing then.

But it is a hard truth in the Glangowlas of this Ireland, even now, that traveling showmen, in the eyes of small farmers, are no better than beggars.

Was it destiny too - surely it was - that prompted old Gilligan to headline the first show for the packed Glangowla hall that evening with *The Red Barn*, the greatest of all the old melodramas, the story of a Romeo and Juliet kind of love which tried to cross the barriers of class and creed. And all the seven members of the family who had, earlier in the show, provided the stream of variety acts - dancing, singing, comedy, juggling - all came together in the sad story of Maria Martin and her murder in the Red Barn.

And young John Gilligan, who had earlier played *In the Mood* and *Sorento* on his hoarse saxophone... and sung, too, like Sinatra... was the young love

in the play, his eyes often straying to the face of Mary O'Malley in the seventh row. But never, of course, seeing the heavy menacing heads of her angered brothers in the shadows at the back of Glangowla parish hall. Never, no never, no more.

And probably, as he spoke his lines, his thoughts were of the meeting he was to have with her later in the night, show over, stars in the sky, the moon walking softly on the road to heaven. And the curtain came down to thunderous applause after his own father, as the avenging ghost, spoke the immortal melodramatic lines: "An eye for and eye, a tooth for a tooth, blood for blood."

The court case has passed into folklore now. It was an ugly business and it ended with the two O'Malley brothers in jail for life and with the Gilligan Traveling Show never ever again taking to the roads of Ireland. And with tears.

And the old people of Glangowla still cross themselves each time they pass the old sycamore tree at the top of the hill. And there are still many who remember the morning that young John Gilligan was found hanging from one of the thick lower branches, traces of the makeup of melodrama still on the eyebrows of a blue face in the dawn. And a smashed, sad saxophone in the dewy grass.

To play no more, no more.

Beware The Chilling Chapel Cough

he Cough came in to the chapel two minutes after the Sunday Mass began. It slid into the back bench inside the narrow chest of Plunket Dillon, whose Morris Minor had suffered a flat two miles away. The Cough remained inside the mean and ribby bachelor chest of Dillon long enough for him to insinuate his damp self into the bench and then it emerged in one short little rush. A kind of half-apologetic, sleaveen kind of cough. You would expect nothing much else. Little that is good or wholesome ever emerged from the throat, chest and mouth of Dillon. He's a gossip of the male variety, he does not smoke or drink or go out with any class of a woman. He will die wealthy in a small miserable way, on a farm stocked with heavy cattle but no children. His father was a Blueshirt.

She fought it to the last, fair play to her, despite her frailty.

From Dillon's person, in the erratic manner in which Chapel Coughs navigate on a January Sunday morning, the Cough descended upon Foley the undertaker, the most respectable and respected man in the parish despite his trade. Foley is a big, comfortable, fat man with a barrel of a chest, and he accommodated Dillon's virus for only a second before throwing it out from him in a grand strong basso rejection which rang the rafters. The Cough got little comfort there. It hung above the congregation for half the length of an Epistle.

Descending again, stealthily, as might be expected, it seized upon poor Andy Breen, kneeling beside the canon's confessional box in the darkest corner of the chapel. To fall on Andy Breen, 80 years this February, was a mean stroke considering that Andy buried his last sister 48 hours earlier, is a heavy drinker and smoker and was feeling low of himself. Having attacked Andy, kneeling beside his grandson, the Cough, in a foul manner entirely, played puck with all of his innards above the waist. It explored every wheeze in his pipes, swelled the veins of his poor old neck, racked the yellowed insides of his ribs. It drove Andy up from his knees and drove his right hand into his pocket to fish out the handkerchief. It reddened Andy's brow and made his whole head shake.

Meanwhile, as he wheezed and barked, the Cough, in the vile manner of its kind, copulated with phlegms and vapors inside Andy's vitals and bred a whole generation of other Coughs. Emerging from Andy's mouth, escaping through his handkerchief, these Coughs infected all the benches immediately around him. The Fagan family began barking almost in unison - man, wife, two children. Next to them Miss Sinclair conceived a reedy Cough in the key of C Minor. Paddy Considine's production was a rasping thing of untold discord. Wee Hughie Dolan, a full seven benches nearer the tabernacle, emitted a wheeze, young Lonergan yipped like a she fox in heat. Maggie O'Neill, the heaviest matron in the chapel, spluttered through six chins.

Dillon's bad bastard of a Cough, damage done, retreated back to its host chest where it rested, gathering strength and substance, for the full duration of a Gospel. Then, fortified and rested, it jumped out of his narrow mouth again just as the collection plate passed by with its load of silver coins. (Dillon placed only 10 pence on the plate.) His thready Cough, following the wooden plate, attacked Rasdale (a young blade whose Christian name I do not know) and, inside 10 seconds, revealed to the entire congregation that Rasdale had been out late last night, judging by the sound of his pipes. It also cruelly revealed that he was smoking too much, was unfit for the fags, and, in fact, caused him great damage. This was because young Joan Montgomery, who had fancied him for some time, and dated him twice, heard the Cough, identified the throat, and remembered her grandfather's verdict on the Rasdales: "Riddled with consumption, every man of them dead before 50." And she decided, there and then in her kneeling, not to date Rasdale ever again.

Having mortally wounded Rasdale, and separated him forever from a 90 acre farm and good house, the Cough then struck at Canon Moran himself in the pulpit. This Cough knew, as all such Coughs know in January, that the poor Canon is delicate these latter years and is frequently aware that his health is risked every Sunday by the viruses released by the massed children of God during his sermons. As the Cough hit him in his thin throat, causing a canonical concussion around his tonsils, it effectively did the devil's work. He had been about to preach a mighty sermon on the need for temperance and this sermon would have turned the tide of the life of poor Benny James, who had been hard at it lately. Instead, however, like a flash, the Canon realized that he would have to have a hot punch himself inside the next hour to kill the flu and he decided, instead, to preach about chastity. Benny James, who knows not the sins of the flesh, will be an alcoholic before the year is out. And he might have been saved but for the Cough.

It jumped at Hilda Morgan in the fifth bench from the front. Hilda is 47 years old, dressed as 29, and she does not wear a Cough as well as she wears a green hat of the dragoon variety. The hat almost fell off and Hilda was mortified even as the Cough put a stop to the gurgle of the infant Flaherty, caused Granny O'Sullivan to reach into the handbag for her mints, and then slyly slid down the throat of Timmy Dowd, aged 17 who had a pimple on his right cheekbone. Timmy already knew that the whole parish was looking at his teenage pimple and the Cough, by attracting attention to him, turned him beetroot red down as far as his ankles. It is possible that he will not attend Mass next Sunday just because of the visitation of the Cough.

The cough rested again inside its virulent host during the scufflings of Communion and the announcements. Then, when things had settled down again, and when the Mass was building towards its sacred finale, the bad bastard of a thing emerged again and went in search of its real victim. It leaped across 17 benches, gathering strength inside the chest of a farmer and a fitter and young Mrs. Murnaghan before finally leaping with full and foul force, down the porcelain throat of little Mrs. Margaret Frances Fahey, 78, the retired school teacher. Never a blacker deed.

She fought it to the last, fair play to her, despite her frailty. She put her lacy little hanky to her delicate aged little gray head and, for a long time, she trapped the bloody Cough inside her small little old chest. But in the end, almost as Mass ended, she was racked by a savage bout. Her head and neck and thin shoulders jerked and rocked with the force and velocity of what the Cough did to her. Her dignity crackled under the strength of the attack so that she was still sitting there, bowed over in racking sounds, when the Mass ended. The Kilfeathers had to come over to her and help her out of the bench, her gentle eyes streaming, her hands trembling, even a little spot of red blood from her nose on the small white hanky. "I don't know what happened to me," she kept saying over and over. "I'm alright now, thank you very much."

She will never be alright again. She will be dead by next Friday evening at five o'clock, stretched out and cold and small and gone from us. The doctors will blame the new flu virus.

I blame Dillon.

A Mortal Sin That Never Felt So Good

mall Aoife from the house on the hill was making the first daisy chain of this summer, the tongue out the corner of her mouth, her lap full of daisies, and, suddenly, just like that, I was back in the dark confessional box in Arney Chapel, 13 years old, and telling Father Donnelly's big bald shadowy dome of a head that I had committed a dreadful Mortal Sin - I'd kissed a Protestant!

Oh, where are you now Suzy Nixon?

I went into The Crocken early that Saturday afternoon with a new catapult and our dog Friday. I had a red sweatshirt on with a Celtic design on the breast of it and corduroy shorts held up by a Boy Scout belt that was the pride of my life because it had a leather loop you could hang your penknife from, and I had two new rabbit snares. The sun was shinning and it was May. The Crocken was a bog a mile from our house and it was full of rabbits. Friday was too fat and slow to catch them, but he could smell them out and chase them a bit, and the general idea that afternoon was to deploy dog and snares together in the hunt. I had no socks on, just bare feet in sandals and the leather insoles of the sandals were warm against my toes.

You had to cross a field to get into The Crocken and then you crossed a fence into a grove of ash and beech trees, their leaves whispering, beyond that the 50 acres of the rough bog, scrub and undergrowth and neatly cut bog banks, and old cutaway bog banks, crumbling away, all their turves

> **She was a Protestant and she lived only three fields away from us at home and I had never spoken a word to her in my whole life.**

stolen already, and here a whole warren of rabbits. You could see their padroads twisting and turning through the heathers and the whitey grasses studded with bog cotton, their burrows, their droppings, little green pellets.

There was nobody working in the bog at that time of year and that was perfect. I put down my two snares at what seemed good places and then unlimbered my catapult and sent the old dog scurrying across the bog behind the snares to drive the quarry into them. He actually put up a hen pheasant, whose explosive whuzz from right under his nose startled both of us as breaking pheasants will do all your life. I fired the catapult at her… quite illegal too… but missed by a mile.

But we caught a rabbit. Friday drove him out of the whins and he ran straight into my new snare on the edge of the grove, to begin a frenzied thrashing about through the heather and grass and that, I thought happily, was that, advancing towards the snare because rabbits can never get out of snares. I could taste him already, with carrots and onions. We ate a lot of rabbits, like everybody else, in those years. Few white meats taste better.

Boys of 13 are both cruel and gentle at the same time. I got the rabbit by his poor kicking back legs and took him out of the snare and held him up, and he twisted himself into a tight terrified knot. I started to give him the neck chop with the side of the hand that puts them out of misery, and I did that without a conscious thought in my head. He was a dinner thing, and my hand was probably chopping down already when Suzy Nixon said from right behind me, "Don't kill him. Don't," and there she was right beside me, with a big book in her hand, and a cotton dress on her with roses on it, and she was a Protestant and she lived only three fields away from us at home and I had never spoken a word to her in my whole life.

Suzy Nixon was a Protestant and Cormac MacConnell was a Papist and this was the North in the '50s and we went to different schools, lived in different worlds, prayed in different churches at different times of the day and her father was a B Special, a bad black bastard too, according to Sandy my father. That was why I dropped the rabbit out of my hand with the shock and called her a stupid Orange bitch straight afterwards as the old dog went mad after the fleeing rabbit, no hope at all of catching it again of course, and Suzy Nixon, frightened out of her life by being called an Orange bitch with such vehemence, dropped her book, with flowers dropping out of its pages, and clapped her hands up against her face and started running away from me into the bushes.

And of course she runs straight into my second snare. And of course she goes down like a ton of Protestant bricks, unable to get her hands down from her face to save herself, and the next thing there she is lying motionless in the heather, face down, and I'm terrified at the thought I've killed a B Man's daughter and simultaneously notice, because her dress has gone nearly up over her head, that she's wearing red knickers the color of my own shirt. It was the first time I'd seen the beauty of a girl's bottom with a pair of knickers over it.

I ran up to her and the first thing I did was pull down her dress and the second thing I did was say sorry. She was reviving already, she was moaning and snuffling, and my new snare was tight around her ankle, the goldy wire nearly the same color as her Protestant skin. Without thinking I reached down and held her ankle and loosened the snare and she was bleeding a small bit from the snare and I had a clean handkerchief and I took it out of my pocket and dabbed it. The blood was very red against the white.

Twenty times I said I was sorry when I was doing this, because her father was a B Special and they went out at night with big rifles and stopped young Papists and roughed them up and, Jesus Christ, I was only 13 and I'd called her an Orange bitch for doing me out of my rabbit.

Suzy Nixon turned over on her hip when I was dabbing her ankle and the tears were still on her face, but she had stopped crying and she was white with shock, I suppose, but she said she was all right. I said I would get her water from the spring and she kinda snatched her leg back from me out of my hands and I gave her the handkerchief and went off to the well 30 yards away, where the bogmen always left a tin porringer for drinking from and when I was coming back I picked up her big book and brought it to her. She had moved and was sitting with her back against a beech tree and she was still whiter faced than even Protestant girl's faces usually are, and she had stopped crying and had wiped away the tears.

She had blondie hair, very fine and straight, and brown eyes, and she said sorry, sorry, sorry too because she'd lost me my rabbit and I suppose because I was a Papist and there were always Papists going out at night to bomb customs posts and shoot policemen every now and again.

I hunkered down beside Suzy Nixon and said it was all right, and I think we were both relieved that things were not worse and, anyway, there was nobody else in the bog to see us. She took the porringer and drank out of it and the color came back a bit into her face and the next thing Friday came up and licked her face and that started the two of us laughing and then we were sitting together talking and even though I knew she was Nixon I did not know her name, nor she mine except I was a son of Sandy MacConnell's.

She was Suzy and she was 15 and she was in the bog getting samples of grasses and plants for some botany project at school.

We talked about a lot of things. It was kinda exciting to be talking to a Protestant girl with brown eyes and blondie hair who you knew was wearing red knickers and the feel of whose leg you'd never forget. And I don't know how exactly we started kissing except that she started it, because, I suppose, she was two years older than me and a Protestant, and it was just that, kissing and no more, with our mouths tightly closed, our two heads against the tree, not even our arms around each other except once she put her hand up on the back of my neck. She had a soft dry hand. She had lovely brown eyes. I will never forget the feel of her lips. It was my first kiss. I had never even kissed a Catholic girl at the time. I kept my eyes closed most of the time.

We were there for maybe two hours, just like that, kissing and talking, and we did not want to go away. There were a lot of daisies growing on a bank beside us and she made a daisy chain, with her quick Protestant hands, and she put it on top of my head. "Now," she said, "you don't look like a wee Papist at all."

And then Friday started to bark at something or other and we thought there was somebody coming and we jumped up frightened we'd be caught, and went away quickly in opposite directions even though, as it transpired, there was nobody coming at all.

I remember, going home, thinking a jumble of thoughts which included the fact that I'd have to tell Father Donnelly's big head that I'd kissed a Protestant, a real Mortal Sin, and thinking, too, no matter what kind of sin it was, that I'd have to find a Catholic girl to kiss awful soon, because it was nice. And is it not sad that I never thought of kissing the B man's daughter again?

Three days later in the post there came a brown envelope which was addressed to me and it contained nothing except a whiter than white handkerchief, folded Protestant style, laundered to the last.

And that's why, when I saw small Aoife making her daisy chain, that my mind flickered with images that are awful sad, really.

Oh, where are you now Suzy Nixon?

Pennies For Heaven

West of Spiddal in Connemara they still have Death Offerings in some parishes. They have a different name for it here, the Irish name Altoir, but it is essentially the same system which prevailed right throughout Ireland until about twenty years ago and Vatican Two. I was at a funeral in one of the Offering parishes a few days ago and the sight of the Offerings being taken up immediately after the funeral Mass, as we were going to bury the dead, did my aging heart a great deal of good. Some traditions might have rough edges to them but it is always interesting to see them surviving.

I was never much good at maths but I reckoned one time, when I was fifteen, that if I died on the following Monday I would be worth eighty pounds and fifteen shillings in Offerings to our good parish priest Father McElroy.

They do it differently in Connemara to the way we used to do it. The Altoir is not incorporated into the funeral Mass inside the church, as we did with the Offerings system, the table for the money is just outside the Church door. The money, however, still goes to the local priests, as it always did. I watched the new pound coins and five pound notes fluttering down into a cardboard box on the Connemara table the other afternoon, the faces around the table solemnized by the weight of the old ritual, the undertaker presiding over it all. My first thought, strangely, was sadness at the thought, in the new Ireland, that no Offerings will ever be paid on me.

If you paid on their dead then they had the obligation in time and season, to pay Offerings on your dead.

Sandy's knees were stiffening up when I was fourteen or so, wearing my first pair of long trousers. It is for this reason, and that Sandy had to stand behind his shop counter, that I early became an expert on the ancient Irish custom of Offerings on the Dead. In harder times than these the Offerings represented a major element of priests' annual income. They represented, however, a great deal more than that. They reflected, very directly, the standings of tightly knit communities, the strength of family connections, the sinews of politics, commerce, and recreation, and, maybe, if the dead person was lucky, some measure of the esteem in which he or she had been held during their lives. There was an almost heavenly aspect to the Offerings ritual; there was an almost hellish side too. Representing my dad at local funeral after funeral, paying five shillings Offerings on dead neighbors, I saw it all.

I was never much good at maths but I reckoned one time, when I was fifteen, that if I died on the following Monday I would be worth eighty pounds and fifteen shillings in Offerings to our good parish priest Father McElroy. There would also have been about sixty cars at my funeral, two tractors, a Ford truck, and one pony and car. In our world it was possible to be dead accurate in such matters, even in life. The final figure was based on the size of our family connection, which was large, Sandy and Mary's popularity, which was fairly large, and such other factors as their prominent association with every local organization from the GAA to Comholtas Ceoltoiri Eireann. My own untimely death might add an extra £15 in five shilling donations but, essentially, apart from the tragic aspect of my teenage demise, I scarcely figured in the equation at all. The matter was largely a family one.

In our chapel a table was placed against the alter rails midway through the funeral Mass. After the homily the priest removed his vestments and stood over the table, flanked by menfolk of the family of the deceased. Their role was to whisper the names of those paying the Offerings into the clerical ear as he intoned the list aloud:

"Joe Murphy five shillings
John Gilleece five shillings
Tommy Maguire five shillings
Oliver Howe five shillings

Pat Dooley half-a-crown
Joe McKeever two shillings..."

Boys like myself, representing their fathers, had only to lay down the coins on the table and their fathers' names were called out. The maximum amount paid ranged from five pounds, paid by immediate family members of the deceased, to a minimum of two shillings from proud but poor men. They always brought up the rear of the line of mourners shuffling up to the alter rail and back down again. After it was over, before the remains left the church, the parish priest would announce the Offerings had amounted to the sum of £110 pounds, or £30 or £15 or whatever. In those days it was a big and well-connected man indeed who broke the three figures, whose death could attract more than one hundred cars, jamming the narrow roads around the small chapels with an unending black ribbon.

Woe betide you, in those days, if you missed paying Offerings at the funeral of a neighbor. Not a single name was ever forgotten by the family involved. If you paid on their dead then they had the obligation in time and season, to pay Offerings on your dead. The hellish side of the ritual was to see pensioners with few relations in the parish, knowing that their own end was nigh, attending every funeral in every local parish, and paying Offerings at them, in a pathetic effort to boost the sum that would be paid over, soon, in the dark shadow of their own coffins, trestled on pine beside the altar rails. And ye know already that if Jack Joyce died last week, the Offerings amounting to £80, then the family of Joe Murphy, dying three days later, would be deeply wounded if Joe's death Offerings amounted to a lesser sum.

Often enough they did. Joe might have been a saint, and a scholar, but unless he had scores of cousins and brothers and sisters galore, and earning grandsons, then the Offerings would be smaller. No way out of that.

It sounds primitive, does it not? But those, too, were the days when the wives of the men who went to pay Offerings at funerals had to go to the same alter rails themselves after the big Mass on Sunday, to be "churched" after the births of their children. Many's the time, as an altar boy, I held a candle beside the priest as he "churched" the mothers, ritually forgiving their bodies for any sexual satisfactions they might have had during the business of procreating more little Catholics for the Holy Roman Church. Times indeed have changed. It is remarkable that, even as a child, I can remember thinking that the whole business of churching was extremely wrong. I never thought the same about Offerings.

It seems so far away now. But it is not. You can travel to some of the coastal parishes of Connemara tomorrow, and in the Archdiocese of Tuam, after the funeral, as always it was, the coffin on its way to the grave will pass a table and the money will whisper its own homily to a soul.

The Rock Outside O'Hara's Door

hen the fire on top of the rock had already been burning for a night and a day, Jack O'Hara came out his door, went over to the big rock, and put his hand on it. He placed his hand at a point on the rock about six inches from where it grew up, naturally, out of his own front street, about 20 feet from the doorstep.

The rock of granite, flecked brightly with quartz, was taller than himself at its highest point. It had the shape of a small, blunted volcano. There was a split in it, about five inches wide, from halfway up the face of it that was closest to the kitchen door. The rock had always been an obstacle on O'Hara's street, but there had always been greater priorities than shifting it. Now, when Jack O'Hara put his old hand on it, the slow burning fire had heated it even that far down.

The fire had been placed on the very summit of the rock, where the cleft was widest. Its gray ashes from the dead turf were falling down on the street. A mild wet wind kept the heart of the fire glowing red. Jack O'Hara put more turf on it and went back to stand in his kitchen door. He is a slight, hardy man in his late 70s. His wife is long dead, and the children almost equally long gone from him. He has a brother in New York, and a sister, very aged now, in a retirement home in Florida. She married a landscape gardener from Sweden shortly after she went to the Station. They prospered. Margaret always had green fingers.

One time, when the O'Hara children were young, Margaret actually grew flowers on top of the rock on their front street. She got soil from the spud garden, and turf mold from around the stack, early one spring, and she grew

bright flowers on top of the rock. The boys were against it because they had been used to playing King of the Castle on the rock. You climbed up and tried to keep the other fellow pushed down. Then you were King of the Castle.

Standing there, aged 11, looking over meadows and ploughed land, an O'Hara boy could see the sea, could see the spire of town, could even see, on a clear day, the castle of King Guaire the Generous at Kinvara. But their mother would not let the boys up on the rock any more once the flowers started to bloom. "Lovely!" she said to Margaret.

Their father, Luke, seeing the flowers ablaze on the rock that first summer, cocked his head to one side, and said that 'twas remarkable to coax that much growth from such a small amount of earth on top of a rock.

"If I could do as well with the rest of the acres," said Luke, "we would be worth a fortune." They were not worth a fortune, but they were all right. It was a good house.

Their mother always claimed that her wedding ring was within the rock, down the crack. She lost it when Jack was four, the youngest, and she turned the house upside down looking for it for days, but concurrently claimed that she threw it out with the dishwater, up against the rock, and the ring went down the crack.

Leo lost a Christmas toy gun down the crack, that was certain, and Jack himself lost an Egyptian marble, a gorgeous glowing ruby of a marble, down into the black space. He was 10 at the time. He was sitting on the rock, as the children often did in summer, admiring the beauty of the marble he had won at school, and it slipped through his fingers, winking in the sun, and down into the crack it went. Down into the duskiness of Mother Earth. The same year, in the early autumn, Luke lost a grand fishing bait, a silver spoon with a green glass eye, down after the marble.

And Joey Donnelly, coming to help with the bringing in of the hay, lost his pipe the same way.

That bastarding rock. Luke hated it. "I'll blow it out of here some of these fine days."

He was embarrassed by it, especially when the hay carts were coming in with the hay, because it took canny driving to get around it and up the back yard to build the big rick of hay. He felt it reflected on the quality of his place, always well kept, that the great thing squatted outside the door.

But it was too close to the farmhouse for gelignite, and there were always more important things to do. Lelia often cursed it for having closed on her wedding ring, but used it to dry dish cloths, and to air her clothes from time to time. In all the family photographs of the O'Haras now browning in a box in Jack's parlor, there is the rock in the midst of them. Often there is a sheep dog sitting on it. Up where Jack lit the fire.

Jack O'Hara remembered seeing his sister courting Hughie Toole up against the rock two years before she went to the States. He was up in the garret, under the thatch, and he was very young at the time. He had to get up to use the big chamber pot under his bed, and he heard a foot crunching on the brittle gravel of the street, and looked out the window. Hughie Toole had Margaret up against the rock - there was a moon - and he was kissing her.

Jack thought that he should tell his father and mother, and went running downstairs to waken them. "Mammie!" he whispered urgently as they awoke. "Hughie Toole is courting our Margaret outside on the street, kissing her and everything." Luke and Lelia laughed at him, and brought him into their bed for a while, and told him it was all right. When Margaret came in about 20 minutes later he was still in his parents' bed, warmly in the middle, and Margaret came to the bedroom door, saying that she was home, and that she had had a good night at Delaney's Hall. "Oh, we heard all about it," chuckled Luke, "and out on the front street, up against the rock as well."

Now I have known Jack for years because he's involved in coursing hounds, and I write about that. When I called the other evening, he was lining up three buckets of cold water before the rock. I had heard of the fire and water operation before, but had never actually seen it being done. It seems that you have to know something about the grain of the rocks, and where to throw the water exactly in order for it to work properly.

"Watch this," says Jack. He used a shovel to sweep the remains of the fire off the top of the rock. Its red eyes flared angrily as he knocked them down to the earth.

"I've nothing better to be doing nowadays," says Jack, "so I figured to myself I might as well burst the rock. I have to get space for the hearse to turn on the street when they come for me." But he doesn't expect that for a good while, you would know from the vitality of the man.

With the fire gone, he took one bucket of the cold water, and hurled it right at the top of the cleft where the fire had been sitting. The second bucket went the same way, after the other, but he sloshed the third lower down into the hissing maze of steam, about at the level from which the cleft began.

The rock grumbled. There was a groany, crackly noise, and then it burst. Half of it tottered, and then fell down at our feet. It lay there like an old giant, steaming from the top where grass had grown for generations.

"'Twas an easy enough job to do in the end," said Jack O'Hara in a quiet voice. He got down on his hunkers, and began scratching about in the area where the bottom of the cleft had been. He could find no wedding ring when I was there, though he might have found it later. He found the mackerel bait, though, almost immediately, the remains of the toy gun, and the bowl of Donnelly's pipe. And he found his Egyptian marble. He held it up to me to see, rubbing off the dust with his thumb.

"Isn't it lovely?" he said. Indeed, it glittered like a ruby in the sun.

The Carpenter's Son

The Irishman, like all his breed, was a rover. So at the beginning of winter, with his dark-haired wife and 11-year old son called Fionn - named after a hero - he came down the dusty road to the village of Bethlehem. And it was long ago.

The carpenter's son, whose name is on the tip of my tongue, a slight blue-eyed boy, was by yards and yards the best runner.

The boy Fionn had a lively way with him and the villagers took to him before they warmed to his wild-blooded father, who looked like the fighting man he was.

The Irishman had white slash scars on his face, the relics of old, wicked wars. He had scars on his back, too, the villagers saw later, a web of whiplash scars that testified to a time at galley oars. He had a small finger missing. And he wore a knife.

And his eyes were green and flared, like a cat's. But oh, he was a sweet blacksmith, a mender of plowshares, a farrier of horse and mule and, since Old Simon had died in the summer, Bethlehem was glad he came and gave him good trade.

He rented the house and forge from Simon's brother Joshua, next door to the carpenter Joseph. Within weeks the village sounded right again, the anvil ringing in counter point to the hammer on the wood. The families became friendly, especially the mothers and the boys, who were like apprentices to their fathers. And it was good.

Evenings, when the pace of the day slowed, the artisans of the village and the womenfolk would be gathered in communal chat around the well. The boys, having brought the herds from the hills for the night, would play

> **"You see I'm 13 tomorrow and I might be able to do a bit of magic for you if you promise not to tell anybody."**

games. Fionn was the best jumper. The potter's son, Simon, was the best wrestler, felling them all in the white dust.

The carpenter's son, whose name is on the tip of my tongue, a slight blue-eyed boy, was by yards and yards the best runner. They had great fun, there, long ago, under the reddening evening skies, in peace.

The tradesmen had an arrangement of free service to each other. One evening, early, Fionn dashed into the workshop of Joseph the carpenter in a dreadful state. Only the son was there.

"Where's your da, quick?" Fionn said.

"He's away fixing a wheel for Zack. He won't be back until after tea," said the carpenter's son, sensing something wrong.

"I'm lost," said Fionn. "I'll be skinned alive. Lordy, I'll be hammered. I'm after throwing my mother's wooden soup ladle, her big wooden spoon, into the fire by accident. It was the only thing she had left from her home and she thought the world of it. I'll be killed. I wanted your Da to make me another before teatime. You couldn't do that I suppose?"

"No," said the carpenter's son, which they both knew was the truth. "Anyway, there's no wood here, only a block of hardwood and Daddy has the tools gone with him."

"Lordy," said Fionn, or words to that effect, and he stood there miserably with his friend on the carpet of wood shavings. "Me Da has a wicked temper. I'll be destroyed."

He turned to go, a broken boy, and his shape was in the door when the carpenter's son said, "Wait a minute," or words to that effect. "I might be able to help you. Close the door."

Fionn closed the door.

"Is there anybody watching?" asked the carpenter's son.

"Nobody."

"Well," said the carpenter's son, "it's my birthday tomorrow and so, if the hardwood block is a bit smaller when my Daddy comes back, he mightn't be too cross. You see I'm 13 tomorrow and I might be able to do a bit of magic for you if you promise not to tell anybody."

"I promise," Fionn said.

So the carpenter's son took the block of hardwood and held it behind his back. In a voice nearly like a man's, he said with his eyes closed, "Wood

is almost eternal. It lasts beyond the dreams of emperors and kings, longer than memory." And then he took his hands from behind his back. In his left hand the block of wood was a bit narrower. In his right was a wooden spoon, a soup ladle, exactly the same as the one Fionn had thrown into the fire.

"If you tell anybody," said the carpenter's son, "the murdering I'll do on you will be worse than anything you'll get at home." Or words to that effect.

It was not until Fionn was an old man, back home in Ireland the green, that he told the story. The ladle stayed in the West of Ireland, a priceless possession of that family for countless generations until a daughter brought it to the States in an American trunk in the 1930s. It was accidentally lost in a house-moving in the 1950s and nobody knows where it is today. It could be anywhere.

That old ladle could be in your mother's kitchen, in the jar with the other ladles. It's certainly out there somewhere, all the way from the time when one boy, on his birthday, did a little bit of magic for his friend. And that's the story. And it is time to sleep.

Sounds Of Life In A Seashore Seashell

Down comes the early of the night to fit like a duckshell over my world. Homewards go the wild and airy seagulls, jerked high over the swell by the magic of their own callings. Into port comes a Spanish tramper, lurid lights around the wheelhouse as cheap looking as a whore's bracelet against the purity of it all.

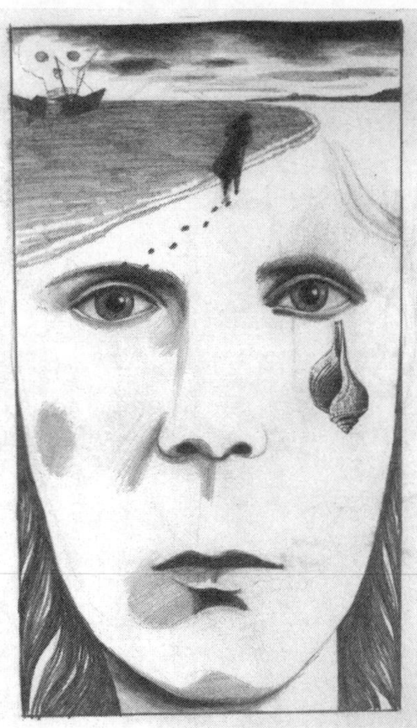

The sun has emigrated to America, far and hidden to the west, but left just a tinge of orange memory inside the rim of the deepening blue. The stoney hills of Clare, across the bay, mingle and meld closer together, not like lovers going a-walking, like old men making it easier for fading sight and hearing and smelling to see and hear and touch and taste all of the evening that is left in it.

I heard yesterday of a lady of the past who used to walk the curves of the cove I'm walking now, for years and years upon years. She was married at 17 to a Claddagh fisherman, a man from the fishing village which still preserves its separate soul outside the clutch of Galway's younger Norman walls. She married him and lost him to the ocean in the one month of June, when this century was young.

He got up out of their warm bed under its thatched roof in the Claddagh and he took his curragh and went out to fish. He never came back. There was no storm that week, the sea was calm, he had not been drinking or carousing, they were very much in love. But he never came back. Neither

the first nor the last from the Claddagh for whom some morning's tide will never turn for home. They never found him

The man who told me of her is a wise man. "If they had been married longer, if there had been children, she would have been all right. She would have grieved for him and then it would have been back to her life. She might have had children to raise in hard times. It would have taken her out of herself. But they had only been married three weeks and a couple of days when he was lost."

So she became Susie the Shells.

She went back to her own family, who minded her in her time of grieving, but she never was herself again. That is both an old and a new story. The family, like almost all Claddagh families of the time, were in the business of earning a living from the sea. The men fished the tides of the sea. The women sold the fish and also went out along the shores collecting winkles and other shellfish for sale to the shellfish dealers who sent them in damp bags to Dublin and even to London.

Susie, who was not beautiful at all, but a strongly made woman with black hair and hands that are still remembered along this coast for their delicate smallness by comparison with the rest of her, would help the other womenfolk pick the buckets and bags of winkles from the ghostlines of the tides day after day. But then she would go walking further out along the coastline, for miles, picking up seashells here and there, in an intent fashion, discarding some, keeping others, placing them in a bright tin can she would carry with her.

"Many's the time I saw her down here, walking away for herself, when I was a boy and she was a middle-aged woman, an old woman, if you like, to me at the time," said the man who told the story to me yesterday.

"She wasn't astray in the head, she was a hard-working woman, but there was something different about her that even a child could pick up straight away. It was my father told me that she was Susie the Shells, and then he said, 'God help her,' and I remember that struck me at the time. I saw her picking up the shells myself, mostly mussel shells and cockles - the bigger shells - and she'd look at them closely for a bit and then either drop them down on the strand again or put them in the can."

Susie would collect her shells maybe once a fortnight, sometimes twice a week, sometimes she might not be seen on the strand for a month. There was no pattern to her collecting, except that she was always out on the shore after heavy storms. "You would be certain to see her the next evening, when she had her work done, walking along the sand in the weed and wrack, picking and discarding all the time."

She would bring the shells home. She would sit down outside the house, the tin can beside her feet. Then, with her small hands, one by one, she would pick up the shells, the blue elongated mussels and pearly cockles, and hold them to her ear. She would listen intently, her face empty of all emotion, to most of them, and then throw them away carelessly. But every now and again, and how often I do not know, nor did the man who told me the story, her face would change to an expression of great pleasure, a complete transformation, and she would go into her house with the shell still held to her ear and close the door behind her.

"She always claimed that she could hear the husband's voice talking to her through the shells. That was how she got the name she had. She always claimed that she could hear him as plain as day, though she couldn't talk to him, that she knew what happened to him and that he was all right.

"When she was an old woman she fell down one hardy evening, over there beside them rocks and she was shaken up a bit. My father brought her up to our place (about 300 yards up from the tideline) and my mother gave her tea. Would you believe it was the first time they were ever rightly talking to her? I don't remember it myself, I think I must have been at school. But I heard about it.

"My mother said she was a lovely woman, well-spoken and normal in her ways. She had two cups of tea and slices of sweet cake and my mother was surprised when the old lady said to her she was sure everybody around the shore thought she was mad. 'Not at all,' said my mother, 'hasn't everyone got their own road to walk.'

"She told my mother that she could often hear him often, talking away to her. She said he told her that what happened to him was that he was fishing away, the sea as calm as could be, and the next thing that happened was that a huge basking shark jumped right out of the sea, high into the air, and crashed down on top of both himself and the curragh and broke the boat in bits and killed himself. And that he was thinking about her at the time it happened. That's what she told my mother."

The story is not so strange as it seems. I was on Aran two years ago and saw the dorsals of the great harmless plankton-fed basking sharks glittering in the sunlight. Leathery and primitive and huge. And the Aran men told that one of the mighty sights of the ocean happens in those waters in the high summer. The sea lice, in their millions, can attack the sharks and drive them demented.

When that happens, like the way cattle run from flies, the great beasts will sometimes throw themselves high into the air in an effort to shake off their tormentors. And the Aran men have lost boats and lives in the way.

I picked up a ribbed cockle shell from the wrack and weed a while ago. There was still enough residual light for it to almost glow in my hand, ghostly and mysterious and delicate as the mind. I held it against my ear, hearing the great roaring silence only, and thought of Susie the Shells.

Man-Eating Plant Takes Revenge On British Empire

et no man or woman in the room call me a liar until I am finished. Let ye not rashly rush to judgement on MacConnell when he says that Charlie Canavan is now some class of a hybrid or tribrid involving the fly-eating Venus Plant, some class of a cactus, and, possibly the breed of mangrove which has extensive roots and can prosper on almost any soil.

> **By the time we had the first drink drunk back on the mainland, Charlie Canavan was halfway to the Equator.**

Let no man or woman call me a liar, either, when I say that Charlie Canavan, in the rainy season, is also covered with purple flowers, is worshipped by the Papinosato people in New Guinea, and devours a lamb or a goat kid for his breakfast at least once a month.

And, recently, it is alleged, devoured much more than that. Though he wasn't quite able for the steel tips and the sparables of the Major's boots. He spat them out.

Still the acidity of the digestive juices which Charlie Canavan's innards applied to them before he spat them out resulted in them sparkling in the New Guinea sunshine as brightly and purely as the facts which I am now about to spread before you all. And let no man or woman in this room call MacConnell a liar.

A person with limited vision would say that Charlie Canavan died eight years ago in the County Sligo. Such a person would point to his name appearing on a death certification and, in gold, upon a tombstone in Ballymote cemetery. Such a limited person would also hammer home their argument with the fact that, at Easter each year, ranks of the Old IRA

Charlie said that he did not wish his bones to be laid to rest in an Ireland which was still not free from the center to the sea.

assemble around Charlie's tombstone, speak strong words, and discharge a volley over the plot.

They would also point to the fact that Mena Canavan, a devout Catholic wife, is married again. That is fair enough, in a narrow way of looking at things, but, in the case of Charlie Canavan, publican and Republican of this country, the focus of fact is far too tight. MacConnell will give ye the true facts.

The facts are that Charlie, being Republican all the way through, and a bit of a romantic to boot, gave very precise instructions to his wife and his old comrades, Messrs. Killoran and McDermottroe, before the advent of what a person of limited vision would call his Death.

Charlie said that he did not wish his bones to be laid to rest in an Ireland which was still not free from the center to the sea. That was the Republican half of him talking, below in Sligo General Hospital.

The romantic half of him added that he should be cremated at Glasnevin Crematorium in Dublin, the ashes placed in a large brandy bottle, and a note placed within the bottle bearing words to the effect that the ashes were the property of Charlie Canavan, were, indeed, all that remained of Charlie Canavan, and the finder of the bottle should bury them in any area of his choice as long as that area had never been under the control of the British Empire. "And throw the bottle into the ocean off Tory Island," says Charlie Canavan, "because I always wanted to travel."

'Twas done. On a November morning, I remember it well. I was there. I am kind of related to Charlie on my mother's side and I always liked the fierce old man with the blazing eyes and the narrow gash of a mouth. Indomitable is the word. There is a place off Tory Island called the Devil's Acre because about six cross-currents try to kill ships there. It was in the middle of it that McDermottroe let off the brandy bottle with Charlie's ashes and the note. The bottle hit the right kind of rip tide and took off like a shot. By the time we had the first drink drunk back on the mainland, Charlie Canavan was halfway to the Equator. Says Killoran, he always wanted to travel.

I ask ye fair and square: Was Charlie Canavan dead, in the broad sense of the word, during any part of this process? The cremation is merely a purification process, surely a rendering down of the basic genetic material.

Was Charlie dead, and he spinning madly in a tide off Tory Island, centrifugal forces exerting themselves upon his atomized essences? I think not. Was Charlie dead, and he travelling first class, snug and safe, towards the Equator? I think only our friend with the blinkers would claim that there was no life there.

Priests have a magnificent grapevine. I know a lot of clergymen and they know that MacConnell is a man who truly understands the mysteries of Life and Death. It was six months later that a priest phoned me from Meath, that had a brother in Malta, to say that Charlie's note had been read by a parishioner of his off Malta in the month of March.

Since Malta was very definitely still shaded by the British Empire it was felt, in that parish, that Charlie should be released to travel further. 'Twas done. I'm sure he enjoyed Malta.

I next heard of him from a nun in Australia, who picked the bottle from the surf herself, and she too, being a Kerrywoman, knew that Australia, where our alleged felons were tortured by the British, was no place for Charlie either. So she cast him back into the briny, gently, and she wrote that the bottle seemed to bow and genuflect in the water at her, before it headed south. Always a man with good manners, too, was Charlie Canavan.

There was silence for a long time thereafter. Other matters intervened in my life and I didn't think about Charlie Canavan all that often. But then, recently, again through the Columban Fathers, didn't I hear tidings of Charlie and they were interesting indeed.

I suppose, in his ferocity, it could be said that Charlie was pagan. It is true, in New Guinea, that the only remote tribe who resist the Columbans successfully are the Papinosatos, amongst whose thousands of warriors there is only one Roman Catholic, and wasn't it against his canoe, significantly, that Charlie's bottle rapped its glass head on a bright morning in their autumn four of five years ago. The Catholic man in the tribe indeed is important only in so far as he told the news of Charlie's arrival to the Columban and the Columban told me.

Anyway the Papinosatos don't see that many brandy bottles full of ashes. They never before saw a note in Killoran's handwriting either. They could not read it but they knew, because they were fey and spiritual in their own way, that they were dealing with something beyond their ordinary visions.

As they were pondering upon the significance of their find, squatting on their hunkers around the opened bottle, observing Killoran's handwriting upon the note, a toucan in the banana bush overhead was cleaning his significant beak against a branch. Seeds of several varieties of plants, including the Venus Fly Eating plant, a Cholla Cactus type, and a Mangrove Tree, fell down into Charlie Canavan's ashes.

Charlie Canavan was a man who ate bacon and cabbage all his life so his ashes would be high quality nitrogenous fertilizer. A Papinosato tribe council lasts three days. By the time it was almost over a strange and wonderful plant had already begun to sprout inside the brandy bottle. Life was bursting forth again.

The little wicked jaws, like Venus plants, were replicas of Charlie Canavan's in his Republican prime. Inside a fortnight, as the Papinosatos watched in awe, the plant that was Charlie burst the brandy bottle in smithereens and plunged its roots into the rich red earth of New Guinea. In two months time it was six feet tall, thorny and scaly, and its voracious mouths were snapping at passing parrots.

It assumed neo-deity status for the Papinosatos and brought great honor to the fisherman who brought it home. They erected a small fence around it and Papinosatos now bow their heads each morning as they pass it by on their routine way to their small wars. They never lost one of those since Charlie Canavan arrived in the village.

The Columban Fathers may not like it but it is true that now, each month, the Papinosatos throw Charlie the sacrifice of a lamb or kid. According to the one Roman Catholic spy in the camp the lamb doesn't last more than 20 minutes. It is sucked in and devoured.

Charlie is ten feet tall now, covered in purple flowers, has about 60 slashed wicked mouths, and is putting on weight. And there isn't a bird within a mile of where he proudly stands. Was he ever dead? I don't think so.

Last summer a British botanical expedition arrived in the area. They were led by a certain retired Major Percival, whose ancestors were rabid Black and Tans in the bad old days. He wore big brown boots and a handlebar moustache and a pair of Zeiss binoculars. He was about 25 stone in weight and every sentence started with "By Jove."

On the Twelfth of July, according to the Columban's spy, the major began questioning the tribesmen about their veneration for the strange green plant with the purple flowers in the village square. They told him as much as they could about Charlie's arrival and showed him Killoran's note. He roared with laughter, walked inside the fence around Charlie, slapped one of Charlie's five thorny backsides, and bellowed "Another bloody Paddy!"

There was a thorny class of a rustle and Charlie had him by both jugulars before you could say "By Jove." The Zeiss binoculars fell to the ground but all else disappeared. Gospel truth. The next morning there were belching noises from the plant that is Charlie, and the following morning, the ground was littered with sparables and steel tips from the boots of the major descended form the Black and Tans. Maybe it was the most unusual ambush in the history of the Fight for Freedom.

Let no man or woman in this room rush into hasty judgement and call MacConnell a liar. Let ye, instead, ponder upon just how wonderful a world this truly is…

This Judge Didn't Know What Hit Him

Driscoll leaned against the bridge at Toonagh at a quarter past nine in the morning waiting for the silvery car from Donegal to come along any minute now. He had everything in readiness. Driscoll was 24 that autumn morning, in his youth and prime, but his brain, like all the Driscolls, was that of a wise old man of 84. He hid it behind a face which would do justice to a freshly minted priest. He had blueblack curly hair, a pair of wide open blue eyes illuminated by simplicity, innocence, and goodness towards all men, he was wearing his Sunday suit on a Monday morning, and he had everything in readiness. Driscoll leaned against the cold parapet of the Toonagh bridge with his hands in his trousers pockets and you would know, looking at him, that he was a very decent, simple country boy.

Even though he was waiting for it, the speed with which the silvery car from Donegal arrived on the scene almost took him by surprise. One second the world around Toonagh was empty of all but a twisted road, rushy fields, two black bullocks, and a sycamore tree spinning its wetly winged seeds into the morning.

It's the only good thing that can be said for the Hard Stuff, said Driscoll, for I wouldn't drink it myself if you paid me gold guineas.

The next second the big, silvery car from Donegal was swishing down towards the bridge, was passing by Driscoll's toes, and was powering into the sharp left hand bend off the bridge. Its rear red lights flared as the driver jabbed his brakes just before making his turn. It was a very expensive car, low and powerful on the road.

The mountain sheep around Toonagh are divils. They are likely to go wandering off their own fields any time of the year, but especially in autumn when the grass growth slows. When they scramble over the Toonagh stone walls they often knock rocks down on to the road. These can be very dangerous for drivers, especially if the stones are on the wheeltrack area of a sharp bend. You don't see them until it is almost too late. If you are lucky, then you might be able to swerve clear. Otherwise the suspension and maybe the wheel are destroyed. A good driver with good reflexes will maybe manage to swerve clear. The Donegal driver was good. The silvery car swerved sharply away from the stone in front of it.

The yellow clay around Toonagh is deadly stuff. It strangles crops in their infancy, only grudgingly yields thick-stalked grass for the cattle, and is lethal altogether when it gets on the roadway, usually from tractor wheels, because it is as slippery as black ice or oil. It was most unfortunate for the Donegal driver, having swerved around the rock, that he hit a small patch of Toonagh clay on the road. It was wet, as well, and extra slippery. The silvery car lost its clutch and swerved into the far ditch. Its powerful engine was roaring in anguish at the point of impact.

Driscoll was moving away from the parapet of the bridge even before the crash. His blue eyes wide with concern, his boots clattering, he ran quickly towards the car from Donegal. It was embedded in the hedge, engine still roaring, when he reached the passenger's door and pulled it open. The driver, a genteel looking man in his fifties with white hair and gold-rimmed spectacles, was as pale as a ghost. Are you alright, sir? shouted Driscoll. Are you alright, sir? Turn off the engine, says Driscoll. Are you sure you are alright? Lord we better get this car off the crown of the bend before someone else crashes into us. Are you hurt, sir? Here, sir, here, take a swig

out of this and it will steady you up. Driscoll quickly dug into his pocket and produced a small brandy bottle, the one that cradles a couple of glasses. Swig this, sir, quick, 'twill stop any shock getting at you.

The shocked driver, still shaking his head reached out and took the brown bottle. His hand was trembling. He took a strong quick swig, grimacing slightly as the booze hit his throat, and then another smaller swig. That's better sir, said Driscoll, now you'll feel better. There's little enough damage done to your car, just a scrape or two to the body. Let's get you out of here before somebody crashes into your ass.

Driscoll was brilliantly helpful during the next five minutes. He put his shoulder to the rear of the big Donegal car to help it clear the ditch where its wheel was lodged. He hopped into the passenger's seat and showed the driver, still ghosted in the face, where to drive into a gateway to collect himself. He examined the body of the car and said there were only a few dents, nothing major. He produced his bottle again and the driver took one more swig. Some color began to come back into the driver's face. He began to recover quickly. Driscoll went back down the road to get rid of the stray rock that had caused the whole trouble. He even put grass down on top of the slippery clay patch that had compounded the problem. Every minute or two he asked the Sir if he was alright. The Sir from Donegal was profuse with his thanks, was recovering quickly. You are a great man to move so quickly, to give me such help, said the driver from Donegal. No trouble at all, said Driscoll.

Driscoll told the driver he had thumbed down to Toonagh that morning to, and he grinned innocently, "see a man about a dog." He had to go back he said, to Ballyfernon and, if the driver did not mind, would appreciate a seat in the big silvery car. The driver was delighted to oblige. He said he was going to Ballyfernon too, it was 16 miles away, and would be delighted to give Driscoll a seat there. They started off again, the Donegal driver handling his vehicle gingerly for the first couple of miles. They talked of the hazards which wandering sheep and clay could cause decent motorists.

Driscoll said apologetically, after two miles, that he was sorry it was not brandy that had been in the brandy bottle. You got the greyhound's rub, he said to the driver, speaking from his heart, a drop of the Hard Stuff Itself that he had come down to his cousin's house to administer to his uncle's track greyhound. The bitch was running that night, he said to the driver, and she was so tender in the toes, otherwise a grand speedy bitch, that they had to rub her always with poitin before her races. It's the only stuff that works on hounds, said Driscoll, no matter what they say. The heat of it gets into their sinews and supples them out, said Driscoll. It's the only good thing that can be said for the Hard Stuff, said Driscoll, for I wouldn't drink it myself if you paid me gold guineas. And I'm sorry, said Driscoll, that I bottled you with what was left of it but I had nothing else and acted on the spur of the minute.

I was glad to get it, said the driver of the silvery car from Donegal.

Such trouble, continued Driscoll, that the same Hard Stuff causes. Do you know, said Driscoll, that I have a summons in my pocket for Ballyfernon Court today for being caught with a bottle of it, just for the greyhound bitch? I'll be drawn up before some black whore of a judge and fined a hundred pounds and maybe sent to jail, even though every man in the country knows that if you have a delicate hound with tender legs the only cure is the bloody Hard Stuff.

The driver, laughing a little, said to Driscoll that he should get himself a solicitor.

No, said Driscoll, I can't afford one of them whores on top of the fine. I'm blackened already, all believing that I was drinking the stuff myself, so I'll stand up and say Guilty to the bastard and take whatever is coming. I can do nothing else. Maybe though, said Driscoll, the bitch will win the stake tonight and I'll get the cost of the fine out of it.

Driscoll asked the Donegal driver to drop him on the edge of Ballyfernon. Driscoll said to the driver that he was to go into the shop and order some shopping for his mother, in case the whore of a judge sent him to jail. The driver, with more profuse thanks, dropped him beside the chapel. Driscoll watched the big silvery car go towards the village and the courthouse. He took the empty bottle out of his pocket and threw it in the river. He smiled a wicked smile. He thought of how well placed his rock had been, how strategically he had located the patch of Toonagh clay so that the judge's car would slide off the road. He reckoned he had nothing at all to worry about in an hour when the Ballyfernon Court started. He laughed out loud in the morning.

A Polish Tin And Its Many Uses

My fingers are idle on the keyboard. They will go wherever my zany mind drives them… my mind is not in the humor of driving along main highways this moment so ye will have to take what ye get and maybe elasticate your imaginations (at which ye are very good, being Celtic), in order to make the "jumps" between one mental padroad and another.

When a mother sent a son or daughter away to America she would go to the cave and say a prayer and light her candle and dispatch it along the underground river.

So we are far from Connemara, which is dark this minute outside my window, one trawler coming into port under tired lights at bow and weary stern, and we are on the Cavan border with Fermanagh. There is a river here, sluggish and mysterious, and you and I are standing on the edge of it watching an old woman with a headscarf on her head putting the stub of a candle on to the bottom half of a Nugget polish tin. It will be a small boat for her bright light.

"Why," I ask, and I am only 10 years old, "why do you send the candle sailing away into the darkness of the cave?"

And she says that it is an old pishogue in the townlands and region of the farmlands above the murky cavelands. When a mother sent a son or daughter away to America she would go to the cave and say a prayer and light her candle and dispatch it along the underground river. It would speed up on the flow of the water, she said, and then it would disappear around a bend, still flaring brightly, and that was a good sign.

> **He twisted and he turned the little machine's brass knobs, did the wild man, and then, from out the space where there was once a penny there came a silvery Irish pound coin, fresh as if from the mint.**

So we stand, you and I, children of big eyes, there beside the wise matronly superstitious bulk of her, in a green coat that smells of mothballs and woman, and we watch her son sailing away to America. First the candle is bright and slow. Then it wobbles a bit because the little tin boat catches the main power of the dark underground flow.

Then it races away, its flame bending backwards against the forces of the world. Then, maybe 40 or 50 yards away, it is overturned by some kinky eddy, long before it reached the end, and the sight to the mother is like a gale of pain in the darkness.

"Oh Lord," she said. "Oh Lord above." And she just stood there. And all our lives since you and I have wondered what happened to that Cavan son of hers that went away in a tin boat…

…And, far away from the Marble Arch Cave, and 50 years earlier, it is a winter evening like this and a young man who is now an old man… but with a great memory… tells you and I about how he had a date on a Tuesday night with the woman who would afterwards be his wife and he could not go because he had not a shilling to his name. And his father, who went to the fair to sell bullocks, and who should be home with some shillings for him, has not come home, maybe got drunk after the fair (the only times he got drunk), so he is sitting there beside the open fire, cursing his luck.

And he has an older brother in the bedroom off the kitchen, a brother dying slowly and hackingly from the then common scourge of consumption. So the brother, only weeks away from his own ending, at 23 years of pain, calls him into the room.

Under his mattress he has a shiny Nugget polish tin. It contains some white powder, like borassic, which he had been given to prevent bed sores. Under the powder he had three half-crown coins, a lot of money then, and he gave them to the would-be lover, still powdery from their hiding place, and he said to take them because he would never get the chance to spend them.

In two months the Health Board men had to come to the cottage to fumigate the death room. They burned the bedding and the fumigation was with a white powdery stuff, just like what had been in the tin, and it was only then, when it was clouding the whole place, billowing like smoke, that the man who was a young man then, an old man now, went down on to his hunkers and howled with the grief of it all…

…And one of the tinker McGinleys came into Roscommon town one time, five years ago, a tangler and a tinker with a shock of yellow hair, a Viking face. "Look at this," he said (to you and I, there in the edge of the crowd), and he had a little timber pressing machine in one hand and, in the other, a Nugget polish tin, shiny too, its polish long washed away, and inside it old pennies, once 240 of them in the pound note, they rattled like wild bones. And said look at this, the rogue, and he took one of the copper pennies, it with the image of a clocking hen on it, and he screwed it into one side of the press. And into the other he poured a bead of mercury or two from a bottle a wide-eyed boy handed him.

He twisted and he turned the little machine's brass knobs, did the wild man, and then, from out the space where there was once a penny there came a silvery Irish pound coin, fresh as if from the mint. How did he do it, we wondered, you and I, and the wide-eyed boy wandered through the crowd with a tin box collecting awed offerings. A man from Tulk wanted to buy the magic machine…

…And my father Sandy said to me that the first time he knew arthritis was beginning to cripple him was when he could no longer open the tins of shoe polish. It was before Mr. Nugget put a little lead lug on the side of the tin. You turned it and its thin edge went under the lid edge and it opened easily. Before that it was so difficult.

And the tin was the first thing that defeated the ailing fingers of Sandy. Later, his hands all twisted, he would admire the functional beauty of that little lead lug. "Do you know," he would ask, magnificent blue eyes twinkling, "do you know that the man that invented this little yoke made a million pounds, became a millionaire…"

…Old Tommy Reynolds, every time he came into our shop, would take a tin of Nugget polish in his hands. He would look at you and we would get into fierce trouble with our mothers, you and I, if we uttered the sentence that he spoke so slowly but always asked us to say fast. And it was, "Polish It Behind The Door…"

My fingers are idle on the keyboard again. This all started because my shoes need polishing before I go out for a pint…

Paddy (London) At The Funeral

hen I was going out the Dublin road, Paddy (London) was standing at the spot where the bright Continental backpackers have been hitching lifts all summer.

In their brightly patterned sweaters and parkas they resembled the butterflies of the golden days just as sharply as Paddy (London), a gaunt crow of a man, blackly angular, underscored the frosted reality of November. It's a long, long time from May to the Month of the Dead.

"Are you heading towards Dublin?" he asked me when I stopped, and, yes I was, a part of the way, and he sat stiffly into the front seat beside me. He had a brown leather case with him with a brown leather belt around it for extra security.

His clothes were dark and conservative, bottomed by strong black boots. Paddy (London) was about 50, I reckoned, with a strong brown face, and hands that had worked so hard, all those years, gripping so many shovels and picks and blocks, that they were ten years older than the rest of him, already a little arthritic and awkward.

We didn't exchange names or anything formal like that between then and the time I dropped him in Athlone. We didn't talk that much either. He just said briefly that he had been home to bury his father, a very aged man, and that he was going back to the building sites in London.

The family had all got back for the funeral, he said, from America and Africa, where he had a sister, a missionary nun, and Home was greatly changed. His mother was still alive. His eldest brother had the place, married, doing very well for himself. That's about all he said.

I dropped him in the center of Athlone. In the rearview mirror I saw him pick up the old case and begin to walk resolutely along the next mile of the road towards London town. And I thought to myself that I knew him so well, though he knew it not, because we are of the same stock.

I thought of all the hundreds of death notices I read every month, as a professional exercise, where a parent has died and the family are listed down below the dead name, as a sort of testament, and the list always seems to include a Rev., maybe even two, a Doctor sometimes, a Professor, a Sister or two in darkest Africa, a solid, sensible son at home on the land. And Paddy (London).

I think, when the father of Paddy (London) died, that Father Charles from Los Angeles and Monsignor Tomas from Rome arrived in Shannon Airport almost together, having harmonized their schedules. They rented a largish car at the airport and booked into a hotel overnight, sensibly, because Doctor Philomena from Toronto and Sister Mary Dolores from Kenya wouldn't get into Shannon until the small hours of the morning. They met their sisters in the whitelight of dawn Arrivals at Shannon.

When they hugged you could see that all their hands were younger than the rest of them, white and cultured hands, educated and articulate hands quite unlike those of Paddy (London). Those of Father Charles were very firm and controlled on the driving wheel of the hired car that made little of the long last miles home.

They met their mother on the doorstep, still brisk as a bee in her eighties, and, for maybe a minute of the clock, hugging her, they were children again but, very, very soon, even standing by their father's deathbed, his rosary twisted in the white fingers, the masks were back on. The Mass the brothers celebrated in the kitchen for the neighbors a few hours later was read by voices resonant and composed. Their mother's face, in the corner, was then close to Heaven. She had always been the driving force in the house.

The father had been the muscles in the fields, a gentle but almost remote presence from early days, heavy steps on the street, a huge pair of Wellington rubber boots, the rare smell of fair day whiskey, the scent of the sales of bullocks that bought them the education that took them away from him, clever heads around school books, long before they physically left home at all.

I think Paddy (London) arrived just after the Mass was over. He stood almost shyly at the kitchen door, the case dangling in his big broken fist. The nun and the doctor and two priests made a huge fuss about him, hugging him

> **He stood almost shyly at the kitchen door, the case dangling in his big broken fist. The nun and the doctor and two priests made a huge fuss about him, hugging him the way they hadn't hugged each other, almost too profusely, but they had all looked sharpquick at him, at the doorjamb, to check he was sober and dressed well enough.**

the way they hadn't hugged each other, almost too profusely, but they had all looked sharpquick at him, at the doorjamb, to check he was sober and dressed well enough. He was indeed and this sent his mother's face to Heaven altogether.

There was only one awkward moment after that as far as the family was concerned. It was when Paddy (London) made an almost animal sound of pure grief when he went to the deathbed. You're not supposed, nowadays, to cry like that, from the heart turned inside out. A man isn't supposed, either, to put his weeping head, especially with old pubfight scars on the cheekbones of it, down on the pillow beside the corpse head of his daddy.

Nor to clutch the rosaried hands, broken themselves by the acres and the years, with his own brown broken ones. Nor to grieve out loud like that. They had to close the door and send Father Charles inside to comfort Paddy (London). That was the only bad time.

That evening, before the funeral, I know that Paddy (London) left the rest of the family at home, talking about oak caskets and funeral breakfasts and important family things like that, and he went down to the pub in the village. When he went into the public bar, not the carpeted lounge, the working men who were there, drinking pints of Guinness, all said, "I'm sorry for your trouble," and shook his hand.

He bought drinks for them all, especially those who were of the same vintage as his father. In this circle the talk was all about his father in the old days. He heard stories about his Da that he had never heard before. There was a fight one time, in the Blueshirt era, and his own father, according to the storyteller, "Beat the full of the yard of Blueshirts."

On another occasion, he heard, his father had cycled the full length of the narrow parapet on the village bridge, a young fellow full of wakeporter, on a Raleigh bicycle. Paddy (London) minded himself. He drank only three pints and a half-one and walked home early.

The other brothers and sister, with relatives and neighbors, were sitting around the fire talking when he came in. Again he got the sharpquick glances to see if he was sober. He had a mug of tea and a sandwich and went to bed.

There was a bishop and a lot of priests who had been classmates of his brothers to concelebrate his father's Requiem Mass next morning. There was an organist and a soprano from Limerick. The church was crammed and the oak casket almost hidden beneath wreaths of flowers.

There was a panegyric from Father Charles. It was a quite magnificent verbal tribute to their father. There were passages of it that Paddy (London) didn't quite understand himself, so magnificent was it. His mother's silvery head beside him bobbed contentedly in the golden flood of it.

There was no mention of Blueshirts, thought Paddy (London), nor of cycling along the parapet of the bridge. At the graveside, a little later, he was the only one to shed a tear. Even the grandchildren with their fluttering curls were riveted to the composure of their elders.

He went to the funeral breakfast in the hotel, sitting stiffly between two clerical classmates of Charlie's who were condescendingly benign. They asked him would he work on the Chunnel to France. One asked about wage rates on the sites. As always, to such people, he lied upwards. They later began to talk through him, right through and past his awkward rigidity and broken hands, making clever jokes about celibacy and such matters.

The next morning he packed and strapped his case. He said good-bye to his mother, crying a little again, not squeezing her smallness too tightly, and he said a quick goodbye to the priests, the Doctor, the Sister. He had a lift, he said, with a mate, all the way back to London so there was no need to drive him.

He gave an English fiver to each of the three nephews. He walked down the lane alone, not looking back. He got a lift into Galway with the milkman. Then Paddy (London) stood at the verge, like a crow blackly, where the butterfly backpackers had been all summer, and that's where we began…

Playing The Virgin Mary

 wonder does Mrs. Mary Kate O'Dolan regret what she did? I wonder has she any qualms of conscience? I wonder does she see the ironic aspects of it all? I wonder does the child know what happened, or why? She is only 13. Perhaps she is too young to catch all the nuances surrounding the casting of the school's Nativity play. I hope she is.

> **It is always the prettiest and tallest girl in sixth class who is selected to play the Virgin Mary in the Nativity play at the start of December.**

Mary Kate O'Dolan is the sixth class teacher. She is an excellent teacher, a good living woman, a dedicated professional educator, wife to a policeman, mother of two university students, Statia and Brid.

Mary Kate O'Dolan's students invariably do well for themselves in their subsequent lives. None will do better, however, than her own daughters. They come home from their lectures each evening, disappear into the sturdy bungalow on the outskirts of the village, never appear again until the following morning. Block and stocky and severe-faced already like their mother. They wear low sturdy shoes, with neat folders of notes under their arms, never missing the bus. One wears spectacles and is going to be a doctor. The other one will be a scientist.

Their father is a sergeant in the police. He is a righteous man with a straight back. They say in the village, quite wrongly I'm certain, that he would summons his own mother if he had to. All of the family are members of the parish choir. If you listen very closely you can hear the solid chorus

of their decent togetherness almost drowning out the rest. A lovely family is what they are called, a lovely family, backbone of the parish.

Each year Mary Kate O'Dolan, as a labor of love, creates the school Nativity play for the Christmas concert. She does it very well. She actually wrote the script herself, about 15 years ago, and nothing ever changes except the cast members. Her fine daughters, all unaided, create the costumes for the Nativity play. Her husband, with a hammer, constructs the set. He brings home timbers each year to his own garage and stores them until the next Nativity time. With the innocence and beauty of the children, the skill of Mary Kate O'Dolan, and the stimulation of the Nativity season, the play, which comes at the end of the school concert, is always very moving in a simple way. Especially at the very end, when the Virgin Mary stands center stage in a spotlight holding the baby safe from all harm. And all the school, and the assembled parents too, softly sing *Silent Night*.

Statia O'Dolan plays the piano impeccably in the background, Brid plays the harp. Their father holds the powerful torch that creates the spotlight. Mary Kate O'Dolan does all the backstage things that have to be done. A lovely family, I tell you, the backbone of this particular parish.

It is always the prettiest and tallest girl in sixth class who is selected to play the Virgin Mary in the Nativity play at the start of December. It is always, is it not, a simple choice. There is always one child that physically shines out from the rest. It was always a simple choice, that is, until this year.

Fiona Hughes is the loveliest child the school ever saw. She is lovelier than any painting you ever saw of the Virgin Mary on any church wall. She has long black hair, green eyes, and ivory skin. She is three inches taller than any other girl in the class, slender and graceful. She is also, academically, the brightest child in the school, a gifted student, and gentle and sensitive in her nature.

Fiona Hughes also bears only her mother's name. She is illegitimate. She is the only illegitimate child amongst the 104 in the rollbook.

When the casting time for the Nativity play came yesterday, after regular school time, all the children in sixth class crowded around Mary Kate O'Dolan's desk. It is the time of year for high excitement. Already, of course, the children would know who the principal roles would go to. Hugh Logue, who takes drama and elocution lessons, would certainly be Pontius Pilate, Jimmy Dunne, the tallest boy who was in GAA play in the spring, and was absolutely brilliant, would certainly be Joseph the carpenter. Fiona Hughes would certainly be the Virgin Mary. Sarah Lally, who reads the lessons at Mass with a voice like warm honey, would certainly be the narrator.

It was only the minor roles, like shepherds and kings and innkeepers and servants and Roman soldiers and maidservants, that were up for grabs. Everybody reads and acts during the annual audition and Mary Kate

O'Dolan, that lovely teacher, has ornamented the basic tale with enough characters to give almost every child in the class some kind of role. The angel that comes to Mary, for example, is always flanked by three or four lesser angels that never appeared in any Gospel I read.

I wonder does the child know what happened? I wonder does she know why it happened?

"Won't Fiona be a lovely Virgin Mary?" said her friend Cathleen Mullally to Mary Kate O'Dolan, starting it all off.

"Oh yes she will," chorused several of the other girls. Fiona is extremely popular.

"I think, children," said Mary Kate O'Dolan, smiling the wide smile she smiles at inspectors and visiting parents, "that Fiona would be even better as the innkeeper's wife." And, she added, "She is such a good actress, with such a fine strong voice."

"But Mistress," said Cathleen Mullally, taken aback, "Fiona looks just like Our Blessed Mother. Look over there." And they all looked at the holy picture on the wall. And indeed it was true.

"No children," said Mary Kate O'Dolan, with the firm voice they all knew very well. "Josephine Sullivan will play the Blessed Virgin and Fiona will be the innkeeper's wife. She will be very good in that part, excellent."

Fiona Hughes said nothing at all during this exchange. She was standing beside the teacher's right arm, looking at the script on the desk. The innkeeper's wife had just one line to say. She says quite crossly, to her husband the innkeeper, "I don't see why you should let those strange people sleep in the stable tonight. They don't look very respectable to me. You should have sent them on their way." That's all she says. She wears a coarse brown dress, according to the script, and has her sleeves rolled up as if she has been working in the kitchen of the inn in which there was no room.

"Josephine Sullivan will be the Virgin Mary," said Mary Kate O'Dolan. She said it very firmly. Josephine Sullivan is, indeed, quite pretty. Her father works in the bank and her mother teaches fourth class. Josephine already begins to look a little like Mary Kate's own daughters. She will go far.

I wonder does the child know why she was not picked to be the Blessed Virgin. I wonder. I hope she does not.

It's Do Or Die For These Dogs

It was a bright morning with the special October sheen to it. That is the peculiarly brilliant spectrum of lighting one gets in the West of Ireland when a thin sun is trying to work through air heavy with the purest veils of mist in the world. You get unusual colors without any names between the edges of the hills and the skies that arch above them.

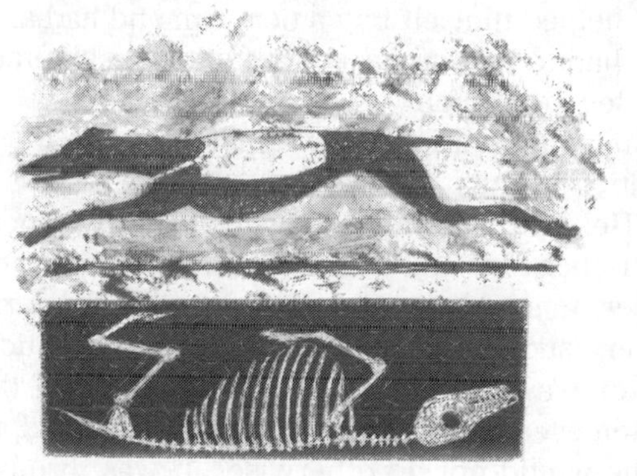

When Dillon picked up Mullarkey and the greyhound the light was such that the hound, lean and sharp looking, looked kingfisher blue rather than black. They put the hound in the back of the van, carefully, and then set off for the coursing meeting.

"We are getting old, you know," said Dillon to Mullarkey, as they jolted out the mouth of Mullarkey's lane on to the main road. "This," he added, "is the 23rd year we have gone to this coursing meeting."

"And only one win in all that time," said Mullarkey, who is serious about his coursing. He always has a dog, usually a black one with good breeding in it, for one of the opening meetings of the new season.

"Ah but that was great," said Dillon. And it had been great. It had been about 15 years earlier when they were both in their 20s. The hound, as always, was called Mullarkey's Fancy, and it had been sired by Golden Crozier from Limerick, one of the best sires around. In the final, Mullarkey's Fancy had been against a bitch from Galway belonging to one of the Divillys, and it had been great. Even Mullarkey's cold narrow face had been ablaze with pleasure for a week after that. Their dog had cleanly taken the critical

> **Dillon produced the bottle of poitin, with about 10 minutes to go, and they both kneaded the fiery spirit into the dog's tensing and quivering legs.**

first turn, having left slips like an arrow, and then had taken the second turn as well.

Dillon would never forget the pleasure of seeing the horsebacked judge raising the flag which indicated that they had, at last, produced the winner of the Cup. They tried every year. They had won no less than £1,000 and, with bets, had cleared another £1,000 between them.

Driving along the briar-edged roads, blackberries plump and luscious against the golden leaves of October, Dillon reflected that the win had paid for Mullarkey's wedding. It had helped himself buy a new van and had also funded his share in the dog that had to be purchased the following summer after Mullarkey's Fancy broke a leg in Clonmel.

Mullarkey was always the real owner but Dillon invariably had a share as well as providing the transportation to the meetings.

Mullarkey was the trainer. He did things his own way. The two men, neighboring farmers, had been friends since infants' class. They had played football together, drank together, married in the same year, shared farm machinery and equipment. Every such friendship has a special chemical mix. In this friendship Mullarkey was very definitely the dominant of the two. Dillon's wife, Maureen, often even used Mullarkey, whom she liked, to influence Johnny to do things he would not do otherwise. It was through this method, for example, that she had cajoled Dillon to get out of cattle and into mushrooms.

The hound stood behind the back seat, shivering in the highbred way that hounds do. Its head, thought Dillon, looked a little bit like Mullarkey's. It was lean and predatory. "How is he in himself?" he asked.

"He's well," said Mullarkey. "He'll have no excuses at all if he loses because he's trained to the last ounce. I gave him a loosener last night and he was going as sweet as a mouse's heart."

"Time," said Dillon, "will tell."

It was another 15 miles to the meeting. Before they went into the field they stopped in Joe's Pub, the coursing pub for the whole region. It was crowded to the edge of the front street with men and dogs, all of whom, whether on two legs or four, they knew well.

Coursing is a small, tight world. They had two whiskeys each and Dillon bought four bars of Cadbury's chocolate to slip into his overcoat pocket in the field.

The coursing meeting, naturally, was picketed by the anti bloodsports protesters. They had come down in a yellow minibus from Dublin. Most of them looked like professional people, teachers and doctors. There were also students. The coursing enthusiasts, brushing by them roughly enough, were equally obviously mainly country-based folk. The picketers tried to establish eye contact with Mullarkey and Dillon as they drove through the gate into the coursing field. Mullarkey cursed them under his breath.

The field was a natural amphitheater close to the sea. The coursing area was surrounded by almost perfect limestone terraces, now occupied by about 2,000 followers of the ancient sport. There was a tented village near the entrance and a crackling public address system.

Both men looked closely at the race that was on when they arrived. They had heard that the hares were not so strong this season. If the hares were not strong the slipper, the man who released the pairs of hounds in pursuit, usually gave the hare a good lead.

As they watched, a hare was released and began to streak down the course towards the escape at the far end. The slipper did give her a good lead before slipping the hounds, a brindle and a black. Like lightning the hounds overhauled their quarry. The brindle hound turned her into the mouth of the black. The crowd sighed a unique sigh of regret. The mounted judge raised his flag to show that the brindle has won. Before it died in the jaws of the two hounds, the hare cried like a baby, a mewing sound.

"Bad hares," said Dillon.

"Aye," said Mullarkey, "I don't like the length of the slip he's giving them. It's easy for a dog to get unsighted when puss is as far down the course as that."

They had an hour to wait before the big stakes in which Mullarkey's Fancy was entered. They spent the most of that time fussing over their hound. Dillon produced the bottle of poitin, with about 10 minutes to go, and they both kneaded the fiery spirit into the dog's tensing and quivering legs.

Dillon could feel the hard, compact, springy muscles under his fingers. Mullarkey had the dog in good shape anyway, he thought to himself.

When Mullarkey brought the dog down to the slipper for this course against a greyhound from Ennis, Dillon went down to the bookies standing on their boxes on the edge of the area. Their dog, he noticed with pleasure, was amongst the bookies favorites to win the stakes. He bet £50 for himself and £50 for Dillon, slapping the notes into the bookies' hands and taking the white tickets in return. Then he went to the ropes to watch the race.

Everything went wrong from the start. The slipper rejected the first hare that was released, considering it too weak to be coursed. When he did release the dogs after the second hare he had given the quarry much too long a lead. Mullarkey's Fancy was always behind its rival on the long run down to the escape. The rival dog from Ennis turned the hare. Mullarkey's Fancy slipped and fell as the hare turned towards him. The other dog chased the hare to the escape and the judge raised the flag to show it had won. Dillon closed his eyes with annoyance.

Mullarkey always went for home the minute his dog was beaten. They were back on the road again, silent and angry, inside the half-hour, accelerating past the bloodsports picket. When they came to the crossing below the town Dillon hesitated.

"Go ahead up the back road past the dump," said Mullarkey.

"Maybe we should give him another chance," said Dillon. "He slipped and did not get a fair chance."

"He had his chance," said Mullarkey.

Dillon sighed. He stopped the car at the town dump. Mullarkey got out and took the hound out of the back of the van. He took off its collar and threw it back in the van. The hound shivered, its eyes sad.

Mullarkey took the shotgun from under the back seat and went out of Dillon's sight behind the workmen's tin shed. The shot came almost immediately. He came back and threw the gun into the back of the van. They drove off.

Twenty-three years competing, thought Dillon, and 22 trips to the town dump on the way home.

Boxing Helps Make A Happy Home

Joe McEvoy worked in the family hardware shop. He was a big softish class of a lad, heavy round the waist from good feeding, good behind the counter, less good out in the yard where the heavier lifting of timber and sheet metal had to be done. He was the only son of a thriving business and when old Andrew Pius McEvoy died, Joe moved into the little office at the end of the counter effortlessly, and did not do any more heavy lifting work about the yard. He had three men working for him, two trucks on the road, a good coal business as well as all the rest.

They shoved back the setee and Father Coyle, a useful boxer even then, showed her how to spar.

Inside the house his mother Margaret looked after him like he was cottonwool. She fed him well, pandered to his every need, just as she had looked after his father for 41 years. Margaret was an almost invisible woman, seldom seen in the shop except to call Joe for his dinner. She would then be accompanied by the most delectable aroma of steak and onions, bacon and cabbage, cloved apple tart for dessert.

Joe McEvoy employed Margaret Harty to help him run the office after about two years. Margaret was the eldest daughter of Owen Harty, a farmer from the outskirts of the town, a quiet and decent man. He was the kind of customer who kept McEvoy in business, honest and dependable, always paying cash for his coal and fertilizers and the timber and blocks he occasionally needed for new sheds or the additions to existing ones. Harty had four daughters and it was good for the family that Margaret got local employment instead of having to emigrate. Margaret was a clean-featured sturdy girl with red hair, a ready quick smile, and a good head for figures. She did well in the office. She did even better than that.

When the older Margaret had a seizure on the stairs on a Monday evening, just before dinner, it was the younger Margaret who competently took control of the situation, sending shocked men and messages scurrying in all directions, getting the old lady into bed, soothing Joe, and a few days later, splendidly handling the funeral arrangements. She did it all so well that Joe fell for her with a bang and they were married inside 18 months.

It seemed a natural development, suitable in every way. Inside two years there was a baby son in the cot and Margaret was firmly in control of the office at the end of the counter. Everything seemed to be fine. The keel of the business was running level and true as far as the outside world was concerned.

It was something of a surprise, therefore, for Father Coyle, the young sporting curate, to receive a late night telephone call from Margaret McEvoy one weekend asking him to meet her for lunch in Limerick the following day. It was a private matter, a bit delicate, Margaret said.

Father Coyle was the life and soul of the parish. He kept coursing greyhounds. He played football for the parish team. He played tennis and squash. He was also the trainer of the local boxing club which was gaining quite a reputation in the region. He was amazed to discover that it was in this capacity that Margaret wanted to talk to him.

"Father Coyle," says she, "it's as simple as this. I want you to teach me how to master the rudiments of boxing. I don't want you to ask me why. I don't want you to say that women can't box, because I know they can. I just want you to teach me how to defend myself against a blow and how to give one back that's twice as hard and twice as quick."

She looked very determined across the table, sipping her coffee. Automatically the priest noticed that she had good big hands and strong shoulders. All the predictable questions and assumptions rushed to his mouth but he was a wise young man and counted to 10 first.

"Good man," said Margaret McEvoy. "Most other men would have started to ask questions that I would not answer. Now, how can we arrange this thing?"

It was simple enough. Margaret and the priest were jointly involved in a number of parish committees. They involved her in meetings in the curate's house, a rambling old Georgian house with a huge parlor. They agreed, under one pretext or another, that they could manage about one session a week.

The first session was the following Friday evening. Margaret arrived in a track suit, the same one she wore for her jogging sessions, nothing unusual. They shoved back the setee and Father Coyle, a useful boxer even then, showed her how to spar.

We are not to know the details of those lessons, which lasted throughout that winter. The only clue we have to their progress is a conversation Father

Coyle had in January with his close friend Father Tom Rutledge from the next parish. Coyle was sporting a cut eye as the two of them walked the greyhounds on a quiet road.

"Did one of the young fellows land a lucky one on you?" asked Rutledge.

"I can't tell you how I got it," said Coyle, rubbing his jaw with a small smile. "But I wish I could. I was clipped with one of the best right hands I've ever seen, a real class right hand. It's one of those natural gifts that some fighters have. You never see it coming. One minute it's there, the next second bingo, you feel the lights starting to go out."

"The boxer that has that will go far for you," said Father Rutledge. "That's a fighter I would like to see in action."

"I don't know that you will," said Coyle mysteriously converting the conversation to matters relating to coursing greyhounds and the politics of the Catholic Church.

It was the middle of February when Michael Doyle and Francie Scales were in McEvoy's one morning. Joe McEvoy had been out for a few drinks the night before and was in bad form behind the counter. Michael Doyle wanted to pay his bill and, because Margaret was not in the office, Joe went upstairs to call upon her services. He left the shop in bad form and the men heard his heavy footsteps on the stairs and his voice irritably calling for Margaret.

"Jesus Christ, you are never here when you are needed."

Sentences like that floating into the shop. Nothing too unusual about that.

What was unusual, though, was the one sentence the men heard from Margaret McEvoy - "So, you'd like to become a wifebeater would you now, Joe?" - and then the slightly muffled bedlam they heard afterwards. It would have come from the parlor over their heads. Feet shuffled, there was snuffly breathing for about a minute, a few other combative noises, and then, suddenly, a heavy thud. Doyle looked at Scales quizzically but both stood their ground.

In about three minutes Margaret McEvoy came quietly into the shop. She was wearing her tracksuit and was as cool as the breeze. Scales noticed that her right knuckles were a bit skinned and red looking as she signed his receipt and took his money, chatting easily all the time. Joe was not seen outside for two days. When he was, he had a bruise on his chin and a black eye. He said he fell in the yard. The couple, to the best of my knowledge, have been living happily together since.

City Boy Fails The Country Test

She was a country girl and he was a city boy. They met in Dublin on his ground, but also a place in which, after three years of city living, she was now assured and comfortable and easy. Sure enough she always had to adjust internally to the city noises each morning she stepped out the apartment door, and she would also forever dislike the squealing of the bus brakes, but she was adjusted and happy.

A graduate, a whiz with figures, she worked in one of the new financial centers, dealing with millions of pounds of paper money every week. She earned just as much and had as much status as he did.

He was a barrister in the Four Courts, doing well, already specializing, at 30, in difficult property issues. Sometimes they met for lunch in one of the pubs beside the Four Courts, and if you saw them sitting at their table, elegant, intellectually as well as physically engaged, you would be hard put to know which of them came from Mayo and which from the socially rarefied heights of the Hill of Howth.

After a while, because it was closer to the Four Courts, and because they were very much in love, he moved to live in her apartment just off the city center. And after another little while, because they were so perfect together, he asked her to marry him.

He saw with amazement, as he put on his climbing boots, once used on a trekking trip to Tibet, that she proposed to climb the mountain in her bare feet.

She put her head to one side, exactly the way her mother had done nearly 30 years earlier when she had been proposed to, and said that she would probably like to. Let her think about it a little. That night they had a bottle of the best rioja in town… a hearty peasant wine, sometimes special… and he thought, by the light of the dinner candle, that she was worth more to him than all the money he would ever earn from his complicated briefs, worth more even than all she had ever dealt with on the financial exchanges. Her eyes were like sloes still growing in their thorny bushes, blackly bluedusted, but he would not have known that because, to his knowledge, he had never seen sloes at all.

It was in the middle of June he proposed. It was on the last Sunday of July that she asked him, very early in the morning, if he would like to drive down to Westport to climb the Reek before nightfall. He asked if that was Croagh Patrick, the holy mountain of St. Patrick, and she said yes, thinking that his elegant, somehow patrician head looked like something off a Mexican coin she brought back from holiday once. And he said he would like to and they went.

It was a dry morning when they left Dublin in her BMW car, and she drove fast and knew well the long road down home. She had grown up in the shadow of the holy mountain at Murrisk, just past Westport and over the sea.

When they arrived, in under three hours, the afternoon was just beginning, the peak was in mist but the sun was shining and there were thousands of pilgrims making a slow black snake up the edge of the Reek. Clew Bay, with its hundreds of islands, was very blue, the fields around very green, the village crammed with traffic.

He saw with amazement, as he put on his climbing boots, once used on a trekking trip to Tibet, that she proposed to climb the mountain in her bare feet.

"Why?" he asked. "Your feet will be torn to pieces."

"No," she replied quickly, looking hard and trim in sweater and jeans, a light anorak tied by sleeves around her waist, "our family always climbed it in bare feet. I've done it seven or eight times, last year as well. I have hardy feet."

She bought two pilgrims staves for them from one of the stick peddlers in Murrisk, haggling briefly to cut 20% off the asking price, and then, almost in minutes, they were past the stone feet of Saint Patrick's statue at the bottom of the mountain proper and they were climbing. They were meeting a lot of pilgrims coming down.

Men, women and children were all saying that it was very humid above at the top, with some showers as well, but always well worth the effort. Some of the older pilgrims ascending with them, many barefoot too, were saying the rosary around them.

He was wearing a black and yellow track suit which he had purchased in Paris on a trip there and she thought, once again, he looked like a young god of some kind and was proud to be with him. Once she had seen him in court in his wig and gown. He had been different then, speaking with a different voice than usual, emanating authority and knowledge, sometimes striking the table in front of him with a kind of affected anger as he cross-examined a witness. On hearing the pilgrims saying the rosary, he said he had never imagined one would find such an atmosphere in Ireland in 1997.

He began to complain about the pain and suffering of it just after they reached halfway. Something in the heavy air, he said was affecting his lungs and triggering off the asthma that he had always suffered from. She had not known of this, she said, and he said that when it attacked him occasionally in the city, as it did, he just took some medication and it was okay. But it was attacking him on the mountain and he had no medication.

His nose began to run and his blue eyes started to stream with tears. He cursed himself fluently as he climbed and, between the curses, sneezed. She had tissues in her pocket and she gave them to him and, every few yards, he was dabbing his eyes.

He wondered aloud if it would be all right to turn back at this point... they had seen it and felt it... but she said no, she could not turn back, he could go back if he wished. He shrugged, a little testily, and said that he would finish. He did not notice that the third toe on her left foot was bleeding a little or that, barefoot, she had been climbing like a goat, easily keeping pace with him.

Somewhere near the summit, where the going does get tough, the country girl got irritated at the way her city boy was complaining about every step of the climb, sneezing and cursing, and she just increased her pace and left him behind and went to Mass and Communion alone in the Oratory on the Summit, a place wreathed with mist. He did not go to Mass, but sat on a rock and never noticed that both her tough little country feet were bleeding here and there. They descended together in almost silence.

She asked him to move out of the apartment about 10 days later. He never knew what happened.

A Gay Old Life

 was talking to a gay old man the other evening. I use gay in the sense that it was used in the times that I was born, not in the modern sense. This old man, a Galway countryman, a farm laborer all his life, has always been gay in the sense that he has always been laughing, always in good form in public, and was very definitely not gay in the most modern sense of that term.

Intriguingly, Seamus claims that you can only be truly wise if you gain your wisdom from what he calls the "darts and dunts" of one's follies.

In marriage he fathered seven children. After a few more of the many pints that have always illuminated his country road through life, he will get a twinkle in his eye and claim that there might well be another few out there too before he settles down.

This man is now old enough to be pagan and Catholic under the one hat. He is old enough to be wise about the times he was foolish and foolish about the times he was wise. Intriguingly, Seamus claims that you can only be truly wise if you gain your wisdom from what he calls the "darts and dunts" of one's follies. At his age, and he is now nearly 90, he has that kind of life wisdom which in many ways has more of a real weight to it than mere academic wisdom.

He was a cattle dealer as well as a farm laborer, for example. He told me the other evening that he always carried a huge wad of notes even when he had very little cash. He would have a wad for flourishing in the heart and heat of cattle fairs, the haggling and taggling.

You always had to be seen to "carrying" hard cash in the fairs or else the farmers would not deal with you. To this day farmers often distrust the check books - hard cash is the thing.

I asked this bright old spark about the regrets of his life the other evening. We were in a pub and he leaned back behind his drink, relaxed as could be, and the story of his regrets was in many ways an index to the kind of life he has led so long and, I would say, so very fully.

He regrets that when he was a young lad of 18 attending Sunday Mass the parish priest one Sunday went into the pulpit and preached a fierce sermon against the evils of sex. Seamus said that at the time he was sitting on the ritually segregated male side of the chapel and, even as the sibilants of the sermon hissed over his head, he noticed one thing. All of the benches around him, with one exception, were filled with bachelors.

Most of them were so aged or set in their bachelordom in that austere era that they knew nothing at all about sex, except insofar as it affected farm animals. Almost all of them were afraid of women and girls because of the very force of the sermons about sex which seemed to be hurled at them every second Sunday by allegedly celibate tongues.

Seamus regrets that he did not stand up in the Chapel that Sunday at 18. And walk out of the chapel. And in this way signify the wrongness of the way in which a delicate subject was being treated.

Over the years afterwards - and he named them for me - he saw the men who sat around him shamefaced that Sunday aging and dying alone, often in dire circumstances. He believes they were damaged greatly by those Sunday sermons. By an attitude ingrained in them. By a fear.

He regrets not joining the IRA two years later when he had the opportunity. He was too busy as a young farm laborer, earning and spending the few shillings.

A man approached him, a man he respected, a young schoolteacher, and he asked him to get involved. Seamus says that he had a date that night with the daughter of a travelling tailor who had finally settled down. But she was wild. So he turned down the offer.

He says he regrets that now. He says that he watched all the politicking down the years. The more he watched, the more he has become convinced that there are only two ways of solving the Irish problem.

You either leave it alone and accept the fact that English domination of the Six Counties will continue forever. And will not be solved by talking. Or, as he put it bluntly, you go out and you fight for your country. That, he says, is the only way the Irish will ever win back all of Ireland.

He says he had discovered down the years, and by working for eight years for English farmers, that the English only give the Irish what they are prepared to fight for.

He regrets, he says very strongly, treating men and women differently, especially when he was younger, when they were wearing three piece suits or the female equivalent. He says that it took him a half of his lifetime to realize that there were as many bad blackguards wearing collars and ties as were without them. There were also many bitches and witches wearing costumes and high heels as were wearing the apparel of the working woman or the Foxford blanket of the traveler.

He regrets the fact that in the peak of his youth, even when he was working hard with pick and shovel, he went out and about the parish and the town only about four nights each week. On the other three nights on the first farm he worked, he went exhausted to bed at maybe nine or ten o'clock in the evenings.

He regrets that so much now. The young, he says, should burn their candles at three ends. They should sleep no unnecessary hour because there are so many years when you have the inclination to go out but neither the youth nor the freedom to indulge the wish. And money should never be a handicap when you are young. You can have a great night with empty pockets.

I'm personally inclined to agree with him on that one.

He regrets not buying the camel. He was at a fair one time in Loughrea in Co. Galway and there was a circus in town. A man from the circus came to the edge of the fair with a baby camel. It was sickly and spindled on its legs. Its eyes were weak and rimed and its breath smelt foul and if it was a calf it would already be dead.

The man from the circus said that its mother had twins and could only feed one. Any farmer could buy it as a novelty item and feed it on cow's milk, said the circus man, and the circus would buy it back from him at good money when they came through again the following season.

He regrets not buying that camel. Like all stockmen he has a great fondness for animals. He saw the circus man taking the baby camel back again to the huddled caravans and tents with the forlorn air of a man who knew that it would die soon. And he regrets, whatever might have happened to the deal, that he did not buy the baby camel in Loughrea.

And one time he drank a half-bottle of poitin that was moonshined in Longford, above all places, and man does he regret that. And he regrets that he was not able to give his wife, Susan, still alive as a cricket, an easier life than she had in the early years.

And he regrets, long before that, not sleeping on the mountain with a willing farmer's daughter who came out to him as he worked putting up a fence. She had a tin can of cold tea and brown bread just with butter, and she had a wish for him in her eyes. But he was afraid to lose his job. She went to America afterwards and he never saw her again.

And he regrets almost stealing two black bullocks from a man one time on the edge of a Mayo fair because the man that was selling them was a little bit simple-minded. He regrets that.

And mostly, said my gay friend, mostly he regrets that he is now old.

His eyes flash with memories, and he says that he would love to live it all over again, the good times, the bad times, the times that were in between. And he would certainly buy the camel next time around!

Book II

The Terrible Tragedy Of Maggie Meehan

They held Maggie Meehan's inquest in the small courthouse overlooking the townland where she had lived, loved and eventually died. The coroner, a big placid doctor with large calm hands came out from the city, and sat where the judge normally sits. The Police Inspector and Sergeant were there. Six local farmers had been recruited to act as a jury. Joe Tobin, the smallest and oldest of them, was the foreman. They had to delay the start of the inquest for ten minutes because Dr. Tom Delaney, who was to give the medical evidence, was on a case on the other side of the mountain. While they were waiting for him inside the sunlit courthouse, all the other parties companionably chatted and smoked. The courthouse was gerrybuilt of galvanized iron and timber in the early Fifties. Its windows are large. They give an almost unrivalled view of the whole townland where Maggie Meehan lived, loved and eventually died.

The courthouse overlooks the slated house where Maggie Meehan lived for all her 58 years, thirty of those with her late husband Dinny. Dinny died three years ago of a heart attack in the night, cold beside Maggie in the bed in the morning, one arm across his face. From the courthouse the jury could see the bedroom window where it happened. Being an intimate rural

> **She had been plunging downhill, all knew, for six months. Once the image of tidiness, she had become untidy and unkempt. She had not been to Mass for the previous six weeks.**

community most of them knew the inside of the Meehan house almost as well as their own.

Joe Tobin, the foreman, was a special friend of the Meehan's, running the neighboring farm. Joe had helped carry both coffins out of the small house in the summershine below the courthouse. Maggie's had been very light. She had always been a slight little woman. The Meehan's had only one son who went to the bad and hadn't been heard of for years. This complicated the inheritance of the home and small farm. It would probably go in the end to a nephew in Dublin.

The Meehan's cottage is built on a flagstone of granite, the same shelf of stone as that on which the courthouse itself sat. It has a green door and three front windows. The flowerbed in front, the jury men could see, has gone to seed since Dinny died. A wide drain, of the type called mearing, a natural split in the flagstone, begins about one hundred yards below the house and runs right past the courthouse. Its waters sing a dull song. It was in this drain that Maggie's body was found last June on a Tuesday morning. The drain is well away from Maggie's normal path around the house. It is in an area in which none of the jurymen had ever seen Maggie all her life, because she was a pure housewife, never far from the kitchen. She was wearing her bedroom slippers when found in that drain, face downwards. She had been there all night.

Dr. Tom Delaney arrived, shedding papers in all directions as usual. And the inquest began. The jury was sworn in, using the one battered Bible of truth in the townland. All the brown hands together. The first witness the inspector called was Owen Patton, the local postman, who actually found the body. Owen Patton said he spotted that Maggie was missing from the house when he delivered her single letter that day. He saw her terrier dog barking at the drain. When he went over he saw her body there. He took her out at once, but she was dead. Answering the inspector he said he had been talking to Maggie briefly the previous day. She was then in her usual

form. He reported finding her body to the police at once. He formally identified the body to Sergeant Watters.

The jurymen looked out the courthouse window, almost in unison, as Dr. Delaney gave his medical evidence. He has a blurred Southern voice. The body was that of the female Maggie Meehan, so identified to him by the sergeant. On examination it was somewhat undernourished. It was without external marks of violence of any kind. In his opinion death had taken place about 24 hours before his post mortem. Death was due to asphyxia from drowning, in his opinion. Could he leave, please, because he had an urgent case. Yes he could.

The jurymen watched the doctor's black car dart away past Maggie's house. Every local man there knew that Maggie Meehan had been on tranquilizers prescribed by the Doctor since Dinny's death. She had been plunging downhill, all knew, for six months. Once the image of tidiness, she had become untidy and unkempt. She had not been to Mass for the previous six weeks.

On the street of the cottage, as they watched with flat black stares, they saw the black and white terrier. He had refused to leave the house after the funeral. Joe Tobin reflected quietly to himself that it would be merciful to shoot the dog. Maybe Hugh Nolan on his left would do it. It seemed the right day for it. Everything being wrapped up. Decently. The dog was old, anyway, and miserable.

Sergeant Watters, in his evidence, loud and booming, said he investigated Maggie's death after it was reported to him. There were no signs of a struggle at the scene or anything to suggest foul play. The house, which was unlocked, had not been disturbed. There was a considerable sum of cash there under the mattress. As the Sergeant spoke, Joe Tobin's mind flashed over the image of the filthy kitchen floor, once so clean, the unmade bed, the smell of stale food, a dead geranium in the window pot, a broken cup on the floor.

The coroner summing up, placidly, told the jurymen it was open to them to return a verdict in accordance with the medical evidence. It had been, he said, a terrible tragedy. Joe Tobin, looking quickly at his neighbors, nodded that this was a verdict they wished to return on Maggie Meehan who had lived, loved and eventually died in this townland. The Police Inspector O'Reilly, on behalf of the police, and Joe Tobin, on behalf of the jury and the coroner, then expressed sympathy with the family on Maggie's death. It was all over in 12 minutes. The courthouse was locked again in 20. Nobody had permitted the word suicide to even enter their heads.

That night, just as darkness fell, Hugh Nolan gently shot the terrier.

A Match Made In A Chapel

t was possible to do what Ned Whelan did because all the families have their own fixed place in the Chapel. If it had been a different Chapel to St. Canice's, and if the Whelan bench had been on the other side of the Chapel, which the sun doesn't strike properly at ten o'clock in the morning, then it would not have been possible at all. But Ned Whelan is an expert at that sort of thing. He always was.

> **She was the type of woman that clapped men on the back or shoulders in a matey kind of way, and got away with it.**

There's stories told about men asking him to "show off" their stock at horse fairs because he's so good at it. If the horse Whelan is showing off for sale is on the small side, he will always bring it up on the highest point of the Fair Green, for example, to add height to the perspective. If the animal is blocky and without grace, he will make sure to position it beside even heavier and more graceless nags. And if the colt is a really good colt, like McGovern's last year at Ballinasloe, Whelan will lead it boldly through the heart of the fair, strutting beside the proud head, whistling high in his teeth to prick the animal's ears and senses.

Yes, Ned Whelan is expert at what he does, but, nevertheless, it would not have been possible to do what he did in a different chapel to St. Canice's.

It also would have been impossible with a different class of daughter than Margaret. But Margaret was always special, and especially close to her father. She was closer in humor and spirit to Whelan than any of the sons,

and often went with him, as a child and a young girl, to the horse fairs of Ireland. They laughed a lot together, Ned and Margaret, and she could drink a pint as good as any man.

She was a big, plain girl of the type that used to be described as strapping, with Whelan's strong, straight back and gaze about her. She was the type of woman that clapped men on the back or shoulders in a matey kind of way, and got away with it. She probably got on better with Whelan's horsy associates than she did with most women. There was something too direct about her, too, for a lot of the young fellows in the parish, that and the sheer size of her: five foot nine in her flat shoes. So, she was 29 years old at the time we're talking about, teaching in the local national school, and no real prospects of marriage at all.

So the new sergeant comes to the two-man barracks in the village. He's from Carlow, where they know nothing about horse fairs. And the first thing Margaret Whelan noticed about him was that he was low-sized, as policemen go, not as tall as herself. And the next thing she noticed was that he seemed to be a nice man, and they were scarce in the parish, what with migration to the cities and emigration. And the underlying reality was that he would be the last sergeant to come to the village because the station is to be closed down next year. And another reality was that there were three young women in the village, including another teacher and a bank clerk, who were all younger, prettier, and infinitely more petite than she was.

On the Wednesday evening, Margaret and Ned were having a quiet drink in the Rowan Bush when the sergeant passed briskly by, talking to Susan Magee from the bank. "There's a potential client, and it's an awful shame that a man with your skill can't get the daughter off your hands," quipped Margaret to her father. And the two of them chuckled. "If I had four legs instead of two," said Margaret, a little wryly, "you would have been able to dispose of me long ago."

Ned Whelan entered into the spirit of the thing like a shot. He's very quick on the uptake. "I could clinch that deal in a week," says he, "if only you'd be led and said by me down to the last detail."

Right, says the daughter, and they had another drink on it with a lot of laughing. "Now," says Ned Whelan, "you are under starter's orders, and the first thing you'll do tomorrow after school, is go into town and get the hair cut. And get it out of that rolled-up style, a real school-mistress look. You have a grand head of red hair: make the most of it, with a pair of smartish, black leather shoes with the highest heels you can manage. A filly has to step high to get noticed, you know."

On Friday, Ned Whelan brought the daughter into Galway to shop for some special clothes. And Ned had the order down to a tee! "Green," says he, "above the waist, in silk maybe, like the jockeys wear. And I want black from the waist down, with as high a hem line as is decent, to show off your

> **There is nothing in the world more, well... arresting than a fine red-headed woman saying her prayers in an Irish chapel.**

grand, long legs. The best of bone and substance in there," and he grinned wickedly at the daughter.

"Yes," says he, "and a black leather shoulder bag, the best leather you can buy, soft and pliable like a saddle, with a silvery catch on it. Not a fiddly little bag like you have now, gathered up into your oxter, but a grand big bag with a bit of style about it."

And he gave Margaret £200 towards the costs, out of his own pocket.

"Wouldn't you eat it for your breakfast in a month?" he grinned when she protested. "Won't I save a fortune by getting out of the costs of your livery?" She came back with a cartload of parcels. And Ned had been doing some shopping himself in the meantime.

When they got home that evening, in fine fettle, Ned made Margaret dress up for him, and paraded her up and down the parlor, showing her the paces, as he put it, for the best part of an hour. She had polish on her nails, and he got her to remove it. She had the grand red hair out of the roll but she was combing it back behind her ears, and clasping it there with a catch. No catch, says Ned, let the hair fall free, the freer and wilder the better. And wash it with rainwater and soap on Saturday night, allowing it to dry by itself. Things like that he advised, brooking no argument, and they had a lot of craic between them. The sergeant goes to ten o'clock Mass on Sundays, says Ned, so that's our Mass on this Sunday, just the two of us.

It's two minutes past ten o'clock, with the priest on the altar, when Ned and Margaret come up the aisle together. Ned is wearing a dark gray suit and rubber-soled shoes, and he's maybe a half-pace in front of the daughter. He had made Margaret go out for a brisk two-mile cycle before Mass time, as a final touch, and she really looked better than she had ever looked in her life. The red hair was flaming softly and wildly over the green silk blouse, her eyes were shining with good health, the divided black skirt looked classic, and her high heels clicked proudly on the chapel tiles behind Ned. You would need to look very carefully to spot that, by his shrewd choice of pace and personal bearing, Ned was, in fact, "showing" her.

She was wearing the emerald earrings he had bought her himself, in silver mountings that "ingled" a little bit as she strode behind him, proud as punch, her splendid head held high.

Here's where Ned was brilliant. The Whelan chapel bench is always lit brightly with a shaft of sunlight at ten o'clock Mass. If the morning was bright, and this one was, Ned went into the bench first, moving well in, and Margaret took her position directly under the sunbeam. There is nothing in the world more, well... arresting than a fine red-headed woman saying her prayers in an Irish chapel. And arresting is a word that even new sergeants know all about. Maybe not all...

The sergeant was eagerly chatting up Margaret at the chapel gates as soon as Mass was over. And Ned Whelan went home on his own whistling between his front teeth the way horsey men do when they are in good humor. And once or twice he laughed out loud. And Margaret was still chatting with the young sergeant in the chapel car park. She was laughing at almost everything he said, and her high heels with their steel tip clicked smartly against the stones like little hooves.

Getting Involved In The Troubles

ying on his belly in the hollow between the two small border hills, the armalite flattened out on the grass before his face, Shaun Adams again remembered how angry his Mayo mother had been when he told her he was Involved in the Troubles. He told her about it on a rare visit home a week ago, coming in through the back gate, just as dawn broke over the city. She said nothing at all that morning until after breakfast, watching him gulp it down. Then, with all the acuity of a Ballina woman whose uncles had been "on their keeping" in earlier troubles, gulping their tea too, she questioned Shaun until she discovered exactly what he was into. She had always suspected, naturally enough, but hadn't been certain. Even as he told her as little as he could, sometimes, only nodding assent to the questions, Shaun Adams knew he should not even be telling her that much. It was forbidden.

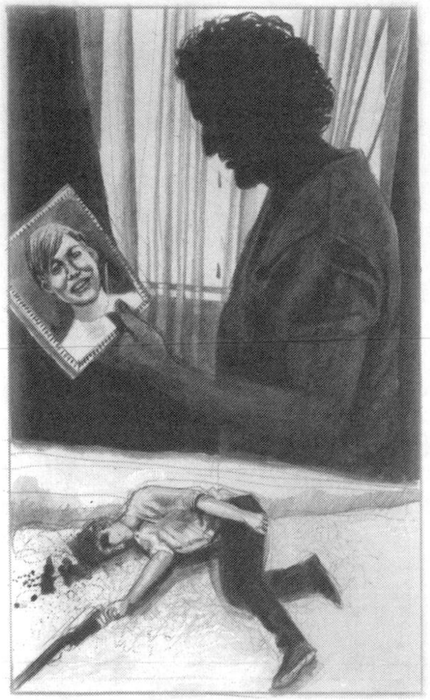

"Ireland doesn't need that kind of killing anymore. It's too much of it we've had, without you getting into it," his mother said, her voice harsh with condemnation. She had a lovely sweet singing voice, too, Shaun Adams recalled, lying on the slopes of an Armagh hill. He remembered her singing 'Down by the Sally Gardens' at his

> **Lying on the hill, ready to kill,**
> **he remembered almost with a shiver**
> **the cold sound of his mother crying,**
> **the cold touch of the holy water.**

sister Helen's wedding. Her face had been smiling and soft then. But now she looked at him as if he were not her son. "No uniform," she said, slapping the table with her small white hands. "No uniform and no dignity, all cowardice. Lying behind ditches to shoot decent men in the back. Is that what Ireland needs from you Shaun? Is it?"

He said it seemed to be. He had no choice anyway. He was Involved. It was, he said, kill or be killed. When he said that his mother began to weep, just sitting at the table, covering her face with a towel. She pushed him away when he went to comfort her. "Go away from me," she said, the sweet singing voice muffled and sharp and crying in the towel. "Keep away from me. You are no son of mine." He went away. As he went out the back door again, automatically he dipped his forefinger into the holy water fount beside the door jam. Lying on the hill, ready to kill, he remembered almost with a shiver the cold sound of his mother crying, the cold touch of the holy water. That night, hours of travel away, he got quite drunk with two of the lads in a small pub in a safe place.

There was a good view of the village and the curve of the road leading into it where Shaun Adams lay in ambush in his jeans and dark green sweater, a balaclava over his face. At this hour of the early evening, just past five o'clock, there was little movement in the village, just occasional elderly shoppers and children crossing back and forth between the three shops. Men going into the single pub. The spire of the church looked very gray and old. It was a bright early Autumn evening, dry and crisp. As he waited for the appearance of the man he was going to kill, Shaun Adams began to feel the first tremble of excitement. He believed he had killed once before, though neither he or the other two lads involved, were certain which of them it was. But this was the first time he had gone solo.

Once again he mentally checked the location of the stashed motorbike that would take him away from the scene. He again checked the armalite. Others amongst the lads fancied heavier rifles. He thought grimly, his fingers moving over the oiled steel, that he had always preferred the armalite. Shaun Adams who was 27 years old, his mother's only son, looked infinitely older and colder as he checked the gun; his mother would not have recognized him then. An hour before, boldly parking his motorbike with its panniers and back pack at the kerb, Shaun Adams had gone into the pub he was now watching. It was still a time of year when stray tourists were common enough even here in the killing fields. There was taped Irish music playing when he went in. Seven men, mostly middle-aged, were lined at the bar drinking pints. None looked directly at him as he ordered a pint of beer with an accent exactly like his mother's Mayo one. "A grand evening," he offered the cool faced barman. He got only a nod in response. He took his pint to the seat beside the window and drank it slowly there. He felt very excited, very relaxed and competent. He reckoned the enemy he would be killing would be driving his blue car into the village in about two hours.

A British army patrol in two jeeps drove briskly into the village as he was sipping his beer. He stiffened and made a slight movement to rise but then sat down again and did not move at all. The jeeps did not stop. One of the men at the bar spat coarsely on the floor. Another muttered something about bastards. The barman polished a glass and looked sideways at Shaun Adams several times. Shaun Adams finished his beer in his own time and left, nodding farewell backwards against the dark silent faces. Once outside the village he doubled back along side roads he knew like the back of his hand to eventually reach his ambush position between the two small hills. It was, he reflected now, almost comfortable. Shaun Adams reflected that his mother would soon get used to the idea he was Involved. He would bring her a nice present next time he got home. Maybe something to wear. He would maybe take her out for dinner in some safe place where he would not be known. And, after two sherries, if the company was right she might even sing, 'Down by the Sally Gardens.' At the thought, a smile flittered across his face underneath the balaclava and that smile was still there when the first of two bullets that killed him struck, almost tearing his head off.

Both the IRA men who had crept up behind him were very good shots indeed. One had been amongst the seven silent men in the pubs who had seen the so obvious undercover soldier, latest of many, come in to drink his last pint of beer. That one was an Irishman too, not a real Brit at all, some of them said later. I hope his mother was proud of him so, said the older of the two men who killed Shaun Adams as the piped music in the background played 'Down by the Sally Gardens, my love and I did meet.'

Hit Right In The Blue Bullseyes

I saw Hogan last week in The Thatchers' Inn. Time is a great healer. He was sitting down in the comfortable corner seat under the football photos when I saw him. It is shadowy there, especially late in the night, from the mockthatch little fringed roof they have over the bar so I couldn't see Hogan clearly. I could discern, however, that he was wearing dark glasses. And he was laughing his old jolly laugh, ringing round the whole place, as if nothing had ever happened. We are a resilient race. Hogan was supping his pint as manly as any man there. Strange, in a way.

And there is a dartboard inside a halved truck-tire up against one wall and it was in this corner, for all the years of my knowing, that Jigs Daly was king. King of all darts thrown.

When I saw Hogan first, about 10 years ago, he was 20, maybe 21, and he was a helper on a fruit and vegetable lorry. The driver was Jigs Daly, a leathery little man in his 50s, with a triangle face under a tweed cap. They made an unusual couple - Hogan, whom people often described as the living image of Jack Doyle, you know the showman boxer they called the Gorgeous Gael, and Jigs Daly. Hogan is over six feet tall and Jigs is not much with five feet. Hogan was always the extrovert, the life and soul of all the bars on the lorry round; Jigs was almost mute. First thing you noticed about Hogan were the big wide blue, innocently sparkling eyes. The eyes of a rascal.

Jigs was married to one of the Devlins, a right spitfire of a lady, and he was the father of about 11 children, maybe 12. Hogan would often quip, in the old days, that they had to sell all the fruit from an acre of big banana trees to keep Jigs' family fed before they could start showing a shilling profit. Jigs would smile silently, almost shyly, at remarks like that.

They were good friends, the two of them. It suited Hogan to be the blarney man of a team that had a big, colorful, rural circuit of small shops to service. It suited Jigs, by his nature, to do little but drive the big truck and collect the cash for the bananas, the chips of tomatoes, the potatoes and onions and bags of carrots. Coming with their relatively exotic cargoes into little country shops at the ends of narrow roads, it was Hogan, with the unending streams of jokes and wisecracks and charm, who was maybe the most exotic element of the entire caravan. He always wore a cravat inside an open-neck white shirt and was always chatting up the womenfolk. A dangerous man with the women was the consensus, a prime boy.

There are about three worlds in the Thatchers'. There's the posh seafood restaurant at the rear, its shiny napery overlooking the river, its velveteen surfaces. That's where the tourists and the wealthy locals go. Then there's the Reapers' Rest, a plush lounge bar with a decor associated with the tools of thatching and reaping grain crops. It has an upmarket clientele too.

Then there was the public bar at the rear of the building. That's the locals' bar, where the real genuine people of the parish drink their drinks of porter and beer and shorts of whiskey and brandy in season. It has the false thatched fringe over the bar and you don't have to be dressed up to go in there and it is the best part of the house. And there is a dartboard inside a halved truck-tire up against one wall and it was in this corner, for all the years of my knowing, that Jigs Daly was king. King of all darts thrown.

There are pubs in Ireland, probably everywhere, which are darts pubs. In this region the public bar at The Thatchers' is the kingdom of the darts throwers. It is not a game I fancy myself, and I am notoriously inaccurate, but Jigs Daly was always the legendary champion of all the local dart leagues.

He had his own carbon-shafted darts, specially stored behind the bar, long before this became popular. I saw him playing two or three times. The darts were unusual - and it is good that they were - in that they had very long, narrow flights of bright feathers combined with very short darts.

Jigs was quite beautiful to watch. He would stand sideways to the board, one shoulder hunched, the little leathery face empty of all expression. His hand would twitch three times, very fast, and all the darts were nestled together in or around the Triple Twenty or whatever else it was he wanted. Jigs was in the All-Ireland finals at least twice in my time. He never won and I quite know why. He would have been fractionally put off his game by the showbiz atmospheres of the big occasions, all the ballyhoo. Nobody ever beat him, significantly, on home ground in his own place. And Hogan was always there close to him, bathing in the reflected glories. They were a lively pair, and good friends.

Jigs would have been happier in The Thatchers' than anywhere else in the world. The wife is a domineering big woman, like all the Devlin women, and some of his young fellows were always in one petty trouble or another. Maybe mitching from school or stealing bicycles. That kind of thing. The apple of his eye was his daughter, Susan, a slight slip of a thing like himself, with black hair and eyes. The summer she was 17 Susan was sometimes down in the pub with her father and Hogan, especially for the big championship dart matches. One of the times I saw Jigs in action I clearly remember Susan keeping the score and Hogan bringing a Coke to her and a pint to Jigs when the tension was highest.

Ye are ahead of me. What happened was inevitable. I heard the scandal myself. Susan Daly was In Trouble, the parish priest was calling to the house, the mother was out on the street of the cottage screaming and roaring at the poor child and there was hell, purgatory, and even worse to pay. That's less than a decade ago but what is handled in an infinitely more civilized and compassionate fashion today was still a scandal back then. With all the trimmings. Especially in a remote western parish like this.

It even had sufficient dimensions and velocity to put Daly's banana lorry off the road for a full fortnight. I even heard about that. But, to be honest, because he had always seemed almost as much a father figure to the girl as Jigs was, I never once suspected that Hogan was the other half of the equation.

What happened was that Jigs came down to The Thatchers' after the worst of the hassle was over and poor Susan, inevitably, went to England. He had not been there for a fortnight or even more. He came in and ordered a half-one of whiskey and talked normally to Seamus the barman. It was late on a Friday evening. It was after 10 o'clock before Hogan came in. Just before he arrived Jigs had commenced a game of darts with Johnny Caulfield. All that is now in the folklore.

When Hogan came in the door he stopped just inside, under the light from the Harp lamp overhead, and then he smiled a wide smile and began moving down towards the other end of the bar where Jigs was. And Jigs, turning back from the board, having retrieved his darts, just stood sideways to him, hunched his shoulder, and his hand twitched twice, so quick you could scarcely follow the action.

"Bullseyes!" is what Jigs Daly said.

The first thing you used to notice about Hogan, as I said, were his two big blue twinkling innocent eyes. Not any more...

A Pub In The Country

I went into the pub in Leitrim at about seven o'clock in the evening. There were two men there, sitting close together in the corner behind a pair of pints. They were both in their 50s, still hardy and active. There were a pair of pints reposing before them on the bar. The froth rings inside the glasses, which were each a quarter-full, showed that one man, the one nearest me, had assaulted his with great force, taking one great draught at the beginning, then a smaller one. The other glass had the kind of frothensic evidence that its owner had consumed it in a handy and tasty fashion. He had taken five swallows of almost equal cubic capacity. He was the one, also, in the most comfortable of the two bar stools. It was the one which allowed him to lean his back against the wall behind him. It was the one which allowed him to talk to his neighbor and friend and at the same time observe all the comings and goings into this country bar twenty-five miles from Carrick-on-Shannon and about ten miles, and two sharp left hand bends, away from Peace.

He was wearing a tweed cap and the back of it was brushing the wall calendar behind him, tacked to the wall. The picture for July showed two men, just like these men, making hay with in a field like any of the

meadows sunning themselves through the bar window behind me. The calendar bore the name of a merchant who supplies fertilizers to farmers to ensure that hay will always grow tall and greenly each summer. "Hello," said the men and "Hello," I said and I called for a pint of beer.

The bar smelt comfortably of the doings of the land outside, of the wooden handles of the hayrakes and forks leaning against the wall of its hardware section off to my right; of the coils of baler twine; of the rubber wellington boots hanging from the roof in an exotic coil; of pipesmoke and porter, the tang of whiskey and that certain aroma which always attends farmers who milk cows twice a day. That's one of the most comforting and rounded scents on Irish earth. I think it maybe comes from the peaks of the caps which brush against the flanks of the cows as they patiently await the release of their burdens.

I sealed myself comfortably into the envelope of the pub's atmosphere and accosted my pint of beer like the gentleman I sometimes am. I realized fully that it would only be a minute or two, five at most, before the pair of farmers would begin to question me in the most delicate way about who and what I was. And why I was there? This kind of common or garden pub interaction may seem a very trivial matter to write about on a page like this. I would argue strongly that it is not. In New York, in the springtime, in pubs catering for Irish people, I actually saw men sitting at bars, their backs to the barfolk, using remote control devices to operate poker machines high on the opposite wall. They were a million mechanical miles away, those men, some kind of machines relating only to other machines. I reckon, here at home, that if ever the day comes when a stranger in a country bar will not engage the minds and tongues of the regulars, then we will have lost a valuable catalyst of our Celtic chemistry. It is curiosity which underpins much of what is called the Cead Mile Failte of this island. How are ye? Are ye from America? What do you think of Connemara then? I see ye are sunk into the Guinness already. Is it from New York you are? And, from that point, it is only a short walk to the point where one can have a good evening of what is called Craic. I have seen friendships develop from less.

So, the other evening at seven in the Leitrim pub, I reckon, if the heart and soul of that parish is still alive at all, that it would be the man with his back against the calendar of all our country years who would throw in the first ball. When he was ready. When I was ready. I reckoned, if things were right, that he would wait until I had lit the cigarette, taken a second swig from the pint of beer, and then, inevitably, relaxed and widened the focus of my face. I reckoned, if I have learned anything from countrymen and the way they operate, that this clever one's opening gambit would be very good, very well-judged, impossible for anyone but a boor to ignore. He would be too good to just throw out a remark about the bad summer weather. He would even be sharp enough to use the lines they often use to strangers in

Mayo pubs, especially to bearded strangers like me - "Excuse me, but would you by any chance be John Joe's eldest lad?" - which is an opening given credence by the camouflage of a beard. Or, what they use in Roscommon, "You wouldn't be the man that Oliver McDermott is expecting because, if you are, he's just gone about five minutes ago. There's a cow calving." The number of times I have just missed Oliver McDermott in Roscommon runs to three figures at least.

"No, men, I'm sorry, I'm just a thirsty stranger passing through."

No man would blame you for passing through this place on a bad day. Nor for stopping for a pint either. Isn't it lads like yourself, passing through, unlikely to complain about a bad pint, that keep Seamus here in business?

And Seamus, behind the bar, polishing the glass, smiling, has heard it all before, admires the delicacy and the beauty of its execution. And if the lads get a pair of pints out of it before the encounter ends… and if I get a story out of it, or maybe a column… isn't that grand too? And that's the way 'tis done. If things are right in a parish which boasts its own country pub with a sound hardware/grocery shop attached.

So I lit up the cigarette in Leitrim the other evening. And I swigged the pint. And I relaxed, looking lazily and easily towards the corner as the evening gilded the world outside, as bushes peered through the window, as the tweed cap brushed the calendar and the sharp eyes glinted. And I counted to ten, inside in my heart, knowing that the ball had to be thrown in, if it was going to be thrown in, before I had reached ten.

Four… five… six… seven…

"Margaret," said the sharp lad to the barmaid polishing the glass, faintly smiling, having seen it all before, "Next time you are down at the shop end of this house, will you bring me back a packet of them disposable razors for I have to go to Carrick this evening for the Removal."

"Mickey," said the second fellow, slowly and lazily as could be, "sure you're not fit to grow a decent stubble any more. I often saw more hair on an egg that is on your chin this minute. Or maybe under the cap either, for that matter, for we never see it off your poll anymore I notice."

And, almost lost in admiration at the subtle way it was done, I turned my bearded face towards the pair of them, and what I said does not matter at all. The place is alive and kicking and ticking. Oliver McDermott and his ilk still walk tall in the West. God bless them all. And if they got a pair of cool pints in the end, the Leitrim lads, I did not walk away empty-handed either.

Betting On Divine Inspiration

The cells of the old monks are empty now in Corcromroe Abbey deep in the Burren. The evening is gold. The rocks are molten silver. The trees that Cromwell said were not strong enough to hang a man seem strong enough, copper-limbed in the evening, to hang a whole regiment of the kind of kings that once rode this way to terrify monks, to split the sky with raw Norman oaths from deep in their throats, to put swirls of alarm into the long gone ancestors of the wild young rooks that now ride the eddies of the winds of autumn.

> **Once he had spent the day in a Chinese restaurant, totally out of nowhere, and the next day bet a small fortune on a horse, a filly simply called Miss Chowmein.**

Stop here, especially at any time of the back end of the year when the anoraked tourists are gone, stop here and walk into the ruins of the old Abbey, and you have to peel away layers of peace before you find the real peace buried deeply below layers of silence. Because the rooks swirl away when you walk there, away over the airy lands of Ireland's most beautiful corner, away and up like forgiven small sins, and then you are alone with the ghosts of the monks that shaped this place.

I stopped in an old cell. I turned on the inside of my head. A voice came. Don't ask me where it came from.

It was a voice without words but a voice nonetheless. I could feel it hammering inside my head. I was quite sober at the time and, indeed, despite what you might occasionally think when you read these pieces, I normally am. I heard the voice.

"MacConnell," said the voice. And then it spoke the holiest name. And then the name of the mother and the father.

For a while I thought I was in bewitchment amongst the old steal-soul stones. But then I saw the figure standing in the corner. An aging man like myself.

"MacConnell," he said again.

I walked to meet him. I had not seen any car stopped in the small carpark at the end of the lane. Two yards away I recognized him.

We were at school together. I remembered his first name, the bench that he sat in, the fact that he used a Conway Stewart fountain pen, chased the nib neatly with blotting paper in his right hand, was very clever, went away foreign early in his life with two degrees hanging over his shoulders.

We had not seen each other for a quarter-century. It was by the most oblique of chances that we met again. He was on business 10 miles away, was driving home like me, stopped on the main road at the sheer majesty of the old abbey, crossed the fields, walked into the cells and there I was.

And do you know what he told me? He is now a professional gambler in England. That is what he does for a living. He told me that he normally goes by the form books of horses and hounds. In this way he earns a good enough living.

But, he said, anyone who stays with the form book all the time will never really make the kind of killings that make the difference. So, he said, sometimes, after a good flat run of what he called ordinary luck, he would throw in a totally maverick day based on whatever different experience he had undergone the day before.

Once he had spent the day in a Chinese restaurant, totally out of nowhere, and the next day bet a small fortune on a horse, a filly simply called Miss Chowmein. She won at 10/1. That, he said, was the way to gamble. You had to throw in the figaries, the oddities.

I was amazed. I asked him how he would come up with a horse's name from the ruins of an ancient abbey in Burren.

Where was he going racing? He was going, he said, to a place called Market Rasen and he would spend at least 30 grand. That was much more than his routine betting. But he was always a gambler. He would stay there, he said, in the old cells of the old monks until a name or names fitted itself into his head. Then he would climb into his car up at the main road and fly out to the Market Rasen the next day and place his Burren bet or bets.

I left him there. We are to meet in Galway next month. Maybe I will do another story on him. I looked at the Market Rasen results the next day. It is, I think, a relatively obscure English track. I grunted from the guts up when I saw the list of winners. There were eight races and eight winners. Most of them had the kind of names that could not possibly be connected with a ruined old abbey in Clare. But, believe it or not, the second race was won by Western Abbot and the last race on the card, may I be struck down dead if I lie, by Empty Cell!

Tied To The Fat Man

The Fat Man comes to the smaller hotels in the bigger towns throughout the provinces of Ireland about twice a year. When times were really hard, about three years ago, The Fat Man made an extra trip, usually about six weeks before Christmas.

He comes from England and, before his arrival in town, the local paper says that he will be in the hotel throughout all the hours of that day. The advertisement always says that The Fat Man will pay the Highest Prices. The Fat Man will also give Free Valuations. The Fat Man will pay Cash. Absolutely No Obligation. Ray Doyle told me, yesterday, that he works for The Fat Man now on some of his trips to the West of Ireland.

Ray Doyle has had a lot of unusual jobs in his time. First time I met him he was selling bananas. He had a yellow van, then, and a big banana of a curved smile, and you met him travelling too fast along the narrow roads leading from the most remote shops.

After the bananas he went into showbusiness for a while, owning one-half of a bad showband with a drunk drummer and a gaudy coach that guzzled as much diesel as the drummer guzzled porter. They never made the big time. In fact, as Ray told me later, they just about made enough to keep the drummer drunk and the van rolling. They played the smaller halls, for the smaller monies, and eventually they disappeared altogether. I lost touch with Ray Doyle for years.

Next time I saw him was at Puck Fair. He was selling ice cream from a little red van, chiming ice-cream music, parked almost under the Puck. The ice-cream, remarkably, tasted excellent. While I was eating my cornet Ray Doyle was telling me that he was now based in Liverpool. He said he had 15 little red vans like the one I was standing beside. He gave the impression that he was becoming a millionaire selling ice-cream to half the population of England.

He had picked up a glass eye in the process, I noticed, and an interesting scar on the left cheekbone. The drunk drummer, he recalled, had given up the drink, joined the clergy, and was now a bishop in Africa. Ray Doyle laughed at the thought. Ray Doyle was always laughing, times bad or good. His smile never forgot that it once sold bananas. Same shape.

I met Ray Doyle again last week in Roscommon. He was sitting at the bar of the smallest hotel in a town that we both knew very well when we were younger. He was not smiling. He was sitting behind a sour looking pint of Guinness and was gazing into it with his good eye and his glass eye, as if he could find the mysteries of life somehow unlocked in there. He didn't see me coming.

It was a cold day outside and he was wearing an expensive leather jacket, looking big and bulky as ever inside it. I approached him from his glass eye side and he didn't see me until I was right beside him. He was startled. It was an accidental meeting. He wasn't just startled either, he was a little bit ashamed. There was no bright red ice-cream van chiming outside the wet hotel door.

After a little while Ray Doyle told me that he was working for The Fat Man. He was taking a break, he said, just for a few minutes, because he just had a bad experience in the room where The Fat Man was trading. A very bad experience.

Did I remember Phyllis, asked Ray Doyle? Yes, I said, very definitely, I remember his girlfriend from the years he owned one-half of a bad showband. She had been very gorgeous and nice, I said, a lovely big long girl with red hair. I said that most of the lads at the time thought that himself and Phyllis would eventually marry. Ray Doyle said he thought so too but in the end she got wit and jilted him. He said, reflectively, that the closest they ever came to getting married was in 1973, in July.

The drummer had been sober that month and they had a summer residency in a ballroom on the coast, beside a long strand. So they didn't have to drive the guzzler of a van. They made good money that month, off the road, in the midsummer resort. One Saturday evening he took Phyllis into town to buy her an engagement ring. He had £200 in his pocket. They walked the street hand in hand but, even then, Phyllis said she didn't want to get engaged. So he brought her into the ring shop and he bought her a charm bracelet instead.

It was nine carat gold. There were three charms on it. One was a rabbit, one was a little wishing well, and one was a little anchor. All in gold. It cost

as much as the ring would have cost. They were very happy that day, said Ray Doyle, and that night too, walking on the strand near the ballroom, hearing the waves fall down on the sand and listening to his own band (or 50 percent anyway) playing to the beat of a sober drummer.

One of the tunes they played, said Ray Doyle, was a popular number of the time called 'The Story Of My Life.' I remembered that one, I said. Ray Doyle bought me a drink. Ray Doyle told me that he had been working for The Fat Man for a while, since ice-cream went out of fashion. He drove The Fat Man to all the small upstairs rooms in all the small hotels and he sat near the window, away from the table a good distance, while The Fat Man did his trading.

I suppose, said Ray Doyle, you could call me a Minder. Even a Heavy. I said it was as good a trade as any. Anyway you can earn a bob or two is the way to earn it.

Ray Doyle said The Fat Man was doing great business in the West just because times were hard. He said that mostly he read the newspapers while The Fat Man was working with people, so he wouldn't even see their faces. Some of the women were very embarrassed, coming to The Fat Man, and they always haggled just a little bit. It wasn't a nice business at all. He wasn't fond of it. But you had to take what you could get.

Ray Doyle said he was taking a break, when I met him, because he had a shock about 20 minutes earlier. The two young children with the woman who came into the room to The Fat Man had been crying. That was why he looked at them, over the top of the newspaper, the Mother and two children standing in front of The Fat Man's table. The Mother was wearing dark glasses. A lot of the women wore dark glasses in that room and hers wasn't the first battered face he had seen either. The children looked abused as well, clinging to her overcoat.

He thought there was something familiar about her, as, like many of the woman before her, she began to sell her bits of gold to The Fat Man, her bracelets and her wedding ring and her engagement ring. And her charm bracelet. It was the charm bracelet he identified her by, as The Fat Man held it in his fat hand, with its rabbit. And its wishing well. And its anchor. To The Fat Man she was just another Irish wife fallen on harsh times. Bills to pay. A bad husband, by all appearances, two children to feed. She was the grist to the mill of The Fat Man.

Ray Doyle said that he hid behind his newspaper. She didn't see him at all. Ray Doyle said that The Fat Man gave her just £190 for all her rings, all her bangles, and for the charm bracelet with the rabbit, the anchor, and the wishing well. Ray Doyle said he needed a drink after she had come. He had to ask permission from The Fat Man. He looked at me straight in the face and there was as much life in his glass eye as there was in the other one.

The Deadly Powers Of Clay

he names of the people that lived far up above the river valley in the airy rocklands were different. The sons were often called classical kinds of names, unusual in rural Ireland in any era.

> **It happened, the inquest was told, because the roadway, at just this point, was covered with slippery clay, almost like a sheet of ice.**

There were several men called Aeneas, there was a Julius, there was even a Homer who died in 1987 at an advanced age, and was finally buried under a headstone which he himself had erected and carved a full decade earlier. "Pray," (he had written) "for the immortal soul of Homer McCormack who died in God's good time peacefully, if a little reluctantly."

The mountain people were always different in their ways in things like this. In every generation there was more than one or two of them that others would call a mad kind of genius. And they all had the kind of springy walk and far-seeing eyes which are given to races who live in high places.

The people who lived below them on the lower slopes were as different in ethos as if they had come from a different continent. Their farms were beaten out of the sticky gray clay, viscous and heavy underfoot, yet strangely fertile, which you often get under the Western mountains. These men and women even looked different.

When you saw them in town they were still walking heavy of foot, as if pulling their Wellington boots out of the clinging clay. They were solidly industrious, sturdy, conservative with level eyes under flat caps. They always called their daughters Mary and Bridget, after our Blessed Mother and the Irish saint, the sons Patrick and Michael and John, and they stuck

together as a community exactly like the clay on which they lived. Hit one Mullaghbawn man, it is said still, and you hit them all.

Talk to one of them, maybe about farming things, and he will always begin his sentences with "we," while the mountainy man above him against the sky, a one man republic, will always begin with "I." It is subtle but telling enough in the context of the story I have to tell.

And the people along the riverbanks, only a few families along the quick silver flow, they are different again. They live on the loamy land, the mixture of the sandy debris from the pathway of the older rivers of ages past and the diluted clays from above. They live with the music of the water, the whispering of the willow bushes trailing their green fingers in the flow, the sighing of the winds from far above. They are a mobile and fluid people, bright in their eyes and in their heads, laughing more in one day than the claymen might in a lifetime, not seeing the dark side of life like the men of the mountains either, but apparently, always the morning sun.

These are the families that produce the musicians and dancers of the valley, the best actors in the amateur dramatic society productions each winter, the liveliest mummers at Christmas, the biggest bonfires on St. John's night in midsummer. Then it is that the sparks and music fly with the claymen on the outskirts of the merriment, sitting together on the green grass, drinking careful bottles of stout and communally thinking that the river-folk are half-mad, but sure, harmless.

It happened last summer, around that very celebratory bonfire, that a clayman and a mountainy man both fell in love with a girl from the river who was playing the fiddle for the festivities. Her name was Marion Madden and she came from a family of singers and dancers. Late in the night she threw her head back, with its flaming red curls capturing all the firelight , and she sang *She Moved Through the Fair*. It was moving enough to capture and shake even the sticky stolid heart of the oldest son of the McLoughlins, already balding at 25, his muscles bulging from digging and tilling the claylands.

And it lit a fire altogether in the head of Theo Fitzsimons from the very highest farm up in the mountains. Theo was typical of his breed. He had come down to the bonfire celebrations on his huge 750 cc motorcycle, in gleaming leathers, a red cravat around his neck, a gleaming silver helmet. He was 27 and a silversmith in one of the best craft shops in the region. His work had won awards both nationally and internationally. He was quite wild, mad for excitement, speed, drink, women, motorbikes, and above all, with his long white fingers, for the silver that he could craft into the intricate Celtic patterns the tourists loved.

He had come down to the bonfire with two bottles of vodka in the panniers of his bike, shared with all and sundry, where the other men had brought ordinary porter and beer in dark bottles. And on this night, and given his nature, maybe only for this night, Theo too went in pursuit of Marion Madden.

It was a cruelly uneven contest. While the poor clayman sat in the shadows, wanting and hurting, and drinking beer that turned warmly sour in his mouth at every taste, the bold Theo swaggered up to sit beside Marion Madden, to throw his arm casually around her, to give her a swig from his sparkling bottle, to sing with her after a little while, the two voices blending like honey, and finally, as the bonfire died down towards its red core, and the warm night embraced them all, to take Marion away up the mountains on his motorbike. It must have been agony for the poor clayman to hear the great beast of a bike snarling away at high speed up into the quiet places where lovers go.

It is a week later, at the beginning of July, and I do not know if Marion and Theo met again in the meantime, or if they had plans to meet again, or anything like that. What I do know is that Theo was killed at the bottom of the mountain when his motorbike skidded. There was a right hand bend beside a bridge and his bike, normally so surely ridden, even at speed, skidded. He broke his bold young neck.

It happened, the inquest was told, because the roadway, at just this point, was covered with slippery clay, almost like a sheet of ice. It might have been from the hooves of straying cattle, the inquest was told, but it seemed more than that, much more, almost like a deliberate smearing of the road just there. It would have taken several people working together, I have been told since, to put so much sticky clay on the road as was there when Theo died. But it is all a mystery.

The clayman McLoughlin was at Theo's funeral with his three brothers, all of whom looked exactly like him. They stood on the edge of the clay grave as the coffin was lowered down, their big hard hands molding their soft cloth caps like potter's clay, their blue eyes as innocent as those of angels.

One Word Leads To Another

t all began with a few words in the Pier View Bar on a Monday morning when a few of the hardier young fishermen were having a few pints before catching the tail of the roiling tide in the half-deckers flabbing lazily and bigbellied along the stone walls below them in the thin February sun. Some would be going out to lift lobster pots and others, further out, after whitefish.

They were talking loudly, in bursts of laughter, the way young men do after a weekend. If all the stories they were telling were even half accurate there was not a virgin left in Connacht after the weekend, and scarcely a pub that had Guinness or whiskey left over. Young men talk like that.

From the window of the bar they could also see the fish processing factory to the left of the Pier. Many of their wives, sisters and mothers worked there in white coated lines, their hairs in nets, processing the fish that the men hauled with hardship from the seas. A lot of work involved filleting and freezing the whitefish for furthering processing elsewhere, and some of the girls were also employed stuffing roll mop herrings into jars of marinade. That line was selling so well on the continent that many of the young girls in the region had been recently recruited to join the line. As the fishermen watched, a few minutes after 11 o'clock, a few of the girls came out for their coffee break. Six or seven of them, the newer employees from further away from the port, headed directly towards the bar to snatch a quick cup of coffee and a chocolate bar.

> **It would take only a few minutes at most for her to be served, and then she would be gone and Seamus knew that he would never have the courage to speak to her again.**

"I'm not leaving now anyway," said one of the fishermen. "You might have a better catch here than out on the cold ocean."

Margaret, the woman of the bar, was already making coffee as the girls approached. They came in through the door, animated, chattering, but just a little self-consciously as is the way of women entering bars in this place. None of them would have come in alone. You always needed to have a few others with you.

They came directly to the bar and those of them who knew the fishermen began instantly joking with them in the fluid Irish of that port. It had a sharp edge to it if you knew the language.

It deflated more than a few stories the young men had been telling earlier.

"You did not get too far with Deirdre even though you must have bought a gallon of Bacardi for her," said one girl to the young man who had been telling the most colorful stories about his weekend. Another was told, laughingly, that the shirt he had been wearing at the disco was so gaudy that everybody had been afraid to dance with him. It was good crack, harmless, just a few young men and women making the best of a hardy Monday morning.

One of the girls, a stranger, stood a few yards behind the others while they were paying for their coffees. None of the fishermen knew her. She had, in fact, only started at the factory that morning.

She was tall and dark, with the kind of Spanish face you often see along the west coast, liquid brown eyes, a kind of shy mouth. A few strands of her coal colored hair had escaped from the front of the hairnet she was wearing, and they lay on her forehead like curraghs resting on a white strand. She was smiling a little at the fun that was happening around her but not taking part. She had a £1 coin in her hand to pay for her coffee.

It was because of this that the quietest of the fishermen, a boy called Seamus Hernon who was only there because his older brother was his fishing partner, knew that she had just started that morning. The other girls paid for their coffee and snack bars at the end of each week when they were paid by the factory.

He made a special space for her at the bar and motioned to her to come up and get her coffee with his head. He smiled a quick smile. He is a shy boy, just past 20, and has trouble talking to girls. He's never part of the boasting on Monday mornings. He was only drinking a Coke.

The girl moved into the space beside him. She nodded acknowledgement of the small gesture. When she had moved into the space beside him they were behind the backs of others by a few feet, almost by themselves in a strange way.

Seamus is shy so he said nothing at all. You could see that the girl was equally shy. It would take only a few minutes at most for her to be served, and then she would be gone and Seamus knew that he would never have the courage to speak to her again.

He looked at her profile against the window. He cleared his throat two times and tried to talk but he was not able.

The girl was not looking at him but towards Margaret with the coffee pot and in seconds she would be gone. All around the pair of them nobody else was having any trouble at all in communicating and having a bit of crack.

Seamus at last made a huge effort. He was shaking a little from the excitement of it and his voice was not his usual when he reached over, just a few inches and gently touched the girl's elbow. She turned her head slowly and smiled at him without saying anything. The smile came with a sort of question.

He tasted the Coke in his mouth and swallowed one last time and he said, "Don't be mad at me but I'd like to pay for your coffee. I think it is your first day." There were a few beads of sweat on his forehead when he said it.

The girl smiled one quick smile and she said just, "That would be very nice of you." And then she said, "Thanks," in Irish.

And then she took the coffee and bar and walked back to the end of the bar with her friends.

It was only a few words. Twenty words altogether, if you count them. It was enough. A few weeks later they went out together for a few drinks on the Friday evening. They talked a lot, maybe 28,000 words altogether. A few months later they were engaged.

They were married a few days ago.

Liz Taylor And The Nuns

here is a convent away out far in the West, close to the ragged edge before the map turns Atlantic blue, and the nuns there pray publicly every morning and evening in their shadow-dusted cloisters for the happy repose of the soul of the late lamented Richard Burton, the film star, and for his former wife, Elizabeth Taylor.

It was the biggest scandal in the history of the convent until the infinitely bigger one surfaced a year later.

I have heard these prayers myself a time or two, silvery tinkles at twilight, from upraised pale innocent faces, turned towards heaven. To look at the nuns there, at those prayerful times, one would never imagine at all that one of them, long ago, was directly responsible for the scandal which blazed across the headlines of the world when Taylor and Burton first fell into their long and passionate love war.

You will remember that it started on the film set of 'Cleopatra' with Taylor in the starring role and Burton, his great Welsh voice ringing like an Angelus bell, playing Mark Anthony. You will remember that their love scenes in that film, echoing the private passion, were so searing that one cameraman afterwards remarked that Burton's plastic armour began to melt and the lenses of the cameras steamed over. You will remember also that it was a major scandal of the time because there were spouses involved.

It's hard to imagine that the nuns praying in the convent in the West were responsible for all that. But they were. At least one of them was and they all pray because they don't rightly know which of them it was. Most believe that it was Sister Bernadette, but there is also a body of opinion which blames Mother Patricia.

The community is not certain because Sol Zimmerman's letter, all those years ago before the scandal broke, was not specific enough for the culprit to be identified without any reasonable doubt.

I'll start at the beginning. Sol Zimmerman was the most famous theatrical wig maker of his generation. He visited the convents in the West of Ireland every autumn to buy the lustrous locks of hair willingly surrendered by the young nuns before taking their final vows. Sol Zimmerman always said that this hair was the finest in the world.

It was invariably long and glossy, had never been permed or tampered with, and had grown in the healthiest environment on earth. Each Fall, when Sol came calling, he was brought into the convent parlour, given tea and cake in the most delicate of china cups, and then was shown the special walnut box full of the lovely tresses of the new nuns. There are several grades of hair for theatrical wigs and the top grade is called Superfine A. I have it on the best authority that the locks from this convent way out West were always Superfine A, and Sol Zimmerman, a man of honor, always paid top prices for such a product.

There were a lot of vocations to the convent then, the box in the parlour writhed with glossy locks of loveliness, almost all of it inkblack, thick, and gently curling and Sol would pay as much for the lot as the nuns would get later in the autumn for a bullock off their farm. He wore several gold rings on his long white hands, did Sol, and he would run his fingers through the box of hair, almost purring with pleasure.

And then, you see, one particular Fall Sol Zimmerman came, greatly more excited than usual, so that he clattered the china cup against his saucer in the parlour as he told Mother Xavier, who always conducted the business affairs of the Sisters, that he had just won the contract to supply all the wigs for 'Cleopatra.'

His rings flashed in circles under a disapproving statue of Michael the Archangel killing the Serpent, as he said this was the contract which would make his fortune. And he needed all the Superfine Grade A hair he could get, especially the locks that were black as coal for Cleopatra herself. And Mother Xavier, for it had been a good season for vocations, triumphantly opened the box and there were the inkblack young pure locks of all the young nuns who are silvered now, praying morning and evening. And Sol Zimmerman actually kissed her hand! Unheard of! Even for a theatrical wig maker. It was the biggest scandal in the history of the convent until the infinitely bigger one surfaced a year later.

Because, you see, about a year later, when the film was shot and the scandal was still shooting, Sol Zimmerman sent a letter of thanks to the convent, in his own handwriting, saying that the two wigs he had made for Miss Taylor had been "totally superb" and he added, probably forgetting that he wasn't writing to theatrical people, "it is said that it was the coal black coiffure of Ms. Taylor that drove Mr. Burton out of his mind with love. I thank you from the depths of my heart."

Which is now why, morning and evening, the sisters pray for Richard Burton and Elizabeth Taylor. And why, hearing and seeing and knowing the story, one is driven to musing about the mysteries of life and love.

A Real Life Suspense Story

he cinema was on the Diamond. It was a typical Fifties cinema with dead red bulbs alongside the live ones defining its single entrance into a small foyer with a worn carpet and old film posters on the wall.

The posters for the three films that were shown weekly, starting at 8 p.m. sharp, always looked garishly bright and promising when compared with the fading ones of the giants of the past… when Edward G. Robinson was young and Jimmy Cagney in his prime behind a magnum revolver, when Sophia Loren was so beautiful she illuminated the entire wall between the small town's realities and the celluloid world you could view from the balcony for five shillings; from the stalls for 3/6d.

In a small town the regular filmgoers quickly become known. They are the ones that go to every change of program, wet or dry weather outside. They are the lovers for the back seats, the genuine cinema addicts, the pensioners. And there are always, also, the lost and the lonely ones, those who do not drink in the pubs around the Diamond and are killing the evenings.

One of these, in this cinema, in this town, I remembered best of all. He was nicknamed Hitchcock. It was cruelly apt on several fronts. He had the portly outline and porcine face of the Master of Suspense. He walked into the cinema every third evening at precisely five minutes to eight with the same short stabbing steps on small feet. And there was something about his eyes which, when you looked closely at him, made you think, as with the real Hitchcock, that there was probably a thin man behind there somewhere, darkly watching the world.

Maybe they called him Hitchcock, most of all, because he had killed his father.

Small towns have long memories. Small towns have a hundred storytellers as gifted, orally at least, as Hitchcock ever was. I was not long in the town before I heard on a pub stool one night the true Hitchcock story. The storyteller was the town's tailor, a leanly yellow-faced man who loved his Guinness and probably needed it too.

I did not believe the end of his life story, either, when I heard it only a few years ago. He died because of his trade. It seems that tailors, when threading their needles for the fine stitchwork on suits, always lick the thread they are using to get a sharper point for threading the fine needles. Over the years a million little fibers go down into their stomachs. Sometimes these form a fibrous ball inside... believe it or not... and these can eventually kill them.

That is what killed the yellow-faced one with the long fingers who looked out through the damp pub window with me as the small cinema emptied out its seats onto the street one Friday night. We saw the outline of Hitchcock. I made the connection and he dryly said that others had seen it already, that the nickname was well affixed for years, and that it was indeed the right one for the man that was in it.

"Why?" That's what I said.

"That fellow," he said, "killed his father."

"Did he murder him?" That's what I asked as Hitchcock, with the wind whipping at his gabardine coat-tails, headed down the street with those short nimble steps that so often propel portly men. It was raining a little.

"Yes," said the tailor, "he murdered him in cold blood." He took a sip out of his Guinness, the story teller, and he added, like a born story teller, "And he never served even one day in jail for it either, isn't that a wonder now?"

Hitchcock's father, he told me then, slowly and with relish, had been a big man in the town. He had owned a wholesale business and a hardware yard. The family lived in a big stone two-story house on the very edge of the town. It was the first house in the town to have a telephone installed, that's how big they were, and they had a Humber car as well with a gold-painted line along the length of it.

Big people, biggest employers in the town in hard times, a wife who played the organ in the chapel, two daughters and Hitchcock was the only son, destined to take over the whole empire. He worked in the place, said the tailor, from the time he was four years of age, running messages through the shop for his father. The father doted on him but was firm with him. The mother spoiled him. As well as being the only boy he was also the youngest in the family.

The tailor remembered going into the shop one time, when he was very young himself, and Hitchcock - though he was not called that then - was in charge of the shop at the age of seven years.

"The war was on at the time and cigarettes were like gold dust. My father had sent me down to the shop to ask, even beg for a Large Player for him. He was desperate, a heavy smoker. I was at school with the young fellow so

I went in and I asked him. I had the money in my fist from my father. He looked at me with those square eyes of his and went into the back office and I could hear him talking to his father. He came out with the packet of Players in his hand. I offered the money. 'No,' says he 'my father says not to take any money, these are a present for your father as a good customer.'

"When I brought the cigarettes back my father was cross instead of delighted. The cute old shopkeeper saved himself a fortune that way when the cigarettes were rationed. Nobody would take charity in those times, you see, so he knew if he gave the one packet to my father for nothing then he would never come back again asking for more. If he had taken the money for them, then I'd have been sent back to the shop over and over again."

But it was years later, said the tailor, before Hitchcock murdered his father. Everybody knew exactly what happened because there were people in the shop when it happened. And it was grisly enough.

What happened was that Hitchcock was carrying a gallon drum of oil across the shop when he dropped it and the sticky stuff covered the whole floor. Some people got it on their shoes. The father gave the son a good slap on the ear, "like we all got at the time and then a kick up the backside" and ordered him to clean the mess up. And did I know what happened next?

"Hitchcock went out to the store. He came back in a couple of minutes and he had a double-barreled shotgun in his hands. They sold guns, too, the labels were still hanging from the trigger guard.

"He had his pockets full of cartridges. His face was as white as a sheet and he was cursing his father for making a fool of him, hitting him before the people of the town. He let fly at the old fellow, behind the counter, at about ten feet and down he went. That was both barrels now. Then he reloaded the gun, talking to himself about being shamed, and went behind the counter and fired two more shots into his father. And he was reloading again when James Treacy, the yard foreman, came in and jumped the counter and wrestled the gun away from him. That's what happened. My own mother was in the shop at the time buying a box of blue tacks. She claimed afterwards she never got over it."

That's what the tailor told me.

"Sure he could have got life for that," is what I said. "He would have too," said the tailor, "except he was only ten years of age at the time. He was a month short of his eleventh birthday."

They were big people. He was sent away to a special school in the north of England for the rest of his education. The shop was sold and he did not come back to the big house until about 10 years ago. It was empty, the mother dead, the sisters gone. He lives there by himself now.

"He seldom goes out," said the tailor whose trade was killing him softly, "except to the pictures."

Down All The Dancehall Days

am looking at the Ballygar notes on Page 22 of the Connacht Tribune and I saw with delight and amazement that they held the Ballygar Carnival again this first week in August. And who topped the bill in the big marquee one of the festival nights but the irresistible Daniel O'Donnell!

There was a time, a simpler time, when the great Carnival Marquees sprouted up like giant mushrooms each summer in virtually every parish in Ireland.

Ballygar Carnival, the eighth wonder of the world, combined with Daniel, the ninth and indeed tenth, represents an earth-quaking occasion in the world of entertainment. I know Daniel played a packed Carnegie Hall recently, but he knows, and I know, and many of you know, that the real pinnacle of success is to top the bill at the Ballygar Carnival.

(Caty, oh my darling Caty, set the scene for us. Create for us a four-pole marquee, of a summer's evening, a full moon blazing, and the whole small town of Ballygar agog with agogery and mad excitement, people streaming from all the streets to pack the marquee, with its sprung maple floor, with fans of Daniel O'Donnell, with fans of life, as she used to be lived, with fans of the great magnificent Ballygar Carnival, the eighth wonder of the world.)

There was a time, a simpler time, when the great Carnival Marquees sprouted up like giant mushrooms each summer in virtually every parish in Ireland. The '60s were the peak of a craze, running in tandem with the showband industry, which saw Marquee Carnivale... often called just that...

> **And the singer, a big handsome guy, is singing the big hit of the season in a white suit, gold rings on both hands, wearing very little Brylcreem.**

running right throughout the summer nights. The big showbands came, the crowds came, the money flowed like strong porter, the porter flowed too in the local pubs, the moons flamed in the skies over harvested hay, over the greenly growing aftergrass of peace, to the sound of music percolating through canvas, to the revelries of Carnival. Ah, but those were the days and nights.

But nowadays, as far as I know, the great Ballygar Carnival is the only big carnival left. The giant mushrooms of canvassed carnival faded from the rural scene as fast as they rose, replaced by singing pubs, nite spots in the towns and cities, discos. But not from Ballygar. This last and greatest outpost of the Canvas Carnivals this summer staged its 47th carnival with, says Ballygar notes in the Connacht Tribune, "the country's top entertainers and music tastes to suit all ages." It's 47 years old! It's as old as I am myself, for God's sake, and going infinitely stronger.

I remember Ballygar Carnival when both it and I were about coming of age. Daniel O'Donnell would still have been in diapers. I'm arriving into the small town at about nine o'clock in the evening with two wild young men from Roscommon, where I was working at the time, writing small stories, and we had a big long Vauxhall car that had something wrong with its fuel line, nothing wrong at all with our own fuel lines, about a jar of Brylcreem on top of our three heads, maybe the equivalent of about $15 between our six trouser pockets. Oh, but that was wealth at the time, I remember, remember it well.

And I remember the whole little town was washed brightly with paint and bunting, a real air of celebration, and we had trouble parking the big beast of a car, for all the traffic that was in town.

Then we were into the nearest pub - I have never been there since - almost in the shadow of the marquee, where a band called The Rhythm Boys from Donegal (too!) were playing... while the real Rhythm Boy was still sucking his thumb in his cot... and we have two pints of Harp each, just because the women wouldn't dance with you in those days if you showed any signs of drink. And the Men's Committee might not even let you into the

marquee, and then we were queuing up to the little paybox, our Brylcreem brilliantined by the raw colory bulbs, and then we were inside the tented belly of the great Ballygar Carnival, and the whole world was there. Quicksteps, jives, old time waltzes, an occasional set dance, and girls in their summer dresses.

Now even at the great Ballygar Carnival, in those days, cosmopolitan and all as it was, the catchment area would not have included the continent of India. And even though MacConnell was already suave and widely traveled, having been both to Dublin and Belfast already, he had never laid eyes on such dusky beauty as that represented by a young nurse, her name indelibly imprinted in the area below the Brylcreem, called Jeya Patel. And she is there because she nursed in London with a Ballygar nurse. And she is very, very beautiful. And she is laughing at all my jokes, her head thrown back, and I'm a very happy little man for an hour of light fantastic great Ballygar Carnivalia.

It's amazing the basic errors even suave Irishmen can make when they are 21 years old. We are living, the Jeya Patel and I, explosions of whirl and twirl, bodies already perfectly in tune. And then, because there is space there, I move up in front of the bandstand, where I never ever moved thereafter throughout my dancing bachelordom, up against the polished shoes of the Jitterbugging Rhythm Boys from Donegal. (Daniel is still sleeping.) And the singer, a big handsome guy, is singing the big hit of the season in a white suit, gold rings on both hands, wearing very little Brylcreem.

And the song is called Things. Remember it? "Things," sings the Rhythm Boy bastard, "like a walk in the park." "Things," croons the sonofabitch, "like a kiss in the dark." And, so quickly I miss it, he winks his left eye at my lovely Patel from India, and I'm one dead turkey. After the tune ends they exchange one quick burst of whispers between bandstand and sprung maplefloor, and then she tells me she has to go back and meet her friend. Ah, I remember, I remember very well.

An hour later I'm standing in the debris of the dance, the ball over, and the boys are packing up their instruments for the next gig. The crooner is nowhere to be seen at all. He is up to things like a walk in the park, a kiss in the dark. I'm standing there alone, all alone, under my melting Brylcreem thatch, and I feel 40 years older and tireder than I feel this minute, and all the bright bulbs of the great Ballygar Carnival seemed suddenly dimmer.

But all that is so long ago, far away. It is with undimmed pleasure that I report that those bulbs are still burning bright in Ballygar, the floor is still sprung maple, the marquee hugely dominating the summer streets, the air of the carnival full of music to suit all tastes, new mown hay, freshly pulled pints, young blood dancing the nights. And Daniel O'Donnel has grown up. Rhodes may have lost its wonder, but Ballygar Carnival has not. I like that.

Strolling Down Memory Lane

Her name was Shauna.

I had forgotten that. Shauna.

I had just remembered a strange little sheepskin coat, fleece out, worn out to the hide at the two sleeve that showed wiry little wrists and small grubby, hard, wee hands. And her brown eyes I remembered, often with tears in them, when I knew her. She was about ten then and she was a blitz kid from Belfast.

I'd forgotten about them altogether because I was only a kid myself then, younger than her, forgotten about them altogether until she came into the newsroom to meet me the other evening. She has been living in the area for years and had heard me on the radio. Because of the Northern twang in my voice she wondered if I was the wee Cormac that once sat in the same desk as her at primary school, so close we could smell the cold morning chalky smell of each other, miles apart because I was the teacher's son and from the place and she was a blitz kid. And from Belfast.

"You were good to me," is what she said when she came in. "You were only a wee fellow but you were good to me. One time you gave me a marshmallow at lunchtime and another time you made me my own paper boat. And your mother was always good to me the year I was there."

She made a beautiful woman, the Shauna, a beautiful, tall, mature woman now with a mane of silver hair, the brown eyes, a silky complexion, the cut of a wealthy lifestyle about her clothes, her bearing, her way of talking.

She's a career woman now, in business in Limerick, married, four grown children. I told her, speaking out my small shock, that I only remembered the cold small hurt smell of her, the coat with the fleece worn away at the sleeves, streaky tears on the cheeks, a damp nose.

She laughed at that.

We went out and had coffee together. I confessed I did not remember giving her the marshmallow nor building the paper boat. She remembered it very well.

When Belfast was blitzed by the German bombers, she said, their whole street was blasted to bits. They were lucky to survive it, her mother and herself under the table with furniture piled on top of it, her father and brother in the coal-shed at the bottom of the garden when it was over. She picked up a bit of cloth that came from her brother's gabardine overcoat, so small, only about the size of a box of matches and burnt at the edges. The bodies were never found.

There was a blur after that, a lot of fat women and old men in uniforms and with torches and notebooks, and that was how she became a blitz kid and was sent to the pastoral safety of Fermanagh, to stay there for years. Her mother had TB. She died about 11 months after the blitz. So she was orphaned as well that night in Belfast when the bombs fell first. I think that Belfast was bombed several times, actually - I'm no historian - but this night, she said, was definitely the first night.

She was awful unhappy in the parish where I was so happy as the teacher's son with my Mammy and Daddy alive, and a shop with bright windows late at night, big jars of sweets in it, and biscuits too. What I never knew was that my Daddy and Mammy kept almost all the blitz kids in our house for three or four nights until they had been placed elsewhere. And what I never knew was that my mother, as the local teacher, was a voluntary placement person, cycling around the parish getting families to agree to take the frightened small ones from Belfast.

And what I never knew was that Shauna, wee Shauna with one black case (she told me), slept in our rocking cradle in the kitchen for the time she was in our house. It was big enough for her, and Sandy would rock her asleep because she was crying all the time. And, like with us, his own kids, there was always a little penny bar of chocolate under her pillow in the mornings she was in our house.

Together the Shauna and I silently remembered the Sandy and Mary.

But Shauna had to go because some boy called Joe who only had one hand stayed at our house. The strange thing is I don't remember Joe at all. That, said Shauna, was because Joe was a Protestant and after a month or so, she

And the worst parts of it were that nobody in that house ever hugged you like her Mammy did or my Mammy did, or tousled your hair like her Daddy did with a hand that was still oil-stained deeply from working on marine engines in Belfast.

knew, he went to a Protestant house and to a Protestant school in Enniskillen. And she had traveled from Belfast in a bus with Joe and they had talked to each other a bit. He was the first Protestant she ever talked to.

She was unhappy all the time in the farmhouse where she was. They were great people - I knew them too - but they were farmers, very, very Catholic altogether. I knew that too, and so hardworking that automatically every hand, however small, was pressed into the family service.

And she never felt a part of the family. In the night at the Trimmings of the Rosary, which were awful long, she would be kneeling on the stone floor against a red-painted plain kitchen chair and the Mammy of that house God rest them all would pray in a singy-songy voice for Shauna's dead Daddy and for her brother Pearse and for her Mammy who was very sick in Belfast.

And after school she had to go picking stones out of a field near the house, even in the winter. That was her job because she could not milk cows like the natural daughter of the house, and she was afraid of even the calves and the hens and the ducks and the dogs.

Sure she was from Belfast. And the worst parts of it were that nobody in that house ever hugged you like her Mammy did or my Mammy did, or tousled your hair like her Daddy did with a hand that was still oil-stained deeply from working on marine engines in Belfast. And the worst part of it all was, and it was accidental, that one winter morning she heard a fierce squealing outside and she looked out the window after scraping the pine tree frosted pane and saw the Daddy was killing the fat pig. He hit it in the head with a wooden hammer and had a spiked thing under its chin, and then he cut its throat so that the blood all splashed out on the yard, the legs of the pig still jerking. And Shauna never forgot that.

It seems that chocolate things were scarce in that good but austere house. That's why Shauna remembered one lunch time when the wee teacher's son sitting beside her in short trousers put his hand in his paper

bag and gave her a marshmallow. The chocolate shell on the top was cracked into a whole lot of bits and she picked them away slowly, one by one, until the white marshmallow was there by itself, sitting softly on the top of the chocolate coated biscuit underneath, and she can still taste it. And another time the teacher's son made her a paper boat just before playtime so that she could sail it down the drain outside the school. Amazing the things you remember!

And I did not.

"The way you describe that marshmallow," I said the other evening, "if I had it in a brown bag now I wouldn't give it to you at all at all, I'd eat it myself."

And we chuckled at that, the two of us, sitting in the coffee shop, side by side, like when we were wee. And then we went back to our work.

I hugged the Shauna outside the office. For a whole lot of reasons. There were tears in her brown eyes again, like I did remember, and maybe in mine too.

And would you believe that underneath the elegant womanly aroma of what she is today, I still caught the sensory memory of a wee girl smell of worn sheepskin coat, cold morning, drying tears, chalk, loss and lonesomeness?

An Unusual Culinary Treat

I had a meal which included spinach yesterday. The spinach was entirely to my taste, not overdone, redolently green, herbaceous rather than vegetable, nestling up against three new seasoned potatoes on the right hand side of the meat. I do not eat spinach often. When I do I think of Lizzie Cooney.

But Lizzie passes the spuds and the lettuce and the scallions and the cabbage, carrots, parsnips, the peas on their trellis, the beans, likewise, the small beetroot. She passes them all and heads for the waste lot just inside the ditch at the end of the garden.

Her head is on one side as she stands in the door of her own house beside Lough Corrib. It is a Mayo afternoon heavy with the sound of young and busy bees and old and lazy frogs. Buzz melds with croak and the belly of the earth is full of hungry roots pushing growth into the midsummer humidity. You can almost see the grass growing.

I know Lizzie well. I have known her for years. In the old days she was postmistress of the local small office with its manual telephone switchboard.

"Lizzie," I would ring from Galway, "I'm looking for 16." The telephone numbers in the villages had only two digits then, sometimes only one.

"You'll not get him on 16," she might say. "I saw him going down the village a half-hour ago. I'd say he's closer to 28. Will I try it for you?"

"Thanks Lizzie. You have a heart of corn."

They say the telephone service has improved in this state in the last

20 years. In a way it has. But there was a heart there in the old days and a human element which is missing now. Reporters loved this human element. You became friendly with the postmasters and the postmistresses with their little switchboards and their immense knowledge.

Lizzie said to me one time when I rang, "The Long Fellow went out in the rowboat at seven this morning. He caught three trout. Two of them were striddlies (minnows) but one of them was nearly as big as himself. Nearly as ugly, too!"

The Long Fellow was General DeGaulle, enjoying a Mayo holiday. Readers loved tidbits like that about the rich and famous. The headline the next day, thanks to Lizzie, read "Big Man-Tiny Trout!" and underneath, "Exclusive By Cormac MacConnell." And readers wrote in afterwards complaining about the General not throwing back the minnows. All good, clean, harmless fun.

Anytime I was passing I would drop a box of Black Magic in to Lizzie. She had a sweet tooth as well as a similar nature, and chocolates were a real treat.

So on this day I'm passing and it is the half-day in the post office, and myself and the mandatory box of Black Magic find Lizzie in the back garden with a enamel basin under her arm. We exchange pleasantries and them she asks me to join Johnny and herself for the lunch, "and I'll give you something to eat that you never ate before, so I will."

"I've eaten many's the quare yoke in my time, Lizzie."

"Not this dish boy, I'll bet. Watch me now."

And into the garden we go together. Her husband Johnny, a lorryman with a hardware shop in the village, was also a handy man with a spade, and they had a good, plain, honest vegetable garden. But Lizzie passes the spuds and the lettuce and the scallions and the cabbage, carrots, parsnips, the peas on their trellis, the beans, likewise, the small beetroot. She passes them all and heads for the waste lot just inside the ditch at the end of the garden.

There's just weeds here alongside a heap of stalks from the potatoes that Johnny has already dug. Thistles and docks and briars trailing their thorned wicked fingers through everything. And nettles. Young nettles close to the ground, and old, strong nettles with angry serrated edges full of sting power.

And it is before the nettles that Lizzie stops and leaves down her basin. And then, as I watch in some surprise, she reaches down with her bare hands and begins to pick the young nettles. She pulls them from the earth one by one, strips them of the leaves, green little fanged things, and discards the stalks.

"Lizzie, are you not being stung to death?"

"If you knew anything, boy, you'd know that if you have rheumatism in your fingers and hands there is not a better cure in the world than nettle stings. I'm getting burned a bit but it's doing me good."

(It is strange that the older people, to this day, describe a nettle sting as a "burn.")

She fills the basin without flinching. I follow her into the house. There is a pan of boiling water atop the gleaming Stanley range. It is, she tells me, slightly salted.

She quickly rinses the young nettle leaves under the tap and flings then into the water. They are cooked inside 10 minutes. She strains them and puts a knob of her own salted butter on top. Johnny arrives home for his lunch spot on time and there is trout from the lake... bigger than DeGaulle's... and new spuds and the young nettles. They taste just like the spinach I had yesterday, only somehow more earthily wholesome. I've never had them since and maybe never will again because Lizzie went to heaven maybe five or six years ago.

I was at the wake. Her white little hands were joined together around a Rosary Beads on her breast. They did not look rheumatic or twisted at all.

I asked one of the neighbors afterwards if the arthritis ever got into Lizzie's fingers. "No," she said, "not at all. Wasn't she knitting up to a week before she died and never dropped a stitch." Old wives' remedies? Young nettles. I tasted them with my spinach and thought that there are strange interconnections altogether between the taste buds and the mental boxes that hold the files of our memories.

Shaftie O'Neill's Cuppa

en that were boys when I was a boy sat and talked to me as the New Year and the New Decade dawned. And for long after the bells rang, and Auld Lang Syne was sung, we sat and talked. And talked. We were drinking the kind of good whiskey which, simultaneously, makes one feel old enough to be a philosopher, young enough to play hookey from school. Or rob an orchard, or fish for the brownest trout in the green pools of all our yesterdays.

And we did all that, aging men, sitting there in a circle of glasses and then somebody mentioned Shaftie O'Neill. "To think that he was as thick as the school wall," somebody said.

"Thicker," was my own contribution.

"I used to have tie his bootlaces for him, when he was 15 years of age," said somebody else, almost with awe. "Well," says Jimmy Meehan, the wisest of us all, "the half of England is queuing up to tie those same shoelaces."

"And if I know Shaftie, he's still wearing the same boots too," was what Mick Boyle said.

And he probably is too. We easily recalled that Shaftie O'Neill was the maverick of our particular school class. He was a wild-eyed boy from the back of the mountain, corduroy trousers bent at the knee, bony wrists shooting out, big black boots, invariably trailing their long laces. An unfocused but friendly smile, uneven teeth and an almost incredible inability to learn anything at all from any teacher living.

He would have looked like the cruel caricature of a laboring Irishman in an English gutter paper - or in Punch magazine.

Every story we told about him, the other night, was funny as the next, all having punchlines, which reflected Shaftie as a classic fall guy. Jimmy Meehan recalled he once sent him to the hardware shop with fourpence to buy three bubbles for a spirit level. Shaftie went.

It is amazing how much any group knows, from many directions, about any associate of the past. One of us could say, for example, that it was his uncle who got him his first job after he left our school. Another remembered actually seeing Shaftie laboring on a site, one summer, near the Manchester United Grounds. He was up to his ears in yellow clay and happier than he'd ever seen him before. And, because I interviewed Shaftie ten years ago, in a big hotel in Dublin, I was able to tell the rest of the story.

It too started in a big hotel in the center of Manchester on a Friday afternoon. Shaftie, then in his early twenties, was at this stage out of the deep drains and was navvying to a Connemara plaster called Coleman Connelly (of whom we shall hear yet more). Anyway it was Shaftie's first day at the job, working eyeball to eyeball to a skilled tradesman and he was doing so badly and so awkwardly that Coleman Conneely, in a gesture which changed his life too, eventually told him to take a break, have a cigarette, cool down.

"That was some break," said Jimmy Meehan, the wisest of us.

Down the hotel corridor wanders Shaftie wearing his empty grin and a pair of well plastered overalls, his bootlaces, we all knew, would have been trailing behind him like a quartet of rattle snakes. He would have looked like the cruel caricature of a laboring Irishman in an English gutter paper - or in Punch magazine. "And maybe that was another break," said Jimmy Meehan.

At the end of the corridor, outside a commercial room, there was a large placard saying there was a Tea Blending seminar for the top tea traders of northern England. Shaftie admits to this day that the only word he saw was "Tea." "I always liked a mug of it." He shambled in rattle snakes trailing behind him.

It was the tea break at the seminar. Every tea expert in England, the master blenders, in three and even four piece suits, were gathered around white clothed tables, drinking the world's best teas.

A paddy in his working clothes looking for a cup of Tay in such a company was like an Englishman's dream come true. "Give the decent Pat

a cuppa," is what Shaftie heard someone say. He never forgot that. "Kenyan or Indian sir," queried another. There was a widespread laughter. "A good cup of tea, please, wherever it comes from," says Shaftie. "You look like a gentleman who would know the difference," says one of the laughing experts. "Aye," says Shaftie, "I would."

And that's how it started. As a laugh at the Paddy with the broken boots, the tea experts of England gave him tastes of several expensive teas and top class blends from all over the world. Great fun entirely. They then asked him which he preferred. Shaftie, without hesitation picked the best and most expensive they had. Then the next best. Then to take the talk away from them altogether he correctly identified the blends and found fault with several of them.

The boots passed from one foot to another. The laugh was on the experts. And it so happened that a man there from one of the major companies recognized the precious gift of Shaftie's perfect tea palate and offered him a job. No more broken boots. No more deep drains. We all know that today he is one of the best and most highly paid tea blenders in the whole world. "And I hear that they only allow him to work about thirty mornings a year and his mouth is insured for millions," said Jimmy Meehan, by far the wisest of us all.

There is a footnote. What happened to the plaster from Connemara who told Shaftie to take a break? Today, he is his chauffeur, his aide, a personal friend who travels the world with him wherever he goes.

Danny Went... Foot First

anny Devitt got drunk at his own funeral in Sligo on Friday. After the funeral, even though he was still whitefaced, and a bit weak from his hospital ordeal, he insisted on going back with all the mourners to the Elbow Inn.

> **"By Jesus," said Danny Devitt, "I'd be a poor man altogether if I didn't get drunk the day of my own funeral. It must be a world record."**

"You should go home for a lie down, Danny," said Hegarty to him as they were leaving the graveyard following the burial. "A small lie down would do you the power of good."

"By Jesus," said Danny Devitt, "I'd be a poor man altogether if I didn't get drunk the day of my own funeral. It must be a world record."

"Surely," said Hegarty, who had been physically supporting Danny all the morning, "Surely enough."

They put Danny sitting in the corner of the pub beside a middling fire. He insisted on paying for the first round, all whiskey. There were eight of them left where once there had been 15. But, said Donnelly after 40 years, eight survivors was a bloody good turnout.

"We are as hardy a crowd as any man could soldier with at his own funeral," Danny said. And he toasted them, a bit of color coming back into his thin face after the first drink. "Ye did the decent thing by me anyway."

"You didn't let us down either when the going was tough in Maloney's Field long ago and Christ above we couldn't let you down - above all men," said Joe Fitzpatrick. Joe had been full-back in that county football final so long ago in Maloney's field when these eight survivors formed the backbone of the only team from the parish to ever win a county senior title.

"Only for you Danny, to tell the truth, there'd have been no cup, no title and no glory," said Andy Leahy. "Sure that's the truth of it."

"Here's to the Harps," said Danny, raising his glass slightly, the two new crutches on either side of his chair like a small set of goalposts.

"Here's to the Harps forever."

And they drank that toast and a few more. The first blazing foundation of whiskey was followed by a fine saucy structure of porter inside while the surviving Harps plucked all the strings of sporting memory. And the brightest memory of all, from the dying seconds of that titanic final against Knockroe Slashers was the goal that Danny scored that won the cup.

"I can still see it, fresh as paint."

"Danny came in from the left, do you remember?"

"Like a lion."

"If Geoghegan had got him with that charge he'd have killed Danny."

"But he missed," said Danny. "He missed by a mile. I can still smell the sour sweat flying off him as he flew by."

"And then you buried the ball inside in the whitethorn bush behind the goal with the right foot... a golden goal," said Hegarty thumping the bar with excitement. "A golden goal."

And with this they all looked at Danny again, as an echo of their youth and pride, and their eyes slid down his thin smallness to the right trouser leg now pinned up neatly from a point just below the knee.

"Here's to my right foot," said Danny. "May it spend its days and nights kicking the arses of every divil in hell until I come up to rejoin it."

And they drank to that with great solemnity. And for a second there fell a proper funeral hush. Because, you see, they had all just attended the burial in holy ground of Danny's famous right foot, the most famous foot of the parish down all those years. I thought it was a remarkably warm and wonderful event myself, when I heard about it this week, and, under the local circumstances, entirely fitting.

What happened was that Danny's eldest son tragically drove a truck wheel over Danny's famous foot three weeks before, a freakish accident which required amputation. Any other foot would have gone subsequently into the hospital incinerator but the surgeon involved was a former Harps player himself, a cousin of Hegarty's, and special arrangements had been made.

These things still happen in the West, thank God. The arrangements involved cold storage and a special metal container until Danny was sufficiently recovered to join his old comrades for the burial.

The curate had seen nothing wrong in celebrating a special mass for Danny's recovery before the burial of the foot in the family plot. Andy Jameson had supplied a small class of a coffin. Everything had been tastefully done. Danny was home from hospital four days before the funeral and had been adamant that he would attend.

The curate had said prayers at the graveside, shook on holy water, the whole ritual, and Danny, pale but composed, had stood there and heard the ashes to ashes, dust to dust bit without as much as a tremor. It was, you know, a very special occasion, something unique.

Things got a bit maudlin in the pub later that evening, of course. The Harps were always a bit wild when they got together. Danny sang 'Danny Boy' naturally in fine fettle and about eight o'clock Hegarty recited 'Dangerous Dan McGrew' and Fitzpatrick went back to his own house, six doors from the pub, and came back with the fiddle.

That was lively. Much later Andy Leahy got Republican, like always, and was all for heading up to the border there and then, to start murdering Englishmen.

"I can feel a kind of tingling in the toes of the foot even though the foot is dead and buried," Danny Devitt said to them all sometime awful late in the night.

"Sure that foot, God rest it, has kept us tingling for the past 40 years and for the next 40 as well," said Hegarty. He raised his glass. "It will never be forgotten." A great obituary. A great occasion. I would love to have been there.

A Smuggler Goes Up In Smoke

Jemmy Smoke died last Wednesday evening. He was 79 and he died easy, warmly slipping away to heaven from his own bed about 10 minutes before midnight. One second he was there with them, inside the lamplit halo of the prayers for the dying, friends and family all about him in the bedroom overlooking the border, the river, the maze of roads of the other side. The next second he was gone.

His old accomplice, Mikey McGrath, getting up from his kneeling stiffly, wiping his eyes, said quietly he could have predicted it. It was always around midnight, down all the years, that Jemmy Smoke pulled his disappearing acts.

If you knew nothing at all about Jemmy Smoke you would have been amazed by many elements surrounding his death and funeral. When they laid him out for the final ritual and exhibition, for example, he was laid out the way I have never seen before. There, on his own bed, overlooking the border of his lifetime, Jemmy Smoke was dressed in a gray pullover and black trousers of the kind farmers always wore. And over that, supplied by Mikey McGrath, was the old trench coat, two or three sizes too big for him, its voluminous pockets, both inside and outside, all limp and empty. And, strangely, they rolled up his trouser legs up to mid-calf and they left his dead feet bare. Even attached to an old corpse the feet still looked slim, well-arched, almost feminine above ankles and calves that looked like those of a man of 30. "Even when he was an old fellow altogether," said Mikey, "he was as speedy as a ghost."

And if you knew nothing at all about Jemmy Smoke you would have been amazed and puzzled at the nature of the crowds that flocked to the house on the hill to pay their respects to the dead. Most of them came from the Northern side of the border and were of Smoke's own generation and of every class and creed. There were maybe a few more women than men and, strangely, most of them said approvingly to Smoke's wife and two sons that it was mighty and proper the way he was laid out.

And there was a very special moment about an hour before they brought Smoke to the chapel when a Northern car stopped outside the door. A tall, aged military-looking man got out, a man with a stern Presbyterian face and short silver hair got out straightaway, and it was Mikey McGrath that met him at the door, gravely, but with real pleasure, and said that Smoke would have been delighted especially to see him there.

The military-looking man knelt for several minutes in prayer beside Smoke's gaunt little face and then he stood up. He touched the trench coat briefly, smiled frostily at the bare feet, and then, remarkably, he took a pair of handcuffs out of his pocket. The key, with a leather fob attached, was in the cuffs. The man opened them, left the key in the lock, and then gently, almost like a ceremonial thing, shoved them into one of the great empty pockets of the trench coat.

"Lord," said one of Smoke's sons after the man went away, "some of the crowd have a lot of nature in them, too."

And if you knew nothing about Jemmy Smoke you'd have been astonished at the special hush that happened, across that hillcupped corner of the Borderlands, when the hearse and the cortege were bringing Jemmy's remains across the border to the chapel on the Northern side. There were policemen and customs officers from both jurisdictions drawn up in some numbers on either side of the sad divide.

The cortege stopped and the hearse went ahead to make the crossing on its own. In a little box on top of Smoke's coffin, plain for all to see, was a strange assortment of items. I did not see them all, for I was not close enough, but they included two plugs of tobacco and several packets of cigarettes, a half-dozen unwashed hen eggs in beds of newspaper, a small box of the kind of hob nails used in farmers' boots, their sharp points reflecting the setting sun, some sweets and bars of Cadbury's chocolates, and, atop anything else I missed, a great yellow bunch of bananas.

And, uniquely, as the hearse passed slowly across the border, at walking pace, all the security people on both sides deliberately turned their backs to it, as one man, and instead of the usual military salute, they applauded. And they applauded even louder, some even laughing, when the hearse, having slowly crossed, suddenly spurted smartly for about 30 yards before slowing down again and waiting for the rest of us.

The policemen and customs men joined the cortege too, every last one of them, and walked the short distance to the chapel. "They were always a bit behind him, bad cess to them," said Mikey McGrath drily - and that brought wry smiles.

And if you never heard at all about Jemmy Smoke you'd have been finally enlightened by the homily that Father Maguire preached at his funeral Mass, the church crowded to the last seat on the gallery, the stained windows all aiming directly towards paradise. "There's another border outside this chapel," said Father Maguire, "and it's the border between this sad world and heaven, and I'm just wondering what the best smuggler of them all is bringing in there now in the pockets of that trenchcoat he used be able to slip out of like an eel if any of the customs men got close enough to lay a finger on him. Saint Peter had better search him." And the whole chapel laughed.

"And it's not right we should have a border here," said Father Maguire, "but as long as it's here there will be border smugglers and none of them will ever forget Jemmy Smoke. He was never in it for the big money, not even during the war. He was just in it for the craic as much as anything else, for the roguery of it, slipping in his bare feet through the fields with his pockets full of tobacco plugs for the Fermanagh farmers gasping for it, hobnails for their boots, sweets and chocolates for their kids, eggs and razor blades and bicycle tubes and tires. And he was never caught."

"And there was one child that was suffering from Saint Vitus' dance," said Father Maguire slowly, "and there were no bananas available in the North for the special diet that might keep that child alive. Once a week, regular as clockwork, Smoke would arrive at that child's house with a bunch of bananas. And sometimes, if money was scarce, he might not be paid for them until the next week. But he always came, life in one of the trenchcoat pockets. And that would never be forgotten."

"There are strange borders and partitions in life," said Father Maguire, "strange indeed." And he paused for a second and his voice lost its clerical frequency and became shaky, human, moved. The child lived, he said, probably because of the smuggled fruit, and wasn't it strange that he went on to become the priest that would stand in the pulpit before them to preach for a wee little barefoot, little rascally kind of savior.

A single beam of afternoon sun smuggled itself through the darkest of the stained glass windows, in the hush, and stole silently down from the rafters to burnish the bunch of bananas atop the coffin of the man they called Jemmy Smoke.

Running With The Hounds And The Hares

he morning rolled into the frosted valley. An orange football of a January sun trundled down the eastern slopes, softening the spiked grass on the uplands, freeing the chilled arms of the stumpy hawthorns from the dewed cobwebs of the night. The radio man said that the fight between Steve Collins and Reggie Johnston had been confirmed for Atlantic City. Hugh and his neighbor Andrew heard the news through the kitchen window from Mary's radio as they laboriously trundled the heavy barrel across the street into the cabin. Andrew, grunting with effort, said that Collins would probably get himself killed. They had seen his Dublin fight on television. He's handy all right, said Hugh, but you are probably right, he does not have the killer punch like McGuigan had. You won't get far without that at the very top.

The hawks in their hunting, he thought, were near as graceful as a greyhound after a hare. There was some kind of beauty about things like that, not that it was easy to put a name on it.

The barrel was full of brine and the fat pig which Hugh, with Andrew's expert assistance, had killed yesterday for spring bacon for the family. Hugh had a big family. They killed two fat pigs every winter, fletches hanging, later, from the hooks on the high kitchen roof. They rolled all the dinners into the shed. It was here that Andrew had stunned the pig, yesterday, with a mallet before they cut his throat. It was the way it was always done.

Tea, said Hugh. They went into the kitchen.

Over the tea, as the sun climbed and blued the bay far below them, the two men and Mary listened heavily to the next item on the radio. It was about hare coursing. There had been a major row at the coursing meeting in Limerick on the previous day, at about the time they were killing that fat pig. Anti-bloodsports pickets had clashed with the coursing followers, blows had been struck, the picketers had attempted to release the hares which had been netted beforehand to be coursed at the meeting by the hounds. A member of the group, very articulate, from Dublin, a doctor, a decent and concerned citizen, spoke angrily about the fact that six hares had been killed at the meeting. Hugh and Andrew, who were members of their own local coursing club, listened intently. When the item was over, Andrew quipped at Hugh that it was lucky those Dublin lads did not know they were killing a fat pig yesterday. Hugh grunted. He thought to himself that he would not bring Mary and the kids to their own coursing meeting next week just in case there was trouble. They loved the day out but it was better to be sure than sorry.

In the bright purity of the day outside they watched a Killybegs trawler hauling in nets, her black stubbiness against the blues of sea and sky skeined above by wheeling gulls. The nets came in heavy, full of fish, silver glints even at that distance, and the hungry gulls swooped in as always, looking for scrapes. Nearer them, over Andrew's land, a sparrowhawk hung motionless above scrubland near a blanched stone wall. Out of the corner of his eye Hugh saw it drop like a stone out of sight. Some field mouse or sparrow, he thought, would not need to worry about the frost tonight.

The hawks in their hunting, he thought, were near as graceful as a greyhound after a hare. There was some kind of beauty about things like that, not that it was easy to put a name on it.

The two men had been friends for years. They worked their farms together, sharing time, tractors, farm machinery, problems. Mary asked Andrew if he would stay for the dinner but he said no, he had to go home. It was a fine cockerel, he knew, for he had seen Mary gently breaking its neck with a wristy twist yesterday, as they were pig-killing. Then she held it by the yellow heels to bleed it, the blood spattering the white stones of the street. I need the loan of the gun, he remembered aloud to Hugh, that bloody fox is hanging around again, I saw him yesterday. She's after our hens. Hugh got the gun and three cartridges from the corner for him. They both knew that if the fox got into the henhouse that was the end of every hen and rooster inside. Have a go at her early in the morning, advised Hugh.

On the radio the anchor man said there had been huge reaction to their piece about the anti-coursing row in Limerick. There had been hundreds of phone calls, the vast majority of them from towns and cities, all opposed to hare coursing. As, said the anchor man, is everybody here in the radio office. We have just had a quick head count. Andrew, standing at the kitchen door with the gun broken over his right arm, his shadow blackly behind him, was looking intently at the corner of the front street, only half-listening, concentrating on something else. Will I do you a favor, he asked Hugh. He put a cartridge in the shotgun, without moving a pace, and fired from the doorstep. Neither Hugh nor Mary moved. The shot rolled over the valley like a small thunder. I got him, said Andrew, without stirring, a big black bastard of a rat heading across the top of the wall towards the cabin. The fresh bacon, maybe, or the bagged feeding stuff, he'd be banqueting all the rest of the winter. Thanks, said Hugh. Rats and foxes and hooded crows, with maybe the odd rabbit and pheasant, were the reasons he kept the shotgun in the house. Killing animals, said the man on the radio, is always wrong.

The working sheepdog that Mary had christened Mandela because of his pigmentation came running from the hayshead at the sound of the shot. He was lean and hard, a working dog for the cattle and the sheep, a farm tool of a dog, never allowed inside the house. On the hill 600 yards away, also disturbed, a hare broke from the field where she paused, sitting up, long legs coiled under her. Both men saw her from the first few yards of her run. A fine hare, said Andrew, I saw her making a fool of the priest's two hounds on Sunday evening, a fine hare. She turned the priest's two bitches inside out and left them for dead. Both men looked out appreciatively at the poised power and beauty of the queen of the valley. Suddenly Mandela whined, scenting or spotting the hare, and dashed off through the vegetable garden towards her. Oh Christ, said Hugh, she's dead. He tried to call Mandela back, shouting and whistling, but the dog, now a black arrow through the bottom rushes and furze, was compressed too tightly against his natural instincts. He was gone on the hunt. The hare began to run further up the valley, speeding easily away on her long loping legs. Mandela was no longer barking. O Jesus, said Andrew, that was too bad, maybe she'll get away though. No, said Hugh, she won't. Ah, said Andrew, with resignation, and set off towards home three fields away.

The hare could turn the priest's greyhounds inside out with her speed and acrobatics, but a wily old working sheepdog is a different animal. As different as a Dubliner and a man from Murrisk. The hare is territorial and lives on the lands of a relatively small acreage. The sheepdog is only about half as fast as a greyhound but he has an unerring nose and a hardy old worker dog will keep chasing and harrying the hare until she tires. And then he will close in.

Hugh was cutting fodder in the hayshead about two hours later, driving the broadblade knife deeply into the benched hay, when he heard the hare begin to cry out on the mountain. She would have begun crying, he knew, because she was getting tired and Mandela was still coming silently along after her. The cry of a hare is like that of a small child, fearful and sore from a hurt. About 20 minutes after that the hare stopped crying and there was silence.

Book III

The Salty Tears Of The Spanish Lady

The statue of the Blessed Mother stood gently in the niched shadows of the seaside church for longer than even the oldest memory in the parish could recall.

She wore a blue robe, her hands were joined, her face was peasant and pleasant, her head was bowed slightly over the old women who would slip in to pray beside her feet at the little side altar. During daylight hours, down all the years, there was almost always at least one woman keeping the Blessed Lady company, there in the shadows.

Often enough I saw them. Through the window to their right one could see the waves breaking on the strand below, the wind combing the tough grass atop the dunes beside McCallion's house, the mounded piles of loose sea sand carelessly discarded by the teeth of the tides.

It is a great pity that sea sand is useless for house construction in this world of sand. There is salt in it. It will not bond properly with the cement.

The statue of the Blessed Mother originally came from Spain. There is a story to it. Some time in the last century the people of the parish, in curraghs and courage of a stormy night, risked their lives to save the crew of a Spanish fishing boat. They saved them all.

When the Spaniards went home they were grateful and they knew the taste of poitin too. On their next trip they brought back the Blessed Lady, half life size, as a token of thanks. People always said that she looked like McCallion's mother, who was slight and small and called Sarah.

I remember her only as an old woman, a bent shape trudging along the strand behind one cow, but she had a lovely complexion, even as an old woman, and a quickly glancing shy smile. She was a nice woman, dead now for more than 15 years I guess, leaving McCallion on his own in the cottage.

The Blessed Mother has suffered too, down the years. Sister Patricia from the convent persisted in trying to clean the church long after she was physically incapable of so doing. She used to tend the statues as well.

The Blessed Mother is made of the soft chalky plaster of all the statues of her generation. Before she was done with her, poor Sr. Patricia, very old and awkward, had knocked the point off the Blessed Mother's nose, had abraded her cheekbones, and had entirely knocked off her right toe.

She would cover up that injury with daffodils in spring, with red roses and the carnations of summer, flaming in the shadows, and with holly and ivy in the Christmas season.

Sea sand is also unsuitable for construction because it retains, in some strange way, the moisture of the tides. If you wash it in fresh water and use it for a cow cabin the walls will always be damp. It's great pity, with so much of it around these parts.

They reconstructed the old church five years ago. They did a great job, stinting nothing. Inside and out. They replaced the ancient Stations of the Cross on the walls with new ones. The time came, eventually, when the Canon and the architect came to stand regretfully in front of the old Blessed Mother with her gently ruined face. They nodded at each other, beneath her bowed head, beside her deformed sandaled foot, and they went away.

In a week a new Blessed Lady statue arrived. She was taller and infinitely more patrician than the gentle peasant Lady from Spain. But she had all her toes, her cheekbones were perfect, and her blue robe was new. Her hands, I noticed, were far more those of a lady than those of a peasant woman. She was slimmer too, not quite so muscular through the shoulders, not so Celtic in the cheekbones.

But then times change, don't they. The old Mother, probably desanctified by a wave of the Canon's priestly hand, was brought outside to the Canon's turf shed to stand there, open to the rain and weather, beside the ruins of the old confessional box that had also been thrown out.

I saw a black cat, one morning, sitting on the Lady's sad shoulder, relishing a rare sunshaft in winter. She looked sad, did the Lady, sad and old in her sandaled feet, one toe missing, her ruined face looking towards the bay from which she had come. I suppose it was when he saw her looking out from the shed, just like that, that McCallion asked the Canon for her.

The canon agreed, because McCallion's grandfather had been at the saving of the Spaniards, and McCallion brought her home in the back seat of the Ford van. The piles of golden sea sand wisp up almost to his cottage door. They do say that if you hold a dribble of this useless sand in your hands, in windy weather, that the more moist grains will adhere to your hand to create the initials of your lover.

McCallion never married. He's the owner of that kind of Celticized mind that trembles on the razor edge between genius and madness. He's notably learned about the sea. He can fill his lobster pots when nobody else can. He put the Holy Lady, gently, face towards the thatch, on his kitchen table and lit huge fires for three days to dry out her poor blue robe that had been flaking.

In the evening shadows, as the winds whispered through the dunes, and the tide shoved its long groping salty fingers into that useless sand, then the Lady's face truly looked like that of Sarah.

On the fourth day McCallion got an old wood chisel and a hammer. Strangely enough he began to cut, delicately and gently, at the top of the Lady's head. The outer skin of the statue was brittle, maybe with the paint, but inside was soft and chalky, and white. McCallion was very careful not to break the surface, but he cut away, slowly and painstakingly, the whole inside of the Lady's poor head.

There were those who saw him doing it, passing his open door, and they didn't like it either. He didn't go out fishing those days and he worked late at night too, his windows burning late and squared against the falling waves. He had other smaller chisels, later, as the work progressed, and eventually the whole head of the statue was hollow. He must have had some kind of filler or putty, too, I don't know what it was, for he also repaired the broken nose.

He did something to the cheekbones, as well, which flattened them out a bit, concealing what Sr. Patricia did. When he was finished that part of the work the Lady looked even more like Sarah looked in the wedding photograph on the breast of the chimney. Outside, as the tides turned, the fingers of the turnings raced at different speeds up along the strand, twisting and turning, melding and mingling, coldly strange. It's such a pity that you can't use sea sand for anything useful.

When the whole head was hollowed out... such a strange thing to do... McCallion was seen out on the strand for two or three mornings. He was carrying a white aluminum bucket and was walking, in an erratic fashion, along the high watermark. It is here that the wrack is twined and twisty around the sea stones, as far as the tides reach up in their comings and wild strange goings.

Sometimes McCallion would hunker down and study that useless sand. Sometimes he would snatch up a handful of it, just ahead of a reaching finger of surf, and dribble a little into the bucket. Often he would stand, for maybe an hour even, just studying the shore line, then go to a certain spot and pick up something again.

If you looked back towards the cottage you could see he had the Holy Lady standing just inside the window that looks out at the pier. Where his mother used to stand. Limned in gentle light. Strange, strange, strange.

It was about a week later that McCallion came up to the Canon and asked him to come down to the cottage. The Canon told me so himself. McCallion said, "There is something that I want you to see, Canon," and the Canon went down, as promised, after the morning Mass. McCallion had the kitchen spotless, as usual, and the Lady was tastefully standing beside the window, her head a little bowed, no sign at all of the work that McCallion had done inside her head, except for the repaired features.

She even had all her toes again. She didn't look one bit out of place, looking out at the sea towards Spain, and the Canon said so. McCallion and the Canon had a glass of good Irish and they talked easily about this event and that until, quite suddenly, with a quiet excitement in his voice, McCallion grasped the priest's arm and said, in a whispery way, "Watch her eyes, Canon. Watch her eyes."

Outside the tide was coming towards the full, racing and roiling, winds and gulls screaming, a world shaking, and, just at the peak of the tide the Blessed Lady began to weep. The great salty tears fell from the bowed face, from the gentle eyes, visibly sparkling in the sunshine as the Canon watched in awe, splashing on the flagged floor beside the sandaled feet. Falling like small rain.

"Isn't that beautiful now?" whispered McCallion. Sea sand, they do say, will drip and weep at the turning of the tide, at the turning of every tide, in an alchemy beyond easy understanding and how was the Canon to know what McCallion had inserted, with sealore and infinite wisdom, inside the hollowed head of the Lady that looked like his mother?

The Cold Little Piano Girls

he cold river catches the rare cold Connacht town in a tight loop. The town, with its stonefaced houses rising up from the clayed riverbanks like the lines of one of the British regiments it once barracked, tries to climb up the one hill almost at its center and fails at the edge of the austere walls of imposing house that is still called The Rectory, though no Protestant rector has lived there for a generation. So the big house, with its cold and lace curtained windows, stands solidly there against the sky, solid and stolid and cold.

The rest of them, like the overwhelming majority of those who are sent to Irish piano lessons from houses like The Rectory, by families like the banker's, would have been exactly the same. There was no music in such bones.

After the British regiments went away in the twenties, the Protestant community dwindled. Finally, the rector too went away.

The Rectory was bought by a Cork Bank manager whose cold face and figure matched it exactly. He had an almost invisible wife, and when he moved in, three ganglingly cowed teenage daughters, all pigtails and spectacles and pale faces, all walking in a line to school with their heads straight and their shoulders back like the soldiers long gone by then.

One day about three months after the banker's family moved in, a lorry delivered a piano to the house. Three sweating big workmen delivered it into the parlor and set it up behind one of the windows overlooking the town, the ascetic loop of the river, the well-drilled garden outside the sills.

By then, already, the girls were taking piano lessons from Miss Sinclair, one of the few Protestants still in the town. You would often meet them walking downhill to her parlored piano in the hours after ordinary schooling was finished. And on Saturdays too, the sheets of music in folders under their thin little cold little gabardined arms. They walked in step, too, just like soldiers.

The piano in Ireland - and probably in most middle-class Europe - has a special position amongst musical instruments. An ability to play it in the classical way is an additional social asset of the kind that banker's children are equipped with.

When this piano was bought, it was bought for £300, which was about the yearly wage for many of the people in the town below. Miss Sinclair, now long dead and buried in the Church of Ireland cemetery, was, for example, paid 14 shillings a week for all the lessons for all the girls. That was in the beginning. Six years later, when the last of the girls left her to move on to boarding school and college, the banker had raised the payment to 18 shillings a week. But by then, of course, only Muriel, the youngest, was taking the lessons. Ruth and Melissa had passed on to third level education.

Piano education of this type, in Ireland and England, is sectioned into grades. All the banker's daughters would have passed all their grade examinations at the first attempt, amassing a raft of certificates along the way. They could play exactly, as on the sheets under their arms, little passages of Chopin and Bach and Mozart.

The eldest of them was sent to a competition once and, though she did not win anything, she was highly commended for effort. But the competition was in Dublin, it cost some money to send her there for little enough return, so the banker did not send any of the daughters away for competitions ever again.

Anyway, I heard one of them playing once when I passed Miss Sinclair's parlor, and even I knew immediately that she was just playing by note and rote with her cold little long fingers, and that she was no musician any way at all. The rest of them, like the overwhelming majority of those who are sent to Irish piano lessons from houses like The Rectory, by families like the banker's, would have been exactly the same. There was no music in such bones.

The big and beautiful piano, always polished and dusted by the daily who came in twice weekly for years, sat solidly and stolidly in the parlor for 30 years until last week. I saw it once or twice. There was always a sheet of music on the stand, even long after the daughters went away and just disappeared from the town forever… to Dublin or England or somewhere… and, atop, in metal frames, were their stiff graduation photographs beside their stone-faced father and mother, amazingly, actually there in the shots but still, somehow, quite invisible, I thought that this old piano, with its walnut logs rooted into the carpet, looked bereft - sad, even - if it is possible for a musical instrument to look sad. I would compare it to the fiddles you saw in a few of the pubs in the town far below, cheap, and almost visibly sweat-marked and resin-dusted and still echoing with the last tune.

The invisible wife died invisibly three years ago. And was buried. The banker, long retired still highly visible in lemon sweaters on the local golf course and in the hotel lobby drinking coffee with men who looked exactly like him, was attacked by Parkinson's Disease shortly after and hunted into a wheelchair. The invisible daughters hired a companion to mind him in his last days. He died last year. He was buried back home in Cork somewhere so that he, too, in the end, passed away almost invisibly. The Rectory, with all its contents, went up for auction.

It so happens that I know the family that bought it, contents and all. The father is a man who began with a small corner shop and traded it upwards, ruthlessly at times, into a small chain of supermarkets. He works hard and works his staff hard and his wife, a Mayo teacher who is twice as driven as he is in her own way, rules her children as totally as any colonel ever did over those regiments that are now ghosts. The businessman has other interests as well, and I have a small involvement with him in one of these. That's why I called to the house last week.

He would not be back for 10 minutes, his busy little wife informed me. She would get me a cup of tea and would I mind waiting in the parlor, even though young Elaine was practicing her piano scales there? No, of course I would not mind, I said, already knowing that there would be two thin arrowroot biscuits on the edge of the saucer of tea was given while I waited.

And already, somehow knowing that the telephone conversation the bright little busy little wife was having in the hall would be about a bridge class she would just be a little late for, Bernadette, because I have to collect the girls from their speech and elocution class.

Small little cold little Elaine was sitting at the piano. About nine years of age, I think, with a pigtail, with total concentration upon the keyboard again after she had said good evening to Mr. MacConnell, watched her little head and eyes pulling the notes off the scale-sheet before her and watched her cold little fingers, one after another, like soldiers on a parade ground, repeating the notes exactly, unmusically by rote and ritual, so that they seemed to invisibly form echoing ranks and files in that big, somehow cold rectory parlor behind the lace curtain windows looking down upon this poor little cold little town trapped in the clay loop of a river forever flowing the same water from the same place to the same place.

And by Jesus, I shivered. And by Jesus, I actually saw that poor old piano shudder upon its poor old walnutted legs. And though I could not possibly do it in the flesh, I wished I could have hugged that poor, poor child.

Observations Of A Townland On A Summer's Day

n acre of the townland of Minna on the Connemara shore of Galway Bay is shaped like a isosceles triangle, its base being of gritty beach, its peak, ascending the rocky hill, the mossed and broken ruins of Dan Josie Stephen's cottage. I'm sitting at the base, looking towards the cottage and the afternoon is shimmering with the haze of a silken summer day. It is as if the sun-drenched thin soil is radiating some kind of atomics of fractions of all the lives that were ever lived here.

There are so many men of the same surname in this place that men are differed from each other by appending their ancestors' names. Dan was Josie's son but, because there was another Dan Josie across the hill, where there is not even a ruined cottage now, it was necessary for the Stephen to be added to him. The other was Dan Josie Pat. This kind of tradition, in a midsummer haze, is the kind of thing that keeps ghosts alive. It telescopes both time and the generations. Stephen was alive as long as Dan was. And Dan is still alive in the old folk's home at the other end of the county.

I saw Dan's face, 18 years ago, yellow and stubbled, being borne out to the white ambulance from the derelict cottage. In the haze of this afternoon you can see it again. And others with it. Even voices you can hear, faces you don't know, horses and carts, forked willows silvered with trout snatched from the Blue Pool of the hidden river, ricks of golden hay more than a century old. I see a man tarring a curragh, both of them light and hardy, in front of a cottage which is no longer ruined and mossed but washed so white that it blazes in the sun. There is a young woman standing in the doorway of the cottage with a child in her arms.

The child, she says to the fisherman, and there is pleasure in her voice, the child has got another tooth.

Fair play to him, says the man, stopping work for a second, the curragh gleaming blackly, he'll be a divil to feed when he gets a few more of them.

There's more fish in the ocean than he'll ever have teeth, she says, isn't that right, young Stephen? And she ruffles the black curls on the child's head that would be known as Stephen Paurig Mary before the curragh was old because there was another Stephen Paurig over the hill and this one's grandmother had been a widow.

There's no logical sequence of time to what you see in a shimmering haze like this. I see a young dark lad, maybe it is Stephen, building a stone wall with large clever hands down nearer me on the shore. I see maybe the same youth lying on the riverbank with his face blanked out totally, a silver gaff in his hand to spear a salmon, there is an old man thatching the house, slowly and deliberately, a scallop of willow twisted in his broken hands, a coffin is carried out the cottage door, shawled women weeping over it, hens stopping in poised steps of curiosity on the rain-drenched street nearby, and there is a woman milking a cow in the open field, her head against the cow's flank, black curls against roan swell, a strang-strang noise of the warm milk jetting into the tin bucket, and there is a tinker on the doorstep, just after that, a man with wild yellow hair, and a golden tongue.

God bless the child, he says to the woman who gives him the porringer (tin cup) of strong tea, God bless the child of the house. Is it the same woman that was milking? I don't know. She stands in the doorway, looking out West towards the Aran Islands, squinting as if maybe trying to see a homing curragh against the sun and there is a child in her arms. I don't know, Josie, if that's your father coming or not, she says to the sleeping child. A black cat sleeps on the windowsill and there is a donkey with his head over the stone wall in front of the house. The air is thick with the hum of insects and bees and birds. The curragh is too far away yet, she says, for me to know for certain.

And there are two youths digging spuds in the spud garden about half-way between me and the ruined cottage. The older one has the spade and the younger one, about 14, is lifting the loosened spuds, all golden and fat, from the sandy soil and tossing them into the basket beside him. He is

> **She stands in the doorway, looking out West towards the Aran Islands, squinting as if maybe trying to see a homing curragh against the sun and there is a child in her arms.**

asking the bigger youth, maybe about 19, when will he be coming back again.

In a couple of years Josie, says the older youth, in a couple of years. He is very handy with the spade, using quick wristy flicks of its corners to toss out the spuds. In a couple of years, with loads of dollars.

Why does Sarah have to go too, is what the younger is asking.

We were claimed out, say his older brother, as if that explains everything, there's jobs for both of us and Aunt Mary will look after Sarah as well as me. It's the way things are done.

They finish the digging and walk back up towards the cottage. The bigger lad carries the basket of spuds against his hip. The shimmering haze swallows both of them up from me. I'm here 20 years and there are not even the faint marks of tillage on the field where I see them digging.

Out of the corner of my eye I see the curragh coming in through the broken water. The two men in it, thickset men in their forties, easily haul it ashore, high above the waterline near me, and take out a basket of herring, some still writhing whitely, a few cod, and about a dozen mackerel. There is another basket against the stone side of the pier... though the pier has virtually disappeared nowadays... and they bend over, grunting, and divide the catch evenly. The older one lights a pipe when they have finished and they talk easily for a while, sometimes scanning the sea before them, sometimes looking up towards the cottage above us. Its door is open wide and there is smoke coming from the chimney, mixing with the haze of the day.

"Dan Josie is getting a bit long in the tooth to be after the young Concannon one. Sure he hasn't a hope," says one.

"Try telling him that," chuckles the other, the one smoking the pipe.

"What's going to happen to him is that he'll finish up with no woman at all, neither chick nor child. His trouble is that he wants a young one with a good few bob as well but he didn't start the chase in time."

"True for you. He's getting a bit too fond of the taps as well. A man like him, all on his ownsome, would need to look after himself better."

They pass by me, heading up the hill. I can smell both the pipesmoke and the fish for a while. Who were they? I have no notion. When was it? What time of what year? Long ago certainly, long ago and far away, but the smell of the fish is fresh. Time gets telescoped, as I said, in a place and hazed space like this one. There's this aging man standing in the place where the spud garden was. He's leaning on a walking stick and he is looking down at the thick green sod of the untilled ground. He's wearing wellington boots, black trousers, black battered jacket, a cap, an open-necked blue shirt in need of a wash, a similar thick vest underneath. There's a black sheepdog at his heel, a bitch, with a young intelligent face. He's talking to the dog. They never came back, he said, Seamus and Sarah never came back. I think he has drink taken. It's probably Pension Day at the Post Office.

The man turns his face to me. I see it is yellow and stubbled. It is the face I saw being carried out to the ambulance from the derelict cottage 18 years ago, alive still, in some fashion, in the old folk's home. The woman in the cottage door, behind the dark figure, tells the man tarring the curragh that young Stephen has cut another tooth. They laugh in the bright sun. I hear the tinkle of it.

This Fella Keeps Coming Back For More

You don't cross a Carson and get away with it. When Harry Carson was at his lowest and frailest last spring, coming in through his own gate on two yellow walking sticks, the thorn tree on the right hand side of the iron gate snagged his dangling belt with its wicked thorns. Harry's independence and vitality were so low at this stage that the thorn bush on the right had the upper hand of him.

But you don't cross a Carson and get away with it. Even if you are only talking about a pair of whitethorn bushes.

When he twisted himself weakly and irritably to rid himself of the thorns the ferrule of the stick slipped and he fell into the hungry wicked arms of the whitethorn bush. It tore his bloated steroided cheeks and his hospital hands of whiteness and stabbed in through his coat and suit at his frailness before he stopped struggling. He nearly died there and then, did Harry Carson, but the ferocity of his anger sustained him.

Lying limply into the heart of the tree, lacerated and torn, Harry Carson cursed the tree. You savage whore you, screamed Harry Carson silently, you might drop your white blossoms this year but by Jesus they'll be your last. For I'll down you, you frigger, and the frigger on the other side of the gate as well. And more of the same, cursed Harry Carson, as he suffered in the thorns and waited for Joe Murphy to come along and release him. Joe Murphy came in 10 minutes, freed him, brought him into the small house, took off his shoes, put him to bed. You'll be alright Harry, said Joe Murphy, though he did not think Harry would be alright.

The worst of it for Harry Carson was that he had been a good hardy man, even up to his 78th birthday the March before. He worked his land, reared his family, served his God, buried his wife, and then gave up the farm to the Land Commission and bought the small house on the edge of the town.

He was ever a small-sized man, but well put together, light on his feet and as tough as nails. He kept his house glittering and his garden full of vegetables and flowers and his independence in age was precious to him. The whitethorn bushes had been growing either side of his gate when he bought the house. He kept them because his wife had loved the fall of the white blossom from them at the start of every spring. Like confetti, she used to say. But when Harry got weak and sick in the winter, all knotted up in his insides, the thorns grabbed him and nearly did for him that night.

But you don't cross a Carson and get away with it. Even if you are only talking about a pair of whitethorn bushes. When Harry woke out of a light sleep the next morning and was struggling to take his tablets, his face and hands scabbed and sore, he looked out through the bedroom window and staunchly renewed his curse against the whitethorns. Ye will fall, and fall hard ye whores out of Hell, swore Harry Carson, and him scarcely able to walk at the time, for I'll down the pair of ye. And he actually shook his white soft fist at the tree that had damaged him. And the tablets within the bottle rattled like white ghosts.

Harry had another setback about a month later. He had to go into hospital again for another operation. Joe Murphy said he would never come home. But Harry came home.

In the hospital, for whatever reason, he had focused his pain and hurt outwards against the two stubby trees. He would close his eyes when the belly pains came and actually see the trees. They had distinctive shapes and he christened both of them in his mind. The one that had grabbed him was Maggie Anderson, the wicked old bitch next to the home farm who had gossiped viciously 20 years earlier when Harry's eldest daughter had got herself into what they called "trouble" and had gone to England. Never came back.

And the one on the right was Joe Murphy next door. Harry had nothing more against Joe Murphy than the fact that Joe Murphy's eyes always looked flatly at him, measuring him for his shroud each instant. And it was Joe Murphy who had seen him in his moment of greatest weakness, having to carry him into bed. Harry Carson hated that.

When they discharged him from the hospital, he came home in a wheelchair. The orderly and home nurse that pushed him down the path went too close to Maggie Anderson's side and the thorns ripped the back of Harry's left hand. Just a scratch. Harry said nothing at all.

The district nurse was a nice young woman called Neary. She had to call to Harry's house every day in the beginning to mend and tend him. Neary

He looked out through the bedroom window. A full moon hung fatly in the sky, under the stars. The images of Maggie Anderson and Joe Murphy looked stark and skeletal, even a bit woebegone, at the garden's end.

was a professional in the matter of death and when Harry came home she thought she would only be visiting him for about a month. But that's a remarkable little man, she told Doctor Costello after a fortnight. He's up and about the house again. He sent back the wheelchair with me last Wednesday. He's eating well, talking about getting up and about again, and he's all for throwing away one of the two sticks. The Carsons are hardy, said Doctor Costello.

Harry had one of the sticks going by the end of the month. He hardened himself up by walking slowly around the house on the one, building himself up in easy stages. After two months he told Neary she need not call again except once a week. He was feeling grand, grand altogether. Each time he went out the door of his house Harry Carson gazed with a malevolence upon the thorned images of Maggie Anderson and Joe Murphy. The real Joe Murphy would see him about every second evening. How are you keeping Harry? Joe would ask from underneath his tombstone stare, slightly puzzled now the stare was. I'm not too bad, Harry would say, I'm living to die and dying to live. Pulling the divil by the tail.

Harry Carson went into the town, three weeks ago on his single stick, steadily down the street, and went into Grogan's hardware shop. He bought a light little bill hook for cutting bushes, and a carbon sharpening stone. The shopboy asked no questions. Harry took a taxi home and spent the rest of the evening looking out balefully at the bushes and edging the wicked little blade. Ever a good man to edge a blade was Harry Carson. At the end of the garden the thorn bushes rattled their fanged bare arms at him. Whores out of hell, swore Harry Carson, his anger giving him a little extra strength. He had discovered that this happened a lot.

He had also learned, from the pit of his frailty, that there were occasional hours, erratic in their coming, when he had infinitely more vitality than the rest of his days. It was a knowledge that he nursed warmly to himself. Mostly he could feel these brief good times by a tingling in the soles of his feet, by a warmed tide of better feeling right through his system. It was erratic and it was brief. But it was there.

At three last Monday morning Harry Carson woke out of his sleep with a jolt. The soles of his feet were tingling. He felt strong. He looked out through the bedroom window. A full moon hung fatly in the sky, under the stars. The images of Maggie Anderson and Joe Murphy looked stark and skeletal, even a bit woebegone, at the garden's end.

Harry Carson got out of bed like a young man. He put on his Sunday shoes rather than the bedroom slippers. He got his bill hook in the kitchen and walked easily out into the night. He sucked in breaths of pure spring air and felt better than he had for years. He slid up behind Maggie Anderson and hefted the hook, stancing himself, striking downwards, and he severed the two inch diameter bush with a single wicked stroke. Inside 20 seconds he had Joe Murphy downed as well, a single canny stroke.

Cursing them both with a fierce joy, Harry delivered knowing supplementary strokes that sundered the two bushes entirely inside 10 minutes. Their limbs fell this way and that, blanched under the moon. With the point of the hook Harry easily nudged them together into a broken pile beside the gate. He never got a scratch from a single thorn. He was not even breathing hard when he was finished. He stood in the moonlight like a young man, full of life. Ye will drop no blossoms this year ye bastards ye, swore Harry Carson, nor draw no more blood from me. I'll live to be a bloody hundred years if I want to.

You don't cross a Carson and get away with it…

The Healing Powers Of A Spud

atch and Josie went down the shore after the storm was over. They saw the Spaniard almost directly because he was wearing a red sweater and because he was lying flat on his back on top of the Corraigmor. Them that are killed by the sea off the coast of this island are nearly always left on top of the slabbed face of the Corraigmor. Like Patch's own father in 1952 and Josie's younger brother only seven or eight years ago. And a lot more than that. It's a harsh place out there.

The two island men did not hurry overly towards the body. They knew there was none of their own missing, nor any fisherman from any of the neighboring islands or the mainland. It had to be a stranger of some class and if he was alive he was alive; if dead, stone dead like many's another good man.

When they were close to the outstretched figure they saw from the color of his skin that he was almost certainly a Spaniard. He would have been a crewman on one of the many Spaniards that poach Irish inshore waters on a daily and nightly basis. He would have been swept overboard during the storm. He was probably dead.

Patch said to Josie, in Irish, that the Spanisher was fishing where he shouldn't have been, that was for certain. And he was surely dead.

He was not. After they turned him over on his side and pumped him a bit he started to cough and splutter and breathe in raspy breaths. They pumped him another bit, roughly but effectively, and then picked him up, without any fuss or excitement, and began to carry him towards the house that always gets the bodies that the sea leaves atop the Corraigmor when it is finished with them.

The Spanisher was shaking and shivering, his eyes still closed, his mouth in agony. He was a wiry fellow in his late 20s. He had an earring in the left ear and a strange kind of silver ring, very thick and heavy, on his right hand. His knuckles were bleeding.

Patch said to Josie he'd almost certainly die, the Spanishers could not take much of the cold water. Josie, nodding up towards the doorway of the house where the old woman was already waiting, also without excitement in her carriage, said he'd die, die surely, and he was thinking at the same time that corpses of Spanishers that came ashore with rings on their fingers had always been ringless by the time the police and the doctors came with the formal papers and the box.

The two islanders carried the limp body into the house and quickly stripped the Spanisher. There were a lot of bruises and gashes on him. They toweled him roughly, with the old woman watching, conversing with them in quick fluid bursts of Irish, and then they put him into the same bed in the front room that the bodies from the Corraigmor are always put into. Patch managed to force a few spoons of whiskey into the man's mouth while Josie was telephoning the guards on the next island that they'd found a Spanisher on the shore. Badly, yes, said Josie, and looked as if he'd die. Yes, said the old woman almost for certain. She said an Act of Contrition into the man's ear, her sharp white nose tapping against the earring. The whiskey was drooling out of his mouth in slabbers. His chest was making strange noises.

They wrapped him up well and turned on the heater in the white bedroom. They heaped two more duvets on top of the shivering fisherman. They did all this with a kind of ritualized compassion. Meanwhile they talked about the Spanisher as if he was already dead.

The guards phoned to say that they'd get the doctor and nurse and they'd be over, give or take, in an hour. There was no report at all, said the guards, of a missing crewman from any of the Spanish boats.

Would he live?

"No," probably not, said Patch. The old woman nodded agreement.

They sat down around the fire for a cup of tea, occasionally getting up in turn to check on the man in the bed. He was getting weaker, said Josie, the last time he came back. "He'll be gone by the time the doctor gets here," said Patch.

It was when they were moving the Spanisher's drenched clothing that the wallet dropped out of the pocket of his jeans. The opened letter inside it still had some legible pieces of the name and address on it. The old woman,

> **The old woman, who had put on her glasses to check out the wallet, made a startled noise when she saw the Spanisher's Christian name was Jesus.**

who had put on her glasses to check out the wallet, made a startled noise when she saw the Spanisher's Christian name was Jesus. She would not have known that just about every second fisherman in Corunna caries the name Jesus.

That changed matters entirely. "No Jesus," she cried, "is going to be let die in my house. We'll give him the spud waistcoat. Quick Josie, get the spuds. Patch, the pot, quickly now."

"It's too late," Josie grumbled, going all the same. "He'll be gone in ten minutes. It's only a waste of good spuds."

But the old woman, highly excited now, fussing over her patient like a son, speeded things up to the point that inside 10 minutes the pot of spuds was boiling on top of the gas cooker. As the spuds boiled she got a clean sheet from the hot press, spread it out on the table and folded it roughly into the shape of a waistcoat. In between times she tried to force several drops of brandy into the mouth of Jesus.

Whiskey was no good any more. The fisherman was shivering uncontrollably at this stage, his teeth chattering. "Always when the Spanishers go like that," said Patch, "they are on the way out. Always."

When the spuds were well boiled, Patch teemed them and then the old woman got Josie to mash them in the pot, skins and all. Into the great steaming hot mess she threw two glasses of the brandy and a full canister of epsom salts, the crystals glittering like sugar. Then she quickly spread the spuds in a thick hot layer on top of the sheet, steam rising, folded the sheet on top of the layer and then rushed into the bedroom.

She had Patch and Josie hold the shivering Spanisher in a sitting position in the bed, his head drooping forward limply, while she slapped on the spud waistcoat, quickly, roughly, and secured it in place with two pieces of cord from the dresser drawer. Then the men let the Spanisher back down on his pillow and covered him up to the throat.

"In about a minute from now," said Patch to Josie, "he'll either be alive or dead. Christ above the heat of that up against your bare skin must be dire altogether. I'd rather die than go through it."

"It saved Pat Hoare though," said Josie, "he'd be dead otherwise. Tis a kill or cure job really, isn't it?"

The old woman, standing by the head of the bed, never took her eyes off the Spanisher's face.

It hit him after about 90 seconds. He roared out loud like an animal, and sat bolt upright in the bed, still roaring, his hands truing to pluck away the huge poultice that was burning him round and round his body. Patch and Josie, on the old woman's instructions, held him firmly by the arms to stop him ripping off the spud waistcoat. The Spanisher's language was his own but there were many references to his own name, for certain, and to members of the family. Eventually, his forehead beaded with sweat, he subsided. Already his breathing seemed stronger even though he was moaning.

Patch and Josie, still holding his hands, sat on either side of the bed. Through the window of the bedroom, across the flat top of the Corraigmor, they could see the Blackbird coming with the police and the doctor and the nurse.

"He will live now," said the old woman, touching the Spanisher's dark curly hair as tenderly as a mother. "He will live. You can't beat the spud waistcoat."

You can't. And he did.

Wandering Into A Wedding

t was a pub in Clare that I had never been in before. I wandered in through the door, at what would have been a quiet time normally, and found that I had walked slap bang into the middle of a travelers' wedding.

They used to be called tinkers' weddings, but in this politically correct era nobody calls the wandering people tinkers anymore.

A wiry man in that comfortable place at the end of the bar nearest the door looked at me with the kind of triangulated sharp eye that has measured the bone and substance of two million horses, and made space for me to order a pint. You would know from the way that he created the space amidst the massing bodies that he knew well I was a settled man, not big enough to cause trouble worth a curse, and that I was unconnected with either of the clans that had just been united by the One, Holy, Catholic, Apostolic and Settled Church.

They stopped serving drink to some of the young fellows, he told me, but I should be safe enough. And I was. The pint arrived and it was good.

It usually took about an hour between the stopping of serving and the start of the first row, said my wiry friend, and when he went to drink his drink, in that safe spot near the door, like a riverboat gambler, the bar lights glinted on the solid gold rings on his fingers.

I have not been at a travelers' wedding for years. The last one was in Co. Galway. It was the summertime and they were having the wedding feast in the open air. There was a long table laden with the best of everything in

They survive. They work the system to their own benefit. They have a remarkably strong family and clan spirit. They still have their own language and customs. They have their race pride.

amongst the caravans, and it was the bride herself that gave me a bottle of sun-warmed beer and a kiss in the middle of the forehead.

They used to be called tinkers' weddings, but in this politically correct era nobody calls the wandering people tinkers anymore.

My wiry friend confirmed this to me. They would not mind at all, he said, as long as tinker was used in a way which was not like a curse. Both of us discussed the wonderful things that his father and men before him could do with sheets of bright silver tin - porringer mugs, buckets, basins, milk cans whose lids fitted so snugly that you would not believe it.

"Not one of them young ones in here would know how to work the tin," said my friend, his rings flashing again, "not a single one of them."

And then he said "plastic" deep in the back of his throat the way settled people used to say "tinkers." A curse. It was the advent of plastic that killed the trade that had allowed the easiest and most productive interaction between the tinkers and the settled of the past.

Ironically, at just this stage, one of the young men who had been refused more drink a little earlier announced rather slurringly that he was about to sing. He stood, swayingly, and attempted, equally ironically, to sing the Cliff Richards song called *The Young Ones*. He managed about three lines before sitting down heavily, silenced by porter and the events of the day, his head moving down towards his knees. I noted, looking at him, that not alone was he about the worse singer I have ever heard, he was also physically the largest traveler to encounter my eye-sight.

The wiry one agreed. The young ones, he said, were getting bigger nowadays because a share of them were housed, well-fed, livin' off the fat of the land. But they were soft, he said, soft as a fat pig's belly, and when it came to fighting you would see that in them. One good skite across the lug, he said, and they were finished, not at all like the men that had gone before them.

I reflected, drinking my pint rather more quickly than usual, amidst people far better dressed than I, all sporting huge wads of notes when they came to the bar, that the tinkers who have become travelers, with every settled hand against them to one extent or another, have adapted remarkably well to the complex demands of this new Ireland.

They survive. They work the system to their own benefit. They have a remarkably strong family and clan spirit. They still have their own language and customs. They have their race pride. A survey this week established that travelers' children, in Ireland in 1997, the young ones, have at least as much self-esteem as any group of settled children.

I finished my pint. I looked at the three-tier cake in the corner of the pub, sweet and solid and covered with white and pink icing, and I looked at the children, dressed to the nines, playing the pinball machines as the rock music belted out in the background. I looked at the indomitable matriarchs in the corner, thoroughly enjoying themselves, and at the young ones, with their blonde hair and hawked faces, and I saluted them all in my mind for their own special kind of bravery.

And then it was certainly time to go. The wiry one just winked at me as I left, a wise and knowing wink that said it all.

Skeletons On The Beach

There was a gale. It shifted the whole belly of the beach. In the morning Mattie Gallagher found a skeleton just above the brineline. The skeleton was lying flat on its back and it was very old but totally complete. The bones were very white and the sockets of the skull gaped blankly at the quieting sky.

Mattie Gallagher is a cool man. He looked at the sight for a second or two and then he cycled into the village to tell the sergeant. This was back in 1970, about a week before Easter.

The sergeant was a Kerryman. His name was Quinlivan. He was a big calm man with a great dome of a forehead. He was also a week away from his retirement. He put Mattie's bicycle in the trunk of the squad car and they drove back together to the beach to commence their investigations.

Mattie indicated the skeleton to the sergeant. The two calm big men looked at it together. The skeleton, they decided, was that of a man who had been a bigger man than either of them.

I must sketch in a quick context here. Back in those days Mattie made a small sup of poitin from time to time. He also fished and farmed. He was a respected moonshiner in that he only made a small quantity of very good stuff and was careful about who he sold it to. He also performed a very significant social service by

> **The two big men hunkered down at the skeleton's ancient toes and Mattie, in the finest of Irish and the most fluent of English, four-lettered the poor divil that had died so long ago and been unburied at just the wrong tide.**

quietly alerting the sergeant if young scallywags tried to break into the moonshining business in his locality. In this way, because these young lads would always make bad stuff and drink it themselves, to excess, Mattie actually saved their lives.

It would be immoral to call him an informer. Nobody was ever prosecuted as a result of his tips. But stills and stuff were found by the police. One find, according to the sergeant later, was actually poisonous. It would have killed.

Both men, standing there over the skeleton that Friday morning, also knew that Mattie's stillhouse was not too far away from where they were standing. It would not suit Mattie, then or ever, to have parties of strange forensic policemen from Dublin scouting all over the place.

The sergeant had begun his last week of service the day before the skeleton appeared on the beach. All else being equal, he wanted that week to be quiet. The lads would be taking him out for a farewell party on the Friday night. There would be a presentation. The superintendent would grace the occasion with his presence. The skeleton being found on the beach meant that 70 documents would have to be filled out, Dublin Castle informed, the Murder Squad alerted, the press arriving like bees. It did not suit. It did not suit at all.

Standing there, the waves whispering at them, the two big men surveyed the skeleton from the same vantage point but, if you like, from two completely different standpoints.

"It's obvious," said Mattie quietly, "that this lad has been lying here since the time of Finn McCool."

It was, too. More probably, said the sergeant, he had been lying there since the time of the Famine. It was in the back of his mind that several skulls and other Famine remains had turned up on the beach even before his 12 years of service had begun in the sub-district.

The skeleton, quite content, looked up at them with his big blank eyes and they looked down at him.

They then looked at the strand round him. Apart from the earlier tracks of Mattie and his dog, there were no other tracks on the strand.

"Seventy documents I'll have to write," said the sergeant, "and 12 or 15 phone calls to Dublin; night duty all week long."

The two big men hunkered down at the skeleton's ancient toes and Mattie, in the finest of Irish and the most fluent of English, four-lettered the poor divil that had died so long ago and been unburied at just the wrong tide. He had customers due the very next morning and no way of getting word to them that if they arrived, as arranged, they would find the strand crawling with detectives.

"It doesn't suit me either," said Mattie.

"Neither of us," said the sergeant. And, unusually for him in Kerryese, he too cast aspersions upon the poor dead bones before him in the sand. Wryly, for a finish, he said he thought he had all his skeletons buried away in cupboards and 'twas a dreadful thing altogether for one to turn up on his last week in uniform.

It was probably this remark which led to the solution which they arrived at in the end.

The sergeant had a jute sack in the trunk of the car. Mattie and himself gathered up the ancient bones, hocus-pocus skull and all, and put them in the bag. Mattie had a bit of fishing line in his pocket. They tied the neck of the bag. The sergeant formally recorded the find and took a brief statement from Mattie stating that due to pressure of business, he would be unable to give further details of his find until the following week.

Mattie signed the statement. They put the bag of bones in the trunk. They decided that Mattie should not come into the village for about a week. They then adjourned to a small stone cabin about 200 yards away and remained inside for about 15 minutes. There was at least one clinking hottley-glossy kind of noise during that period. Whatever else happened is none of your business or mine. Two old associates were saying goodbye. Mattie went home happy. The sergeant drove back to the station. Late that night, when alone, he placed the bag of bones on the very top shelf of the cupboard in the day room of the old station. All sorts of bric-a-brac were up there, like gas-masks from the last war and old ration books and broken batons.

The sergeant returned to glowing tributes that weekend. He had a great last week. Then himself and the wife went back to Kerry to enjoy retirement. As far as I am aware he is alive still. So is Mattie, alive and well and hale and hearty and still making a sup.

The station got its first Ban Garda (woman police officer) a month ago. She was a big strapping girl from Offaly and she had qualified top of her class, male and female. She looked Scandinavian, with a big, freshly scrubbed face and bright blue eyes. In her first week she summonsed more motorists than ever had been summonsed before in this quiet place. In her second week she complained to headquarters about an allegedly sexist remark made to her by one of her male colleagues (all he said, and I quote, was, "Lordy but there's eating and drinking to spare on that one") and, that same weekend, she raided every pub within the sub-district and ruined the most lucrative after-hours trade in Ireland.

Last weekend, late on the Sunday night, in sole command of the station and with nothing happening, this energetic young woman decided that she would spring clean a place allowed to fall into rack and ruin by generations of males. It was 1:00 in the morning before she reached the lower shelves of the big cupboard. It was just before 2:00, everything sparkling at the lower levels, when she reached up to the top shelf.

Mattie's fishing line was old and frayed 20 years ago, the afternoon he tied the mouth of the bag of bones. It needed only one touch for it to break and for the bag to disgorge its grisly secrets, skull and all, down on top of the earnest face below. The resulting scream was heard from one end of the village to the other.

There is no longer a policewoman attached to this station. Her resignation went in three days later when she had recovered slightly. The after-hours trade has resumed in the area and things are returning to normal.

Sometimes skeletons in cupboards have their uses.

Waste Not, Want Not

There was no warning. One minute Yankee Ruane was sitting at the head of his own table, all his gold teeth glinting with health and life and prosperity, and, the next minute, the knife and fork dropped out of his hand, and his face fell forward right into his plate of bacon and cabbage and spuds. Some of the cabbage went into his hair.

> **Waste not, want not, live straight and decent, work hard, drink little, and, in the end, straight as a gun ball to Heaven.**

Maura screamed the Three Holy Names from the other end of the table, and then screamed, "Mick! Mick! Are you all right?" But he was dead. Massive heart attack, the doctor said later. Felt no pain. Straight to heaven, said the priest.

A good and decent man said all the neighbors who came flocking to the house in the immediate aftermath of the passing to comfort Maura. A decent man. Straight as a gun ball.

Maura Ruane was back in command of herself inside 10 minutes. She was shaken, it was true, but she is one of the Currans of Loughtalt, and they are a hardy lot. She is 59 years old, two years older than Yankee was, and the Currans and Ruanes both saw more than their share of hardship down the generations.

One of the first things she did, strangely, after Yankee had been put in the bedroom following death, was to throw out the remains of their dinners to the two collies. Waste not, want not was always the credo of the Ruanes. How else would Yankee and Maura have raised the big family they did?

Waste not, want not, live straight and decent, work hard, drink little, and, in the end, straight as a gun ball to Heaven. And give the ruined dinner to the dogs.

He liked them so well, the gold teeth, that he got other full teeth later, in the back of his mouth, all gold, solid gold, so that when he smiled widely later, or laughed out loud, he looked, said Snipe Lenehan, like the entrance to the Yukon.

Maura had a pound of corned beef and a pound of tomatoes in the fridge, as always, so she was able to give sandwiches herself to the first rush of neighbors to the stricken house.

Her sister, Joan, the hospital matron, arrived inside two hours. It was Joan who took command of the phone, and told England and the States that Mick was dead. Massive heart attack, felt no pain, straight as a gun ball to heaven, and your mother is holding up grand, thank God. The calls were all brief and to the point. Waste not, want not.

The wake was traditional. You could not say that anything was stinted in the slightest. There was food and drink aplenty for all the callers. But Maura herself switched off the hall light in the corridor between the sitting room and the bedroom where Yankee was laid out. Wasn't the door of the bedroom open and two lights on in there?

Yankee was wearing a habit rather than the Sunday suit that some men are laid out in nowadays.

He looked well. He looked, said Jackie Hynes, as if he was sleeping. The four gold teeth in his upper set glinted in the light of the two lights burning in the bedroom beside him. Yankee got those before he got sense, when he was working in the States in the early '50s before marriage.

A cousin was a top-class dentist, and Yankee lost his natural crowns in a trench collapse. He liked them so well, the gold teeth, that he got other full teeth later, in the back of his mouth, all gold, solid gold, so that when he smiled widely later, or laughed out loud, he looked, said Snipe Lenehan, like the entrance to the Yukon. Truth was that Yankee got all the dental work done cutprice by the cousin.

He made enough dollars over there to buy the place when he came back home. He met Maura Curran two years before he came back. She was in service with a Greek family who owned two ships and a villa in Corfu.

Maura did not come empty-handed, either. They had a car, the Ruanes, when few families had cars, but then Yankee made a profit from the car by operating an unlicensed taxi service for the neighbors. Waste not, want not.

As always happens, the family gathered quickly. The four sons and the Ruane daughter were all gathered around the home hearth by early the following evening. Joe and Charlie are in the construction business in the States, both doing well in different cities. Young Mickie has a market garden in Kent. Con is a tar macadam contractor and landscaper in Bristol. They are all big, careful men.

The sister, May, is a nurse in Canada, and after her ordinary working hours runs a private nursing home for geriatrics. She resembles her mother. She's not married. She's the oldest of the clan, and was the first to leave home.

All the sons and the daughter arrived back home almost together. They prayed and cried around their dead father's deathbed for a good while afterwards, and said a rosary out loud. When she was leaving the room afterwards, May turned off one of the two lights. Yankee, she said, looked better that way.

Maura and Joan had already made all the arrangements for Yankee's funeral from the chapel the next morning. He would go to the chapel straight from his own house. Who needs a funeral parlor when you have a home? Anyway, John Joe the undertaker charges the earth for everything.

You have to get the coffin from him, and the habit, and pay for the death notices in the paper, but you don't need to go any further than that. The family bonded sturdily around their mother that evening, and, later in the night, the neighbors left them alone with their grief. Joan had to go back to the hospital to straighten out a few administrative matters as well. They were alone.

After Maura went to bed the sons and daughter had a deep conversation. I missed the very beginning of it so I don't know who raised the subject first. It was probably Charlie, almost certainly Charlie. He had a blunt way of raising things, too, has Charlie, so I imagine that after he spoke first, stating his mind, there was a bit of silence around the fireplace.

The fire was nearly all out at that stage. It had been burning all day for the neighbors, and the room was warm enough, so why waste any more turf. The winter would be in soon, and Maura would need all the fuel that was in it. Waste not, want not.

That's exactly what Joe said after Charlie spoke. Waste, he said, is like a mortal sin.

Young Mickie said that, in a way, he agreed with Joe and Charlie, there was nothing wrong with the way they were talking at all, but what about their mother? What would Maura think?

I think, said Con, that my mother said to us there, just before she went to bed, that she knew we'd do everything that was right. Our mother, he added, is a very sensible woman. She never liked waste of any kind.

There was a silence, and then Joe said that he couldn't do what was necessary himself. He could not be up to it. Charlie said he was of the same mind, sad as he was to say it. Mickie said nothing at all, only looked into the fire with his eyes half-closed. Con, who is the youngest of them all, started to say something, and then stopped. The clock ticked solidly on the mantelpiece.

May was sitting at the head of the kitchen table with her chin in her hands. She opened the drawer in the table. Its contents have not changed in years. Any string that ever came into the house on parcels is neatly coiled there, in little hanks, in case it would ever come in useful. Stamps that were not postmarked, and could be reused. Rubber bands. Things like that.

She found the small pair of pliers where they always had been, in the right hand corner. She took them out. She looked directly at her brothers, and nodded silently.

May walked down the short corridor to where Yankee was laid out. The light from the one lamp beside his head made a square of gold on the corridor floor. She stood at the door and looked at her father's remains.

The golden smile from all the gold teeth glittered forlornly from the cold, dead face. She felt the pliers equally cold in her hand. Waste not, want not is what she thought, waste not, want not…

Mystery Of The Shattered Masterpiece

he was the schooner Glenasmole out of Cork, and when she was running Spanish guns from Corunna to the men who would become the fathers of the Fenians, she was as beautiful as schooners can be, which is to the far horizons of the world in all blue directions. And after the British captain Orme sunk her, with all hands, by foul play, when the last century was young, the Glenasmole was maybe more beautiful still. For the namesake son of the Con O'Donovan who skippered her, and who died with her, made six models of the Glenasmole, perfect to the tiniest detail, and she became the rarest and the most prized of all the millions of the world's ships in bottles.

Until this Christmas, there were only four remaining.

Now there are only three.

That means that each of those is worth hundreds of thousands of pounds more than that they were worth a month ago.

They are identical, perfect, heart-stoppingly striking inside their old thick shouldered Spanish brandy bottles that have just that faint greenish tinge in their glass.

I saw one of them 10 years ago.

The Glenasmole, ready to strike back at some pursuing English warship, is peeled back against the curve of the wave she is riding on. Her sails, even in

> **The detailed provenance does state that the creator of the models, young Con O'Donovan, had "put a curse into said bottles with each model, blowing his breath into the bottle before sealing it, cursing the English seamen who sunk his father's schooner by not fighting fair."**

the miniaturized vacuum of the bottle, are cannily drawing the last sinews of strength from the wind that is even flexing the mainmast slightly. The mouths of her five cannon, loaded and ready in their ports in the sleek oak flank, are as wicked and lethal as the maws of sharks.

Behind each cannon the teams of Cork sailors are crouched, the gunners with the slow matches already lit. The models are pluperfect, even to the narrowed eyes. The skipper, Con O'Donovan, whose son made the models a half a lifetime later, is the best realized figure of all. He has the wheel in one hand. He has a pistol upraised in the other. He is about, you know, to shout the order to FIRE and then the matches will touch off the cannon, all together in a broadside that will thunder and smoke and echo over the oceans of the imagination. A work of savage art; a terrible beauty. More terrible now.

I have often told ye how detailed the Irish folklore is on matters like this. Men know, to this day, how many muskets the Glenasmole ran into Castletown and into Kerry coves before she was sunk. Men know the names of most of the crew crouched behind the cannon. There was Clune and Skyrne, O'Leary, Suffin, Sugrue, Dowd, who had only one arm, just like the model, McCarthy, and the Man from Beare with no name known apart from that and, at the base of the mainmast, with a cannon swab in his hand and a leather bucket, his head taut with excitement, a ship's boy called Mongon. He is there, too, his minute toes curled tightly against the minute decking of the model.

The one I saw was bought by an American textiles tycoon for $220,000 a decade ago, and was cheap enough too at the price then. Later it changed hands for double that, and went to northern England, with its provenance and its price tag, a curiosity for some wealthy man, an investment maybe.

The detailed provenance does state that the creator of the models, young Con O'Donovan, had "put a curse into said bottles with each model, blowing his breath into the bottle before sealing it, cursing the English seamen who sunk his father's schooner by not fighting fair."

It is not detailed, anywhere, what foul stroke was pulled on that early evening out of Corunna and a west wind blowing. But there must have been one.

The Southampton antiques dealer who made the most recent purchase of one of the rare Glenasmoles... and I do not know which one... had been the underbidder at the last auction for the one that went to northern England, I know that for certain. Where he laid hands on the one he got is still not clear. Time will tell.

He had it delivered by Securicor, the security firm, to his home overlooking the harbor that British fleets have sailed out of since ships first ran with the wind. It was in a protected metal container, deeply insulated and lined, and with a combination lock. He delayed all day opening the container so that he could more fully savor the moment.

It was seven hours after the container arrived, and his shop had been closed for the day, his staff all gone home, everything locked and secured tightly against the night, before he went up and fed the combination into the brass lock and took out the ship in a bottle, in its red velvet bag, and sat it down on his desk, and then took off the bag, reverently almost, his big hands shaking a bit with the excitement of the true collector. And then he left down the Glenasmole on top of the desk and just sat there, for minutes on end, just admiring the beauty of it, not touching it at all.

And the three clocks in his office, all works of art, ticked time out of time, and tocked time out of sync, and the Christmas lights of Southampton's great port were multiplied by the facets of a fleeting tide.

The collector, like most people of this city, had the sea in his bones. His ancestors, both as merchant seamen and navy men, were more comfortable on the waves than on the hills and downs. He himself served in the Navy in World War II. His stock, renowned throughout the art wold, has a marine bias to it in consequence. Few would have appreciated the beauties of the Glenasmole more than he did.

So it is good that he admired his treasure for a long time before he picked it up to study it more closely.

He held it by either end, corked neck and thick base, and studied every detail of the model, every plank and every stitch and every sail and every straining line. And he admired the poised perfection of the gunnery teams crouched behind their perfect miniature cannon. And he admired the ornamental timberwork around the poop, authentic to the last whorl and whirl.

So finally he wished to look more closely still at the ferocious face of the captain, there behind the wheel, the arm raised with the pistol preparatory to giving the order to FIRE. And he put his face right up against the cool greenish glass. It made his big blue eyes look grotesquely huge and gargoyled.

And then he died.

They said it was an aneurysm.

They said that it was the shattering edges of the Spanish glass that caused such appalling damage to his eyes and face when he fell right down on top of the treasure as he died, breaking the masterpiece of masterpieces.

But, probably after Christmas, the questions will begin to emerge.

The little Glenasmole is smashed pieces, true, but why do the tiny cannon have scorchmarks on their muzzles? Skyrne and the Man From Beare were modeled kneeling with their slow matches behind the cannon.

Why are the figures now full-length, the painted faces suffused with joy, the arms above the head as if in celebration? Why? How?

Why is the right arm of the skipper Con O'Donovan no longer poised above his head, ready to give the order to FIRE? And where is the pistol now? And why is that hand, too, like that of Skyrne, turned into a celebrating fist jutting forward of the body? Why? How?

And is there any significance at all in the fact that the antique dealer's name was Orme? And that, buried in Naval records somewhere, there is a question mark over some of the methods adopted by one of his ancestors, long ago, on the high seas near Corunna.

Watch Out For Church Spiders

Sometimes fact is even stranger than fiction. Often enough, maybe the freest flights of fiction are based tightly enough upon the facts of this strange and wonderful life of ours. Facts are cobwebs of things, spun with octagonal precision by a Greater Power across the paths that we are taking from day to day, from cradle to grave.

And what happened to her should not have happened to any decent woman kneeling down in the incensed shadows praying for the likes of you and me.

And sometimes, even when our minds and imaginations are very far away altogether from our corporality, the realities of our existence, like a flying gossamer cobweb of a summer's night, will touch our skin. And adhere thereto.

Not all that often, though, does this occur as dramatically or as frighteningly as in the case of Mena Griffin, a venerable and almost saintly Donegal woman who spent most of her adult life on her knees in the cathedral in Letterkenny praying for the likes of you and me. Mena had a particular devotion to the local St. Eunan, after whom the cathedral is named, and it is my opinion, sitting here this minute in the bench where Mena prayed so often, that, in the end, by our mortal standards anyway, St. Eunan failed Mena Griffin. And failed her badly.

And what happened to her should not have happened to any decent woman kneeling down in the incensed shadows praying for the likes of you and me. But it did happen, and that's a fact of life. And it was all stranger than fiction.

This little spider, totally carnivorous until that time, loved the taste of the Spanish oil.

I'm sitting here where Mena prayed and the facts of the matter come back to me. I look all around the vaulted silence, significantly devoid this early evening of venerable spinsters like Mena Griffin and note, not surprisingly, that the only worshippers in the cathedral are either big strong men with the bullshoulders of retired policemen… men afraid of nothing… or hardy wee nimble little men like myself. There's no woman at all in St. Eunan's Cathedral this minute.

That's not surprising at all, given the facts. St. Eunan let the women of Letterkenny down that evening about 20 years ago and it will be a long time before those who still mourn Mena Griffin will forgive him for that. This is also a fact.

Here are more facts. About 21 years ago the ascetic amalgam of priests and lay-people who man the shadows of cathedrals like St. Eunan's had a meeting. This was a routine meeting to decide such matters as replacing a piece of roof-leading here and there, repainting, the provision of new kneelers and such matters of small moment.

It was during the course of this meeting, which was held in a room under the cathedral's old roof that it was decided, without one dissenting voice, to replace the aging sanctuary lamp of the cathedral with a new model.

Mena Griffin was almost certainly saying her prayers in the front bench on the women's side of the cathedral when this decision was made. I find that sad, too. She was probably praying for the sinful likes of you and me. Above her head, as she swayed slightly in her venerations to St. Eunan, the old sanctuary lamp glowed redly. As such lamps are supposed to. Or maybe it was out. It had been extinguishing itself occasionally during the previous two years. That was why they were replacing it. It was replaced inside six weeks.

The new model never went out. It came down from Dublin in a white van and was hung up, in the old chains, by two young men, one of them chewing gum. Mena Griffin was there that hour and prayed for them too.

The new lamp was of the same dimensions as the old one. However, in the critical change, its fuel was different. The kerosene of the old model was replaced by a much cheaper vegetable fuel oil, also much safer. The little wickboat floated on the surface of this oil, imported from Spain in shiny tin cans, and burned beautifully.

Mena Griffin, raising her eyes towards the general whereabouts of God, St. Patrick and her beloved St. Eunan, would not, in her transports of worship, have been consciously aware of the brighter new red flame, but would have been subconsciously spiritually stimulated by it as she prayed for the sinful likes of you and me. Amen.

More facts. When the young man with the chewing gum was lighting the lamp, for the first time, he struck the center chain of the suspension system with his left hand. He knocked a small spider down on to the edge of the new lamp bowl. This spider was an ordinary belfry spider of minute size, masculine in gender, one month old at that stage, leading a quiet kind of cathedral life.

This spider, as soldiers can, survived the fall to the side of the lamp bowl. His eight feet, however, were covered with minute amounts of the new Spanish oil fuel. He licked his feet clean again. Bull spiders do this. This little spider, totally carnivorous until that time, loved the taste of the Spanish oil. He had more, from the rim of the lamp bowl.

It was gorgeous. It was nutritious, full of vitamins. It tasted much better than the celibate kind of church-fly flesh on which he had been weaned. He had his fill of it, and more than his fill, and then happily climbed the chain again to his home in the cathedral roof. He was one happy spider. Below him, I have no doubt, Mena Griffin continued to pray for the sinful likes of you and me.

I'm sitting here now, in the bench where Mena prayed so much, and I'm resisting a temptation to embellish hard facts. I succeed. The next hard fact is that the spider in the roof, very frequently, perhaps thrice daily, descended to eat and drink the Spanish oil in the lamp. This is borne out by the complaints to the cathedral clergy, by the new sacristan, six months later, that the new lamp, though splendid in operation, was… and I quote, "very heavy on the oul juice, Father," and had to be refilled with Spanish oil twice a week. But the stuff was cheap, and there were tins and tins of it, so the complaint was not followed up. Lord, what a tangled web we weave.

It was during Lent, a year later, that disaster struck in St. Eunan's Cathedral. It was early evening in the incensed shadows and there were only three worshippers in the benches. One, inevitably, was Mena Griffin. The second, thanks be to God, was the ex-sergeant Joseph Malone, retired eight years from the force after a career which included two decorations for bravery.

The third worshipper was Aggie Delaney, the parish gossip, then aged 54, who, God love her, has been unable to speak since. It was eight o'clock in the evening.

We must have reached, just this evening, at just this time, the critical point. Our friend the bull spider, to whose person the Spanish oil had reacted in the same way as steroids affected Ben Johnson the Canadian sprinter, was descending towards his vegetarian dinner along the chain. He is, at this stage, a fearsome specimen of a spider. He has several green eyes looking in all directions, hairy legs seven inches long, an appallingly red mouth and a glossy black mane of hair all along his back.

He looks like Satan personified and his entire genetic system has been totally shagged up by his addiction to the Spanish oil. And, perhaps because of his oily feet, or perhaps because of his additional weight, now nearly five pounds, this dreadful creature slips from the chain and falls 20 feet down on top of poor Mena Griffin. Who was praying, as always, for the sinful likes of you and me.

I must not embellish the facts. I resist it. The gross insect struck Mena's shoulder and then fell into her black leather handbag, open on the bench in front of where I'm sitting now. As Mena began screaming, the Bull spider, making grunting noises, devoured her pension book in its brown envelope, her prayerbook containing 30 memoriam cards, £17 in notes, a First Class relic of Maria Goretti and the plastic cross of her crucifix. It then tore the side wall out of her handbag and emerged, again, with Mena screaming at full pitch, to fix her with an implacable glare from all its eyes.

Aggie Delaney, as I have said, has not uttered a single word since that evening. I will embellish no further fact of this episode. I merely quote from ex-sergeant Malone, who wrote it all down later in his notebook. He wrote: "On hearing Miss Griffin screaming, I approached the scene. I saw this huge spider devouring one of her overcoat buttons. I struck this creature with my walking stick to distract it. It was like hitting a stone wall. The spider attacked my stick, biting it. The mark remains until this day.

"I continued to strike the spider, at least 16 or 17 blows, until it ran away. Miss Griffin had then collapsed. So had Miss Delaney. I summoned assistance. In all of my years of service I have never seen so fearful a creature as this. I was very shaken afterwards but went and summoned assistance." Those are the facts.

That brave man has since gone to his reward. Mena Griffin, after a month in hospital for shock, came home to Poulnascobe but never recovered. She was gone inside the year. During that year she never stood in a church again.

Aggie Delaney, as I have stated, survives, but has lost the power of speech. Sergeant Malone's son Corny preserves the walking stick his father used in his last act of bravery. The sanctuary lamp in St. Eunan's Cathedral now burns on kerosene. Evening worshippers, like this evening, are exclusively male.

I get down upon my knees, having first checked the roof above me, and whisper a prayer for the happy repose of the soul of Mena Griffin who, in her time, prayed a great deal for the sinful likes of you and me. And I pray, too, for St. Eunan himself, who was found wanting when needed most. And I contemplate the cobwebs of the Facts of Life.

A Speedy Road To Jail

bout half way up to Dublin they stopped at a country pub that has a snug just inside the front door. Pat Breen and Hugo Treacy, who had been sitting in the back seat of the car, got out first and were installed in the snug, with the serving hatch open, by the time young Andy Geoghegan had locked the car and came in to join them.

Andy and Pat took off their caps and left them down side by side on a shelf beside the hatch. A merry red face appeared there after a minute or two, a jovial man in his fifties...I know him well...and he took their order for three pints. The outside bar was full of men and women all dressed up in their Sunday best of a Friday.

"You're busy today," said Pat Breen to the barman when he shoved three pints through the hatch. "A decent man died. They were all at the funeral," said the barman, giving quick change and disappearing down the busy bar.

Pat Breen handed around cigarettes and the three men slowly relished their pints. Hugo Treacy saluted his companions with his before he delicately extracted the first creamy inch of it.

"Ye are decent lads, both of ye," said Hugo Treacy. "I never came up this road in better company and God knows I've traveled it often enough."

He was a very thin wiry man in his late thirties, very dark-featured, with fine white teeth and a coiled quick power in every movement. He was a citeog, a left-handed person, and he had very sharp brown eyes and a poised hawklike head. Even in repose, in the snug, he looked like a man they might call Speedy. That was, in fact, his nickname back home in the Galway parish.

"I traveled with a lot worse company myself," said Pat Breen, slouching down comfortably. "You're a great man to pass away a journey with, Speedy, I'll give you that." He chuckled quietly in his chest. "I know it's kind of early in the evening but I don't suppose you could rise to a bar of a song yet, could you, to liven up this pub?"

Young Geoghegan raised his eyebrows quizzically, saying nothing, but Breen nodded quickly at him and Speedy Treacy smiled widely altogether, a quick flash of teeth. "I don't know if it would be appropriate, Pat," said Speedy, "but I wouldn't mind at all. But isn't that a funeral crowd out there? They mightn't like it."

"They'd love it," said Pat Breen. "I know this area well. I worked here ten years ago. They'll be singing themselves in about a half hour and not one of them as good as you."

"Jesus," said young Geoghegan, "I'm not so sure it would be right either." He went to the hatch and stuck his face into it, calling three more pints. When the barman came with them young Geoghegan said, "We have the best ballad singer in the West of Ireland here with us. Would it be alright if he left out a blast or two?"

"It would be like a breath from heaven," said the barman. He looked quickly into the snug at the three of them and laughed out loud. "It would be mighty," he said.

"Go ahead, Speedy, so," said Pat Breen.

Speedy Treacy took another delicate sip of porter and looked up towards the ceiling of the snug. His eyes focused on a knothole in the timber ceiling and then they went blank and then he closed them altogether and then he sang. And it was at this point, just on the first line of 'She Lived Beside The Anner,' that I came into the pub, heading down from Dublin, and the big Westmeath farmer in his Sunday suit of a Friday opened the door to let out the song into the pub and I saw Pat and Andy, whom I know well, and Speedy, whom I know by repute, and he was walking towards the stars along the soaring notes of Anner.

He has a wildly powerful voice, like a tenor who stopped the lessons about a month too early and went on the booze, every golden note accordingly lubricated with porter, and it stuck me to the floor.

'Take this message to my mother
Say we'll meet with God above
Likewise to my dear father
Say I send them all my love,
May the angels ever guard them,
Is their dying sister's prayer
And enclosed within the letter
was a lock of nutbrown hair.'

The pub went wild, of course, when Speedy finished, and men crowded into the snug, and women too, to shake his hand, his quick citeog hand, and shower him with drinks, all of us, and I was chatting Pat Breen for a wee while in the middle of it.

Speedy, he said, was the best singer he ever heard. It was always great to travel with him. It was a pity that he was so quick and dangerous with the citeog, that he half murdered his mountain neighbors with strikes of it so quick when they annoyed him, usually over land, and that they were so quick to take revenge on him. But, Lord, wasn't he the great singer.

The best in all Ireland, the big Mullinger mourner said to me after, the best in whole of Ireland. And he sent a full glass of brandy into the snug to Speedy, who at his stage had a black-haired woman sitting on his knee, and Speedy responded with 'The Rocks of Bawn.' Oh he wished the Queen of England would send for him in time. For to place him in some regiment all in his youth and prime. To fight for Ireland's glory from clear daylight to dawn. And never to return again to Plough The Rocks of Bawn. And the power of it tore holes in the cobwebs in the far corners of the pub.

It was when they were still clapping that song that Pat Breen said to Speedy that maybe they should be shortening the road to Dublin. And Speedy said he supposed they should, because he'd hate to be the cause of Pat's fine wife Maggie having to spend the night on her own below in Galway. And young Andy Geoghegan said to me that he'd learned more that day, about his job, than they had ever taught him. And then the two guards put on their uniform caps with the silver badges and they stood up and it was only then you saw that Speedy had been handcuffed to Pat Breen all the time.

They were bringing him up to Mountjoy to serve three months for assault. When he stood up and came out of the snug, all of the crowd shouting good luck to him, he shook the handcuffed arm in the air, with Pat Breen grinning, and Speedy grinned wickedly and sang one last blast.

A lonely feeling, he sang, was o'er him stealing. And the mice were playing in his prison cell. And the Auld Triangle went Jingle Jangle. All along the Banks of the Royal Canal. And then they were gone.

Glasses Geraghty And The Sin Bin

Did I ever tell you the story of how Glasses Geraghty broke the sacred seal of confession and caused total chaos in the parish of Partrymore, away up in the Mayo mountains?

In the course of this work, they threw out the old pine confessional box, all warped and woodwormed, where the sins of the parish had been whispered to five canons and sixteen curates for nearly 200 years.

I don't think I did so I'll rectify the omission now because it's one of the best stories I ever heard. It is also quite a scary one for anyone who ever opened the door of a confessional box and went in, knelt down in the dark, and whispered their secret sins through the bars of the grille to the priest.

Over there you talk about the sky high technology of star wars. That's nothing at all to the mind-bending sciences unleashed on the parish of Partrymore four autumns ago by young Glasses Geraghty, only son of Terence and Theresa Geraghty, from the highest house in the parish on top of Hanging Rock.

Up there the air is clear and powerful. People always say that is the reason the Geraghtys were always so intelligent they trembled on the brittle brink of madness. Young Glasses, whose real name is Gerard, but whose thick lenses early earned him the nickname, is probably the most intelligent of them all. Wherever he is now - and I don't know exactly where - I bet he is doing powerful work. However, it is unlikely to have such startling results as the time he broke the seal of confession in Partrymore.

We have a national competition for young scientists over here annually, you see, and Glasses, in his final year in the Regional College, a straight A student all the way, was a natural four years ago. He was casting around for an exciting project to enter for the competition and it so happened that at the same time the parishioners of Partrymore were carrying out major reconstruction on St. James church.

In the course of this work, they threw out the old pine confessional box, all warped and woodwormed, where the sins of the parish had been whispered to five canons and sixteen curates for nearly 200 years. For six days, in the rain, the old box lay sadly at the gable of the parochial house and on the seventh day Glasses Geraghty asked the poor canon if he could have it, it not being a sacred piece of furniture any more.

The canon was glad to get rid of it. Young Glasses brought it home to the Hanging Rock with a tractor and trailer, dropped it off near his workshop, went to work, and that was when the sport started.

It so happened I had occasion to call to the house in connection with a newspaper story three days later. I dropped into the workshop to see how young Glasses was getting on with his project. I'm not a technical person and much of what the young fellow said to me that day escaped my mind, except I came to the conclusion he was stone mad.

He had the old confessional reassembled and standing in the yard with its doors open. A tangle of cables and wires ran inside, some roughly tied to the grilles. The other ends of the cables were attached variously to the dashboard of an old Volkswagen car alongside the box, to a generator, to a small home computer, to the zinc roof of the henhouse, to a rusty mowing machine, to an aerial protruding through the window of his makeshift workshop, and finally to an old style gramophone on the workshop bench.

"What exactly are you trying to do?" I asked young Glasses who was highly excited. He responded in a language which I couldn't understand fully, it being laden with electronic jargon, but I dimly gathered his thesis was that the spoken work, especially the urgently whispered word, never dies and is somehow imprinted in physical objects nearby such as the grille of a confessional.

He was arguing they could be brought back, these whispers from there, by some complex agitation of sound frequencies. "Good luck to you anyway, young Glasses," says I and left him, smiling under my beard as he was revving up the old Volkswagen engine, causing the henhouse to shake to the foundations and causing some kind of red bulb to illuminate itself inside the confessional. Stone cracked, was my judgement at the time.

It was exactly two nights later, after midnight, that bright flashes emanated from the top of the Hanging Rock and Johnny Enright, the thatcher, coming home half drunk, clearly heard, apparently from the skies, the unmistakable sounds of his one-time neighbor, Shubert Mason, 23 years dead, confessing the lurid sins of a Saturday at the Galway races - sinful day and long sinful night - to Canon Halligan, ten years dead and buried and very cross entirely with Shubert before he came to the Absolvo Te.

Rooted to the road, shaking, Johnny Enright then heard all the sins, scarlet enough some of them, from some Saturday night confessions in St. James Church, in the years after the war. They were all being broadcast clearly through the frosty air.

Poor Johnny broke down altogether when he heard himself, as a mere stripling, confessing about a night with Rosie Murphy after a crossroads dance in 1946. And the tongue lashing he got. Then and there, even at that hour, he went straight to the canon and the trouble started.

I had been wrong, you see. When the canon and Johnny arrived at Geraghty's, at nearly two in the morning, they discovered that young Glasses had indeed broken the sonic seal of the old confessional box. It was some sight. The old Volkswagen engine was revving, sparks were flying out of all the cables, the generator was spluttering and, worst of all, from the gramophone, in some amazing fashion came all the whispered sins of Partrymore.

They were spewing out from the long dead and the living alike and being broadcast from a speaker on the hayshed roof at high volume - science has no respect for secrecy. "I've done it, Canon," shouted young Glasses at the canon the minute he saw him.

And those were the only words he had time to say before the Canon hit him a clip under the ear which knocked him into the henhouse. Then, without a word, the canon and Johnny ripped down all the cables, smashed the gramophone to smithereens, stopped the old Volkswagen, and burned the old confessional box, there and then, to white ashes. Geniuses, I always say, are never given recognition in their own parishes.

Young Glasses, in disgrace and public odium, left home inside the week and never returned. He was last heard of in Turkey. If the Russians lay hands on him, mark my words, ye can forget about star wars.

King Of The Tinkers

The Barretts of Galway are traveling people. Their breeding and bone is of the high and higher roads of Connacht, until recently the old camping sites beside spring wells and close to the curlings and curvings of rivers like the Suck.

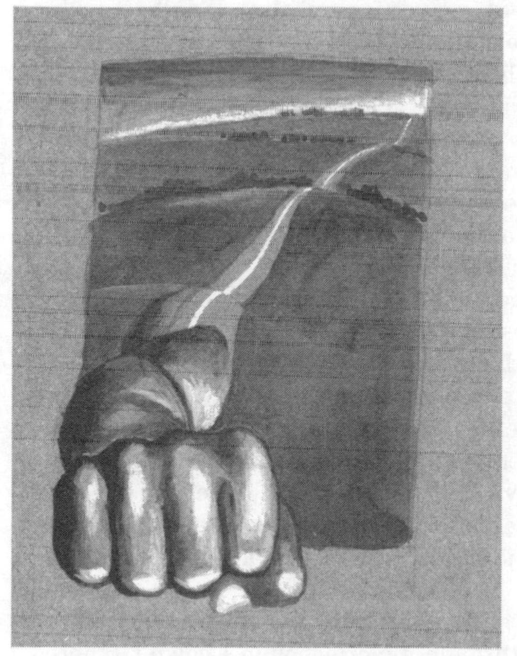

They are one of the colorful clans that once filled whole stretches of countryside with the wildness of their lifestyle, the fiery horses, the roundy caravans, the flat spring carts with their spindly shafts pointed toward the stars near where stickfires crackled and fizzled and drove heart into great iron pots full of the kind of stew that only travelers ever knew quite how to make. Everything in spring water with a fist of salt and plenty of pepper, carrots and parsnips and big onions and rabbit and chicken and mutton, sometimes all at once. I tasted such stews once or twice, and when your belly would be outside them you would be well fit for any road in Ireland.

But, anyway, the times have changed and the traveling people of Ireland, naturally, have changed too. The horse-drawn caravans are gone the way of yesterday, replaced by glittering big caravans hauled behind motor vans and jeeps. The traditional country campsites are deserted most of the year, replaced by concreted and semi-serviced hardstands on the edges of towns and cities. Most of the travelers don't travel all that much anymore.

I think the average traveler is still as much maligned as ever, despite all the efforts that have been made down the years by integration workers. They are still seen as second class citizens.

Like the Barretts of Galway, most of them spend the most of their lives on top of these hardstands. They take on the complexities of modern living as best they can. A fair few of them, it has to be stated, make a horse's hames of it and their violent deeds, especially in relation to rural elderly people, have blackened the modern reputation of the overwhelmingly decent majority. It is the way of things today.

I think the average traveler is still as much maligned as ever, despite all the efforts that have been made down the years by integration workers. They are still seen as second class citizens. Young traveler men are not allowed in most public houses for a drink. Young women are refused admission to nightclubs and discos. There are regular rows, right throughout the country, when local authorities allocate houses to travelers. The would-be neighbors object, frequently violently.

Similar rows erupt when local councils announce plans to build more hardstands or serviced camping sites for the travelers. Such uproars are so common that they are not even headline news any more.

Neither is the fact that travelers, especially after their huge funerals, still are guilty, far too often, of disgraceful behavior on the streets, especially brawling and drunkenness. When a traveler dies and comes to be buried, the local publicans nowadays routinely close their doors. When an elderly farmer is robbed and beaten up, the public perception nowadays is that it was probably a gang of travelers who did it. The facts, sadly, often enough support that perception.

It is reasonably certain that the rising generation of young traveler males include a percentage who, usually through experiences in England, where they regularly go, are tougher and harder and infinitely more criminal in their lifestyles than were their fathers and grandfathers. This group has created havoc throughout the past decade and has done much to harden the attitudes of the settled majority towards travelers.

And so we come to Frankie Barrett, of the Galway clan, who is aged 19 years and who is a fighting man. With a difference.

The fighting men of the traveling people have been legendary over the generations. The bare-knuckle tradition has survived amongst the clans to this day. Annually, with huge bets on the side, the hardiest of the breed fight each other at the Ballinasloe Horse Fair.

I have seen maybe a dozen of these battles. They are hugely exciting, passionate, fiery and brutal. The champions strip to the waist and try to club each other senseless, usually not heeding self-defense at all. The action is fast and furious and the bets run to thousands of pounds. The action gives visiting TV news teams great footage and the moveable arenas cause great policing difficulties for the Gardai.

The fights are as much a part of the traveler culture as the bareback horse races which also enliven this elemental side of the Horse Fair and, in more recent years, the trotting races. Ballinasloe is the great hosting of the traveler clans, year after year, and there are always bleeding reputations afterwards. And much more ammunition, too, for those who claim that the travelers are a lower form of humanity.

And so we come to Frankie Barrett, fighting man with a difference. At 19, living in a caravan on the Hillside estate outside Galway and training in an old truck container beside the family caravan, Frankie Barrett is now the senior amateur boxing champion of Ireland at his weight, whose precise definition escapes me now, but which is about 11 stone.

Against all the odds, always fighting out of the hardest corner, young Frankie has made it to the very top of his sport. Now, as you read this, he is in intensive training for that selection tournament which, if he gets through it, will lead towards the Atlanta Olympics.

I reckon, and so do many real experts, that Frankie Barrett has all that it takes, and maybe a bit more, to make it all the way in the professional game after Atlanta. They call Wayne McCullough the Pocket Rocket, and this Barrett, already, has all the action of McCullough, a harder punch in either hand, and the kind of all action style which should one day make him a millionaire. Not for nothing did he win the special medal for the Best Boxer of the entire Irish championships.

He was fighting a taller, physically superior Corkman in his final. The Corkman was also rated as the better boxer coming into the decider. Barrett, after all, though many times a juvenile champion, has only months ago graduated from intermediate ranks. He is still a learner. But right from the first bell, with immense power and no little skill, the Galway traveler waded into his man. He has an incredible wallop in both hands.

In the first round the Corkman, with excellent technique, was able to avoid the worst of the punishment coming towards him and probably shaded the initial exchanges. After that, however, the tide turned. In the third round, pouring forward all the time, punching from every angle, the young traveler's power and purpose was almost awesome.

He is stocky and muscular, like a boxer's version of Maradona the footballer. He wore a pair of shorts which carried the message "I Know No Fear."

But he was somehow a little more than the sum of all his boxing parts. He has that thing called star potential, which you can see at a distance without being able to precisely define. It is what Michael Carruth, for example, has not got, which Stevie Collins, even though a world champion, has lamentably not got, and which the Pocket Rocket demonstrably has. And so has Barrett.

I can take or leave pro boxing as a sport. On the other hand, if you are an Irish traveler living in a caravan and training in an old truck body, there are not that many highways towards a better lifestyle.

Far too many young travelers of Frankie's generation, still only teenagers, appear in the court reports in newspapers, in Galway and everywhere, for brawling on the streets outside pubs and take-aways. And for more seriously violent crimes.

The settled community are not going to be much help to Frankie until he gets to the Atlanta Olympics. That's for certain. And already, there would be people saying that because he's a traveler, the next fight he could become involved in could be a bareknuckle thing on a street corner over a bag of chips. From all I hear of Frankie Barrett that is not going to happen. I dearly hope so.

This young man, whose glittering shorts say that he knows No Fear, could do a great deal, not just for himself but for his people, by devoting himself totally for the next few years to his sport. He could and should strike gold and fame and fortune. He could become the first real King of the Tinkers. That would be great.

Every Picture Tells A Story

he tourist that I met at Reception in that lovely little hotel in Bundoran called The Foxe's Lair was, she said, from Cincinnati and I never met anyone from Cincinnati.

> **It was a kind of postcard which sells millions here in summer. You've seen it. There was a hardy countryman sitting on his ass cart coming out of a scenic bog in Connemara.**

She was a lovely little old lady and we stayed chatting for minutes at the desk even after Pat McNelis gave us our keys and personally carried our bits and bags away to the rooms. Pat is from Ardara, up where the map of Donegal turns all brown and heathery and, strangely, Marion's husband had been an Ardara man too.

I learned he was a Bonner and she met him when they were both young. He had always been planning to go home but children came along in numbers, and the attendant bills and the years fled and they never made it. So Marion, whose parents came to Cincinnati from Scotland, decided she would come by herself and there, spry as a bee, she was. She was going to Killybegs with her group the next day, she said, and on the following day to Killarney.

I didn't say to Marion that such journeys represented a very small morsel of the Irish nation. It was no business of mine. I said all the useful things I could think of, about Killybegs and Killarney, and then we parted. I was working on the election. It was the next morning, as old friends, we met again at Reception after breakfast and Marion had just purchased a picture postcard from Pat's desk stand.

That single photograph was the only bit of labor the blackguard ever did, and under heaven he has never stopped drawing money and booze out of it since.

It was a kind of postcard which sells millions here in summer. You've seen it. There was a hardy countryman sitting on his ass cart coming out of a scenic bog in Connemara. In the background past the ass's ear, one could see three white washed cottages, two of them thatched. There was a battered cap on the turfman's head, pitched to the left hand side, and a pipe in his mouth.

A small freckled boy in a red sweater, with red hair too and freckles, was seated beside the turfman. A black and white sheep dog was sloping along the side of the road just ahead of the ass. A thread of smoke was barely visible from the nearest of the two thatched cottages. It made a pretty picture, a perfect Irish summertime postcard.

Marion loved it. She showed it to me. "Hasn't he a magnificent face? Doesn't he look content? That must be his grandson along with him, coming home after a day working in an Irish bog cutting peat? Isn't the donkey lovely?" She was a sensible woman, Marion, so I put my elbows on the desk and told her the truth behind the glossy face of that postcard: told her there and then.

"Your man," says I, gesturing at the turfman, "your man never cut a sod of turf in his life. That's the infamous Mick Pat Connor. Mick Pat has kept his hands so clear of manual labor all his life that there are actually tufts of black hair growing on his palms. The nickname they have on him in Derrybeg - where that picture was taken - is actually Hard Labor Connors.

"He's 72 years old this summer, lives well off his sharp wits and that's his house away at the back of the picture postcard, the one that isn't thatched. Look very closely and you'll see his bicycle leaning against the gable.

"The only other thing in that picture that's Mick Pat's is the dog. The dog's name is Guinness, the same as the drink. That's one of Mick Pat's cutest strokes. Himself and the dog go together into Mac's Pub every summer evening when the place is full of tourists. Somebody always asks the name of the dog. That starts a laugh, and when somebody calls the dog by his name, Josie Mac always says, 'Do you mean Guinness for all in the house?' and there's no knowing how many pints that sheepdog has earned for Mick Pat.

"Now Marion, do you see the nearest thatched house, the one with the smoking chimney? That belongs to Joe Taylor. He is a crony of Mick's, maybe the only real friend he has, and Joe does have a bit of a bog and does cut turf. But the reason the fire is burning in the postcard is because Joe turned his ankle chasing sheep the week before the photographer came and so Mick Pat borrowed Joe's ass and the cart for the bog.

"They got $100 from the photographer who came down from Dublin, and they split it down the middle. They had three great nights in the pub out of that picture postcard. Strangely enough Joe's daughter was home from England that weekend and she met a local lad on the second night and now they are engaged so there's romance attached to this postcard as well."

At this stage Marion was entranced and Pat McNelis was standing up at the desk with his mouth open, looking at his own postcard as if he had never seen it before. "The young boy with the red jumper is no native of Derrybeg," I continued. "He was the photographer's son and a right brat. Himself and the red sweater he's wearing were specially imported to sit there in the cart.

"The photograph was actually taken in the month of September when there was no turf in the bog and it was bloody cold. I remember well the young boy was crying most of the time because Mick Pat wouldn't let him hold the reins or give sugar to Joe Taylor's she-ass. Do you know why?

"That's the worst tempered bitch of an ass in Ireland. She'd eat the face of any man, woman or child that would come into range. See the strain on the reins in Mick's hands? Just after that shot was taken, in fact, the ass lunged at the photographer and nearly tore the trousers off him.

"A real bad ass. Joe Taylor got rid of her afterwards and she was 50 tins of cheap pet food by the time this postcard was issued first about two summer's ago."

Marion and Pat studied the bad ass very closely. "This postcard," says I, "is better than a state pension to Mick Pat Connors. He'd be autographing copies of it in the pub every night, sitting up there, full of drink. That single photograph was the only bit of labor the blackguard ever did, and under heaven he has never stopped drawing money and booze out of it since. The word is ill divided."

Marion reached out and took the dozens copies of the card remaining on Pat's hands and bought the lot. "And do you see that little blotch of a shadow on the road there in front of the sheepdog?" says I.

"That's me!"

And it was.

Sandy The Soberer: A Good Egg

I have a splendid eggler called O'Dwyer who calls to my door once a week with lovely brown eggs. I had one of them threeminuted for breakfast this morning.

As I struck it sharply on the left anterior area of its bald poll with the eggspoon, to release the goodness within, I was struck myself, just as sharply, by a memory all compounded and complexified of brown eggs, brown porter, brown sauce, brown bog, an RUC sergeant's flinty brown eyes, and about 25 drunken hens of Rhode Island Red variety.

Yes, and through the whole memory, like a warm tweed coat, the kindly zany aura of my lovely father Sandy whom men once called The Soberer.

There are a few men in America today who are nearly millionaires...according to the stories we get back here anyway... who will remember Sandy the Soberer with a grateful shudder. They're probably teetotalers today but they surely were not on those autumn nights by the Erne when I was ten and a pint of porter was tenpence and the road from Enniskillen was straight enough until you came to MacConnell's Shop.

Then it hooked and crooked, brown soft bogs on either side, and there was hardly a weekend but some poor divil with a few pints extra aboard wouldn't come to grief. We'd hear brakes squealing in mortal agony, inside in our kitchen even, or in the wee country shop, and then there'd be a scrunchysplush noise of a vehicle ploughing into the bog below the road.

And then the hiss of silence... except the once... and then Sandy the Soberer, behind the counter of the shop, would already be swinging into action.

Yes, I know, I know, it's anti-social, even criminal to drinkdrive. And I agree. But, as so often with us Irish, there were extra factors in those days.

The men passing our door all Kicked With Our Feet and were all, to a man, in that unfair era, being well and truly kicked about by the RUC. Furthermore there was an Orangewoman in the locality, with a rare telephone, who never slept, and, as sure as the Lord made little apples, she'd be on the phone to the police to report the drunken Papist. And the police were never far away.

Sandy the Soberer and his aides, family and shop customers, would have 15 minutes at the most to do the sobering-up job and save the man's license. And, Lord above, I well remember those 15 minutes!

My mother would boil the kettle quickly and Sandy the Soberer would reach up on to the shop shelf for a bottle of brown H.P. sauce. It was largely composed of vinegar and spices and was commonly used with meats. Sandy would plunge the bottle into the hot water while his customers, strong men all, rushed out to the roadside bog to retrieve the victim. The bog was so soft they were never injured, not ever, but some of them were very drunk indeed. They would blink under our kitchen light like stranded fish, all pale and slurred and shocked. My mother would check, quickly, that no bones were broken and then Sandy would tip the nod to his cohorts...

I remember it well, we kids loved it, and they would seize the tipsy one and Sandy would bottle him with the lukewarm bottle sauce. We had a cousin Thomas who was often the chief assistant and Thomas had some trick of being able to keep the struggling victim's jaws opened, by pressure on some jaw nerve, until every last drop of the hideous dose had been consumed.

Some men jerked, as if being electrocuted, when the sauce hit their systems. Others went rigid. One or two fainted briefly. Some said, later, that they would rather do six months in jail than ever be bottled by Sandy the Soberer again. But one fact was constant. When the bottling was over, within minutes, when the RUC men would troop into the kitchen, revolver butts gleaming at their waists, the victim would be sober. He might be green in the face. He might be trembling. He might have a fixed stare in his eye. He might even speak in a falsetto voice as a result of all that hot vinegar. But, by God, he was sober and no man ever lost his driving license after being bottled by Sandy the Soberer.

There were no breathalyzers or blowing in bags in those days, of course. The police used to ask the suspects to pick up coins from the floor. They would ask them their name and address and the date. They would, finally, ask them to walk a straight line formed by the tiles in our kitchen. We'd all watch like hawks. I remember it well.

After being bottled by our Sandy, a man could walk a straight line all the way to Moscow and touch the tip of his nose with his index finger any time a sergeant asked him.

After being bottled by our Sandy, a man could walk a straight line all the way to Moscow and touch the tip of his nose with his index finger any time a sergeant asked him. The Orangewoman with the phone must have hated Sandy the Soberer. He never lost.

It was a great social service he performed as well, that lovely gentle man, now with God at the end of all the crooked highways of Life. No man he ever bottled once ever arrived back in our kitchen again. Several told him afterwards they never touched a drink again. In real physical terms they suffered as much from that bottling, for seven days and nights afterwards, they claimed, as they would have done in a month's hard labor. They never again assaulted the brown porter of Enniskillen in such a fashion as to leave them likely to fall into the hands of Sandy the Soberer ever again.

The police were puzzled too. When I was a cub reporter, years later, one of them, then retired, asked me directly what miracles my father Sandy performed with drunken drivers in his kitchen. This sergeant had big hard brown eyes in a soft fleshy face and I remember looking into the well of them and saying, "My father used to remind them of the kind of Justice you gave them. That sobered them up awful fast."

He didn't like it at all. I liked him even less. He would throw down more coins for the suspects to lift than anyone else would. Small big things, like that was his forte. He's dead since. I doubt if he's moving in the same merry circles, though, as my father and the men he bottled with brown sauce so long ago.

The only drunks I ever saw after the bottling operations were the Rhode Island Red hens. It was the only noisy crash too because the load of battery hens, big fat matronly ladies of hens, were being transported in wooden crates by a Fowlman who, forgive me, fell foul of one pint too many and had to be bottled.

The crates burst open in the impact and, long after the sobered Fowlman had survived the RUC and was suffering the horrific after-effects of the bottling, we children were out through the dark bogs and fields capturing the hundred shocked hens. They were easy to catch, having been housed all

their lives. They crouched down in the beams of our torches the very way we were all supposed to crouch down before the RUC. We caught the majority of them.

They were bound for some soup factory, their laying days over, according to the green-faced Fowlman when we eventually got himself and his patched up crates back on the road in the wee small hours.

There were seven of them, though, in a dreadful state of disorientation, on our back doorstep the next morning. They, who had never seen the sunlight, were drunken on an October's morning richness. They were blind and staggering and their speech was slurred and any policemen would have put them in jail. We told the Fowlman about them and, as a gesture of thanks, he gave them to Sandy the Soberer.

They got the free range of our back garden, under the apple trees, a whole new lifetime of joy and freedom, and Sandy the Soberer even got a big rooster from the Cavan border to keep them company. He was like that. And, in return, they began to lay these lovely big brown eggs for us. In nests under the trailing limbs of the whitethorns, sweet, they were as nuts. Eating an O'Dwyer egg this morning, tapping its brittle skull, I tapped my own too. And I enjoyed my breakfast.

What Goes Around Comes Around

hat happened was that Joey McHugh got drunk one night when he was 20. His eyes got red-rimmed, which is a sign of a McHugh maddening for a fight, after exactly seven pints of porter. The spiky black hair seemed to stand up straighter on his head. That's another sign. Then he jumped off his stool in Fegan's Pub, which is an elemental pub today, too, as it always was, and he went off out through the door looking for a fight.

If he had enough money for seven pints he often fought at the weekends.

This was in the North, 40 years ago and times don't change that much. The first man Joey McHugh met was a young RUC constable from Bangor. A red rag to a drunk, green bull. Joey McHugh sailed into the poor young policeman like a day's work. He hammered him within an inch of his life. Then he ran off to Manchester rather than face the inevitable court proceedings.

There is not now, nor has there ever been, much good or goodness attached to Joey McHugh. That's fair enough. It is not his fault. It's in the ancient genes. A few centuries ago the McHugh's were much prized by the Chieftains of that region as warriors, gallowglasses, knifemen. It was known then that they went berserk in battle, fearing nothing nor no man. It is not Joey McHugh's fault that he is what he is. The spiky hair is silvery now and he is stiff. But you don't trifle with him. He is, in a way, a warrior out of season. Born outside his true era.

Joey worked on the buildings in Manchester and lived with cousins. He came back to face the court music a year later when his mother was sick. Time tempered the court's diligence and he was merely fined heavily and given a suspended sentence. One factor of the relative clemency was that

the young constable was a champion RUC boxer, and said that McHugh was the "hardest boyo" he ever met in his life.

"The defendant was drunk and I should have been able to handle him," said the constable frankly, "but I was unable to do so." The constable's name was Balfour.

Joey went back to Manchester. If he had enough money for seven pints he often fought at the weekends. If he drank less, somewhere between three and five pints, he went after women instead. This is not laudable but it is a fact.

On one weekend Joey had an encounter with a young Manchester woman called Celia Boles. It was only one night, but Celia Boles subsequently became pregnant. She was a member of a large and supportive family, a wild girl at the time, and they looked after her. Joey McHugh never knew anything about it. It is possible, since they had been ships passing on a moonlit night, that Celia Boles did not even know where he worked. Her family did not go after Joey, perhaps just as well. Celia Boles had a son. He was a healthy child. They named him Tom.

Joey McHugh came back home after eight or nine years in England and went to work with the building firm of a more successful local man whom he'd worked with in Manchester. Joey was a fine, hard worker, glorying in the tough, physical stuff.

Some time later, he began going out with a local girl called Mary Monaghan. They married in time and had a family of two daughters and three sons. The daughters and one of the sons took after their mother. They have flat, wide, dark faces on top of flat, benevolently willing minds. They are nice people. The daughters are now nurses and the son works in a bank in London. The other son was a McHugh from the day he was born, from the marrow of his bones to the outside of his freckly skin, a full son of Joey's. They called him Tom.

Tom McHugh worked in the hometown, first as a television aerial erector and later as a roofer. He was never unemployed, always a hard worker. He played Gaelic football for a team called the Slashers and never played well, not really, until he got a knock or two. Maybe a bleeding nose from an elbow. Then he could be magnificent.

You know the type. He drank on the weekends. If he took between three and five pints he was inclined to go after the girls. If he took seven pints or more his eyes might get red-rimmed and the spiky hair might appear to stand up straighter on his skull and he might be inclined to fight. That is putting it mildly.

The country, as we all know, went into a spasm of Troubles, punctuated with bombs and bullets. It is not over yet, not by a long chalk and just about everybody is involved one way or the other in the area where the McHugh's live. The remarkable exclusion, given the genetic history, is that the McHugh's never have been. I cannot explain this. They vote Nationalist, of course, like all their community, but a family that might have been expected to be actively Republican, at whatever level, simply never have been. This would be something that would be clearly and precisely known, by both communities, in their hometown area.

What happened was that a new, tough, English regiment came into the town a month ago. There had been a couple of incidents towards the end of the tour of duty of the last regiment. As is often the case, the new crowd clamped down hard when they took over. There was a lot of hassling and searching and holdups at checkpoints. That sort of thing. The temperature climbed a point of two but nothing major. One evening, as so often happens, a soldier who was on a foot patrol was just a little careless and a sniper on the hill above the chapel did what snipers did. It happened on a Saturday evening about seven o'clock. The killing set off the inevitable military response.

What happened next was that Tom McHugh, who had been held up and hassled a lot on his way into town for a few drinks, took eight pints that evening. His eyes got red-rimmed. The spiky, black hair stood up straight on his head. His eyes turned triangular and black under their eyebrows. At closing time, he jumped off his stool and crashed out the door into the night.

What happened next was that the best mate of the soldier killed by the sniper was coming back into town with two other soldiers, having just heard the news. Having been off duty, having visited Belfast, the three of them had been drinking. Two of them were consumed by tears and nerves but not the best friend of the dead one. He was in the back seat, behind the driver, livid with rage. He was simply looking for a focus for it. What he saw was the prickly profile of Tom McHugh, on the curb, shaking his fist at the whole world. He ordered the driver to stop, the brakes screaming, and was out of the car and running towards Tom McHugh before the vehicle had come to rest.

The young soldier roared and Tom McHugh roared at the same time. they leaped towards each other. It would have been an interesting battle, except that the soldier's enraged right fist was full of revolver. He shot Tom McHugh three times into the face and chest, killing him instantly. Then the soldier stood over the fallen body, his chest heaving. His eyes were red-rimmed. The spiky hair was standing rigidly to attention on top of his head. His eyes were black triangles of hate.

He will be tried next month. His defense will plead for leniency on the grounds that his best friend had been shot dead, that he had drank seven pints of beer, and that there had been some provocation. Soldiers invariably get light sentences in the North, no matter what they do, and Corporal Tom Boles will be no exception.

Noirin And The Winking Wastards

The public telephone kiosk is just outside O'Flaherty's pub and O'Flaherty's pub, one of the finest, is just beyond Screenbenagapall, away out where Connemara turns the map brownest, though the hills themselves are yellow with the furze these days, and empurpled with heather, and I never pass O'Flaherty's. The car does need a rest there from all the hills. Ye know well what I mean .

Anyway, I had been within for a while, as the car recovered. I emerged eventually into the golden evening, considerably refreshed in the mind and body, and I was about to continue my journey home when the telephone rang in the kiosk.

It jangled with some urgency. The door of the kiosk was open and, Good Samaritan that I am, I stepped inside and answered. You could know from the static, even before you heard a voice, that the call was for long distance.

"Hello," says I, not being a man to spare words, as ye well know. "This is the kiosk outside O'Flaherty's. The pint is good within, the weather is good without, whoever you are." That, you will agree, is the proper way to answer any telephone.

"Jaysus Christ," said this male voice with a Connemara blas buttered all over it. "Are you the mad whore that writes for the 'Irish Voice' over here? This is Colie in New York. I do read you when I'm not sober. Is it yourself?"

"It is," says I, and added maxima culpas about the quality of the yarns betimes and asked him who he was, exactly like, and he wouldn't tell

> **He had a soft, thick white neck on him, had the Wastard, and I didn't like him at all. Noirin, however, was clearly wavering.**

me, exactly like, because there was the small matter of legal residence (or otherwise in New York), from which he was ringing, and, sure you never knew who was listening.

The boss of the pub was away and he got the use of the phone in the office. He was working in the pub for almost seven months, liked it right well. But you got lonesome. It was mighty, in fact, that a stranger had answered the phone because the work he wanted done was best done by a stranger. The neighbors were too nosy.

"What can I do for you, Colie?" says I.

"Look straight across from you," says he, "and you'll see a house with a slated roof and rose bush at the left hand side of the door."

"I see it." The house was only the width of the road and a small garden and street away.

"My girlfriend Noirin lives there with her mother and father," says Colie. "She has no phone nearer than this one and I was wondering if maybe you'd cross the road and give her a shout for me. If it's not too much trouble."

"No trouble at all," says I like a shot. "I'll get her for you directly. In fact, it's well if I don't see her already out on the street. There's a lovely blackheaded lady there talking to somebody in a red Ford."

"Oh, Jaysus Christ, the Wastard is moving in!" came this anguished cry down the line from New York and it is not feasible, my friends, to print the succeeding ten sentences spoken by Colie. Suffice it to say that they contained many references to the Wastard. The Connemara people, as ye know, tend to use a "W" sometimes where the rest of us use a "B". I said nothing at all. I was looking at Noirin and the Wastard.

He was leaning against the bonnet of the car and she was smiling up at him. The Wastard's hands were flying in all directions. You could see he was stating his case for a date. He was pointing, from time to time, in the direction of local singing pubs and even towards Salthill 30 miles away. He had a soft, thick white neck on him, had the Wastard, and I didn't like him at all. Noirin, however, was clearly wavering.

"What's happening there?" says Colie, just as Noirin turned and went back into the house. She left the door open behind her and Wastard sat into the car. I reported each detail to Colie accurately. It was the least I could do for him.

He said the Wastard Concannon was a well-known ram, no scruples at all, well known for moving in on other men's cailini whenever he got the chance. "Did a light come on there at the end of the house?" says he.

"It did. There's curtains there with a pattern of yellow flowers on them."

"Christ," says Colie, "she's going to go out with him. If I was where you are, Cormac, and I swear I'd wring the Wastard's neck. We'll have to stop her. Would you go over and tell her there's a phone call for her. Would you go over there as quick as you can? No, wait a minute, forget about Noirin altogether. Did you spot a big redheaded lad at the end of the bar when you were inside?"

"Yes," I said, "Big as a house. A lad they were calling Colie, if I'm right."

"Right. Get him for me quick as lightning. Quick now, because Noirin doesn't take too long to get ready."

I had the big red man out of the pub in 30 seconds. He clamped the phone to his ear. I stayed outside the kiosk and kept an eye on the Wastard. The light was still on the Noirin's room and the Wastard had the car window open and you could hear country music coming out of it. The tune was, ironically, 'Your Cheatin' Heart.'

The big red lad came out of the kiosk, having replaced the receiver, and he looked me straight in the eye and said thanks. Then he hitched at the waistband of his trousers and started purposefully across towards the Wastard. I got into my own car and shamelessly watched. The light was still on behind the yellow floral curtains.

The redhaired Colie went straight up to the Wastard, behind the wheel, and spoke so powerfully you could see his jugulars leppin'. On one occasion he struck the roof sharply with his fist. Seconds later the Wastard drove off. He drove off quickly.

The redheaded Colie stood there for a few seconds after. Then he scratched his head slowly. The light snapped off in Noirin's room. She came out to the doorstep. She was wearing a black leather jacket and high heels and looked very well. Redheaded Colie went up to the doorstep, grinning all over his face, towering over her, and spoke to her. I couldn't hear the words at all.

After a couple of minutes, I still watching, she began smiling just the way she had smiled at the Wastard. The redheaded Colie was laughing out loud and once he touched her on the shoulder. O Christ, I says to myself, it's well if he isn't another Wastard. Et bloody tu, Brute!

And dammit if the two of them didn't walk companionably down from Noirin's street to a battered blue van and the two of them climbed in. As he bent down to get inside, the redheaded lad looked straight over at me and winked a real genuine goldplated wink of a Wastard.

The phone rang in the kiosk again. It jangled urgently. I decided I wouldn't answer it and drove off. What would I have said to poor Colie anyway?

Book IV

Confirmations Aren't What They Used To Be

I assisted in the Confirmation of my Dara and my Ciara last week in the church of Mary Immaculate in Barna. The sun sparkled on the Galway Bay outside the church windows, there was bunting everywhere, Bishop Eamon Casey of the Diocese of Galway and Kilmacduagh was in splendid form, his crozier glittering, and there were moments during the ceremony when I was quite moved and very lonely for my children's mother. I had to stand alone behind my son and daughter, at the point where one places a parental hand on their shoulders as the Bishop applies Chrism. It was very obvious that the other gentle hand was missing.

His immobility shows that the MacConnells have become civilized, relatively speaking, since Johnny the Crow's time.

Dara and Ciara looked very well. They selected their clothing themselves. Ciara has superb thick hair and it glossified like a blackbird's wing. Dara is all legs and shoulders, and is emerging as the most handsome of my sons. He is, of course, taking after his father! He remained immobile when the Bishop was actually confirming him as a Strong and Perfect Christian and a Soldier of Jesus Christ, which is a fragment from the old penny catechism book of my youth. His immobility shows that the MacConnells have become civilized, relatively speaking, since Johnny the Crow's time.

In an era when corporal punishment was standard in all schools, with a strap or simple "belt across the lug," this inability to turn the other cheek was very costly to The Crow

Johnny the Crow, so called because his hair was blacker than Ciara's, and his skin swarthy, was an ancestor three or four generations back on my side. He was a very wild young fellow altogether, according to the family folklore, and was in trouble from the day he was born near the small town of Lisbellaw and even closer to the quaintly named townland of Tatymacall. Johnny's main fault, all his life, was that he was unable to turn the other cheek, as Christians have been exhorted to do since the time of the catacombs. It is maybe a national fault as well but it was especially strong in the genetic makeup of Johnny the Crow.

In an era when corporal punishment was standard in all schools, with a strap or simple "belt across the lug," this inability to turn the other cheek was very costly to The Crow. He was not especially bright at classwork, by all accounts, and so would qualify for a few slaps every schoolday. But he never learned how to just stick out his hand and close his eyes like everybody else. He would offer his hand, game as a hare, for the first slap but, the instant it was delivered, he would violently react. Usually, it is recorded, he would kick Master McCusker's shins in immediate response. This was not recommended because McCusker was then in his prime, well over six feet tall, and as strong as an ox. The punishment that poor Johnny the Crow drew upon himself for his reaction to the slaps was very considerable indeed. "McCusker used to hammer the backside out of his britches," is the phrase most commonly used. It happened day after day, week after week.

Walking back to my bench after Dara and Ciara were confirmed, the memory of the stories about the poor Crow came back to me. And I reflected, not for the first time, that it would have been far better for the MacConnell clan if The Crow had never been confirmed at all when his time came. Because they should have known what would happen. Confirmation is not like Baptism or Penance or Eucharist at all. In the case of The Crow, to whom the Lord be kind today, it confirmed nothing at all except the poor devil's single weakness. They should have known what would happen.

The devout and traditional amongst ye will know that, according to the old rite of Irish Confirmation, the Bishops of Ireland approached the child before the alter. Typically in those days of the hierarchy, the Bishop was very old and feeble because of the power of the church in those days, the child was both transfigured and terrified by the enormity of a major occasion in his life. Then, having spoken some words, the Bishop applied the oil of chrism to the child's forehead, gently and delicately, blessing the child. Finally, as a symbolic gesture to signify the necessity for obedience to the church, the Bishop would give the child a very gentle slap on the cheek. A mere touch.

So the Confirmation time approaches for the poor Crow. The class sailed through the religious examination in the school a fortnight before and it is even recorded that The Crow distinguished himself before the diocesan examiner, a red-haired priest from Tyrone called McCann. Father McCann, much given to pastoral parables, and being a farmer's son himself, with an uncle a cattle-dealer, asked the entire class a kind riddle. At that time, in the country, there were quite a number of milking cows with holes, caused by thorns, in their teats. This made them difficult to milk. It was a common practice amongst farmers, when selling such damaged stock, to block the apertures with a combination of solids, including sealing wax or tallow from a candle. Suppose you doctored a defective cow in this fashion, asked Father McCann, and brought it to the fair and sold it, would you be committing a mortal sin?

No, says The Crow like a shot, you would not. It is up to the man buying the cow to make sure she is sound in wind and limb.

And Father McCann was most impressed with that answer. He patted The Crow on his black head and said a fragment of Latin, representing the law on the matter, and meaning Buyer Beware. And said to Master McKenna that The Crow would go far.

So, on Confirmation, poor Bishop McNicol, who was about 90 and feeble, came to the parish to confirm the children of Lisbellaw. And there was The Crow in the midst if them. And, as was his custom, the Bishop spoke first to the parents and made an impassioned plea for temperance amongst them all, and for the highest standards of morality and for the tolerance of all neighbors, including all Protestant neighbors in particular. And he praised the turnout of the children for Confirmation. Sitting in the front benches in their whites and blacks, every face intent and serious. And there was The Crow in the midst of them.

And so the Confirmation proper began. I have heard it described so many times at family gatherings that I can almost see it. The first row of boys and girls went up and they were all confirmed without delay and clattered back to their benches. And then the next row came up. And there was the poor Crow in the midst of them, a triangle of white handkerchief in his breast pocket and his first ever necktie around his thrapple. And then the Bishop came to confirm The Crow. And he prayed over his black head that he would be a soldier of Jesus Christ. And that was grand. And then he applied the gentle oil of chrism to the young swarthy forehead. And that was grand. And then, the Lord between us and all harm, didn't the poor wee old feeble Bishop, and him barely able to stand up, didn't he give the mandatory slap on the cheek to The Crow.

And The Crow downed the Bishop. One stroke. No delay. The right fist came over the top before you could say "Confirmation," and the wee Bishop and his peaked mitre and all his gilded vestments and all his old bones went down in a heap before the altar of God. And his big crozier fell down on top of him. And a candle that was lit. And two prayerbooks. Out like a light, the poor wee Bishop, and his family disgraced and scandalized for at least two generations. In fact it is something that was never forgotten in the Diocese. When I was being confirmed myself, 80 years later, I saw a wary look in the eyes of His Lordship.

Dara is reasonably stable, as MacConnells go. But even when he was being confirmed, and even though there is no symbolic blow to the cheek any more, I was ready for anything.

Death On The Island

n the island every man is the width of a jack plane in the end. The jack plane is the class of wood cutting instrument which has a leveling projection fore and aft. It is just under 30 inches in length. That is the width of all the island men, poor or rich, in the end when they come to die. It is the measurement they use for the shoulders of the coffins.

On the island coffins are never imported from the mainland to lie awaiting death in some hidden shed. On the island there is a superstition about that. It would not be lucky. On the island they never make your coffin before you die, even though your death comes by slow inches, as so often, and it would be the prudent thing to do. On the island they wait until you die before they begin to make your coffin. There is a superstition about that too, powerful as poitin. I like that.

On the island, if a boy dies, long before his prime, or a boy baby, they have another superstition. They do not make his coffin to the size he was when the Lord took him away. No they do not. On the island, for any male that dies, they use the jack plane for the basic measurement of the shoulders. Old men, shriveled with years and gales, are buried in coffins they would have filled in their prime. Babies, only pounds in weight, unlike

And if by chance any short piece has to be taken off a long plank to finish off the coffin then the rest of that plank will never be used for anything else, not even for making another coffin, because that would be unlucky.

on the mainland, are buried in full size coffins they would have been able to fill if the Lord had not taken them away before their time. I like that too.

On the island, a man's world still in 1997 on the edge of the Atlantic, they bury their women in coffins that are nearer their true size, small or large, and the girl babies too in baby coffins. There is a superstition about that also. I am not sure if I like it or not, but it is there.

On the island there are always plain deal planks somewhere, the cheapest and softest of wood, white as the driven snow in the sunlight, with knots on them, here and yonder, like the marks the old teachers used to say mortal sins always left on your soul, even after Confession, and that was the reason for the bleaching thing of Purgatory. That is the way it is.

And so when the death happens the men who make the coffins take the numbers of white deal planks that are needed, quietly under their arms, and they bring them to the house of the dead man, in the two hours after he dies, day or night, and they leave them down in a quiet place in the backyard, in a cow cabin or shed.

And everybody gathering in the death house for the wake knows that they are there, certain as the death that preceded them, as much a part of the cycle as the end of breathing, and whiskey and tea and porter is sent out to them, as it will be, a little later, for the gravediggers. And they will have the simple tools they need for the job, the jack plane, the longest of them, the measure of the width of a man.

On the island, when the wake is on in the death house, many of the male islanders will quietly drift out of the back door to the place where the men are making the soft white coffin with its king-sized shoulders. But not one of them will touch any piece of the wood that is making the coffin, or even the sawdust if they can avoid it, because there is a superstition about that.

And if by chance any short piece has to be taken off a long plank to finish off the coffin then the rest of that plank will never be used for anything else, not even for making another coffin, because that would be unlucky. It will be burned, too, with the smaller bits and pieces that are left over, in the

hearth of one of the coffinmakers. Deal burns badly, crackling and spitting angrily against the heat. Maybe like a soul being placed in Purgatory.

On the island there is no fancy lining for the deal coffin. On the island there is no woodstain for the white wood. On the island there are no fancy mocksilver handles or paneling on the wood. On the island there are no fancy screws for just screwing down the lid of the coffin when the corpse has been coffined. On the island, when you are coffined, they nail down the lid, flush and tight, with three inch nails driven home, powerfully but reverently, by the men that make the coffins. That is the way it is on the island.

On the island they are so very knacky with wood. It is because they are fishermen and boatmen and islanders. On the island, naturally, they make the coffin so well, the planking fitting so flush and neat, that the coffins that are the shape of small boats could float to America if they had to, instead of to paradise. On the island when they finally shoulder the coffins to the graveyard, up the hillside a safe bit from the ocean, the white boat shape atop the black mourning wave of blunt shoulders does look a lot like a boateen coming safely home to pier and mooring and home.

On the island most things are different to the mainland. On the mainland, with its richer clays and soils, passive and heavy oak and walnut caskets, it is not safe to reopen the family plot for six or seven years. Sometimes longer than that. On the island the hungry acidic loamy soils make soft-edged graves that seem to clutch the softwood white coffins almost as soon as they are lowered down to final rest. On the island, all and all and all is dust again, except the nails, by the time three summers have smiled, by the time three winters have snarled, when the swallows that flighted over the funeral are still young and strong. And I like that too.

Back From The Edge

The first time I was in McKenna's farmhouse on the island was when Jacko was 17 and already a bright spark. I recall he reached up to the mantle piece above the Stanley range that evening, when the craic and music was running high, and he took down his parent's wedding photograph from between the sacred heart lamp and a box of shotgun cartridges.

He was the glittering bright spark of his parents' lives. He was a long loose-limbed gimp of a lad when he was in his teens, always up to rascality.

Julie was looking smart on her wedding day in one of those tweed costumes brides wore at the time. Andy was wearing the good Sunday suit, the tie knotted tightly against his big apple and a huge grin on his face.

"Do you see that glint in Andy's eye?" was what young Jacko said to me when he handed over the photograph.

"I do." It was very obvious.

"Well that's me," said Jacko, and his big mother gave him an affectionate cuff behind the ear. I remember the occasion well. He was the glint in Andy's eye, too, if you must put it that way, because he was born nine months and four days after the wedding.

"Every old dragon in the parish was counting the fingers, it was that fast," was how Julie put it that night.

He was the last glint too. There came no child after him into McKenna's. He was the glittering bright spark of his parents' lives. He was a long loose-limbed gimp of a lad when he was in his teens, always up to rascality.

Jollip is a very strong laxative for sows. It works very quickly. Jacko slipped it into a cup of tea that Walter O'Toole unwittingly drank in their kitchen one night. Walter O'Toole, dour and sour, is the nearest thing there is to a fireside bore on the island. He barely made it out of the kitchen after he was dosed with the Jollip. He never bored the McKennas again.

Jacko went to "the bad" about five years ago. He left the farm and his parents and the half-decker fishing boat that earns more than all their acres when salmon are running through and he went off to England with a blondie-haired German hitchhiker with a leather skirt that came in on one of the tourist ferries.

He sent back letters for the first two years; he was Doing Well. For the next two years, he remained on the fringe of the emigrant circle of islanders that is in England, among the fraternity that could help him get work and digs and enjoy his craic and his wildness.

They obliquely reported back home about him. Jacko was still cracked as a cricket and drinking like a fish, their grapevine reported. He was still working on the buildings and he was never seen abroad in the pubs without at least two women hanging out of him. Jacko was okay.

But then, for the past year, there was silence. There was no word of him at all. Julie and Andy did hear he had gone to the Middle East working on an oil project in some desert but they felt the report wasn't reliable. It somehow seemed wrong for any report to suggest that Jacko would be in an arid desert.

Anyway, the story hadn't come back on the reliable tide of news from exiled islanders. It could be probably be discounted. Julie has some kind of saneness about her from her mother's side, from a seventh sense of knowledge and she told me when I called last February to see them that they were not worried at all about Jacko. She knew for certain he was alive and kicking somewhere.

It was a Sunday and Andy said nothing at all to me about Jacko. After the tea, though, he took a long coil of heavy rope from behind the farmhouse door and when Johnny O'Toole, brother of Walter, called by they invited me to go out for the apparently ritual Sunday walk along the cliff tops. There was no rain that day. It was a grand fine hardy evening.

They went straight as a die, the pair of them, to the edge of the island at Aughrismore. Here the cliffs that face towards the sea and wide open world beyond the island are deeply ledged and terraced, almost like a rude staircase toward the buttermilk of the surf far below.

Johnny jerked his thumb down towards the bottom ledge of the cliff, the one just above sea level. Even then I had to look hard several times, before I saw the shivering young ram, gaunt and bedraggled, almost plastered against the black cliff face behind him, compression-boned with terror from the nearness of the cruel sea.

Johnny is a cliffman, wiry as any goat, and I just stood there and watched while the pair of them tied one end of a long coil of rope to the strong stump of a bush near the cliff edge. Without further ado Johnny went off the edge and down towards the terrible sheep as swiftly and gently as a wisp of mist.

Watching him go, Andy said to me, out of nowhere, "The mother is worried about Jacko." And then, from another point of the compass altogether, he said, "The sweetest grass on the whole island grows in those ledges. The wildest of the young lambs do jump down on that wide first ledge, when they take the notion. They graze the last blade of it. It's awful sweet.

"Then they jump down to the next ledge and graze it clean, and then on down and down. Until they come to that last narrow one where that young ram is caught now. They can't get back up themselves. We call that ledge the Crioch, which is the Irish for the Finish. Mostly we come up here on the Sundays, and Johnny or Eamonn Jack go down and save them and bring them home. You'd lose the odd one, but not that many."

Below, Johnny tied the sheep to the rope. We hauled him up. It was easy. He was weak and famished but he had the use of his legs and he made off for himself back towards the safety of the hills when loosed from the rope. Andy dropped it back down to Johnny again and we watched him begin to come up, one quick sure boot after the other, hand over hand. "The young fellow of ours is out on a ledge somewhere," said Andy, "but we'll get him back."

I got a telephone call from a black English northern town calling Workington on Tuesday last. It was hospital social worker there. They had a strange young Irishman in their drying-out unit for winos. He wasn't too well. They had no name for him. And the only document they had, funny enough, was a story written by me in the *Irish Press* about an island where the cliffman saved the sheep from the ledges.

Would I have any notion who he was? Where was the island? Andy and Johnny flew out from Knock Airport to Workington the next morning. I pictured them, in the mind's eye, not flying away up high in their Sunday suits but going down all the ledges of the cliff towards a place called the Crioch - the Finish - to snatch back a famished, frightened wild thing.

And bring him safely back to a place where he was once only a glint in his father's eye.

A Cold East Wind Blowing

There was an east wind blowing on the evening that MacGowan was born in December of 1911. By the time the east wind reaches the December hills of the far west, it is a bitingly cold animal. The valley at Moughnanna, where MacGowan was born in the front room, channels and funnels the east winds, and sharpens their cold fangs against its granite flanks so that they always whip and snarl around the small house with a peculiar malevolence.

The Moughnanna people, like the MacGowans, hate the east winds. The prevailing airflow here is from the west, from the sea a mile away below, and so they all built their houses, like MacGowan's, facing the east.

The winds rattle the doors, accordingly, rattle the sashes of the windows, leak into the kitchens of the farmhouses in razored draughts that tweak at the bottoms of the curtains. Still, on the evening that Oliver MacGowan was born, in his parents' own big bed in that front room, there was a rare fire of black turf burning in the bedroom grate, very seldom used, and the room was warm and comfortable. The midwife was there for the birth, a big, strong nurse called Callanan, and the doctor came later to check that all was well. And it was.

Nobody ever thought to tell Oliver MacGowan that there was a cold and colder east wind blowing on the evening he was born.

The oak tree over the spud garden was still stubbornly clutching on to a bare handful of yellowing scallop leaves on the evening Oliver MacGowan was born. His father stayed around the house most of the time but, still, there were cows to be milked, bullocks to be foddered, jobs to be done.

One time, when the father was going out in his heavy boots, the wind blew two oak leaves into the kitchen against him, rustling in to the far corner beside the bag of flour and the big, bulging bag of Indian meal for the fattening turkeys. The father's hands were warm that evening, bringing the fodder to the beasts in the far field, because the wind knifed at the hacks on the outsides of his toiled fingers. Over his head a few late seagulls came breasting home to the cliffs from the chilled inlands. And you could hear the tide rattling the rounded rocks on the bleached beach of Annagh, grinding them all against each other, smalling and smoothing them.

Nobody ever thought to tell Oliver MacGowan that there was a cold and colder east wind blowing on the evening he was born.

He got married in early April of 1946, when he came back from the war. He would have been married before that, but not much before 35 years, except that he got captured by the war. He had been in America in construction, the second son of the house, and had joined up at the very beginning of the war because his friend Daly joined up. Daly died on some Pacific island, which I cannot spell, fighting Japanese men who were not afraid to die at all. But Oliver MacGowan came home safe, and because the brother from the homeland was marked with the scarlet flag of T.B., and died soon afterwards, Oliver came in for the place, and, later, without much fuss at all, married the Anna that his brother would have married had he lived.

Before that, though, the Health Board had to come to the house to fumigate the front room where Andy died. The consumption was infectious, so it had to be killed in the house after it had its killing done. The Health Board men wore white overalls and face masks, and they filled the room where Oliver was born (and his brother before him) with clouds of white powder. Oliver watched from outside with a hard face. He had used face masks himself, on those Pacific islands I can't spell, when he was using a Paragon flame-thrower against

the Japanese in the dark caves. You got the wind behind you when you were doing that, and the screams drifted away on the edges of the flamed winds. He didn't like to remember that.

He saw the Health Board men, at the end of their work, opening the windows of all the rooms of the farmhouse, and the two doors, front and back, so that the white fumigating cloud drifted away like his brother's last ghosting.

He did not notice that it was an east wind blowing that Saturday, scourging the inside of the house to all the corners, blowing the yellowing leaves from the oak tree into the kitchen. When he was foddering the bullocks that evening, later, the hacks or toilsores on the outsides of his fingers stung in the coldness. It was falling dark, and late seagulls went breasting home towards Annagh, to the sounds of a high tide grinding and smoothing and smalling the rounded rocks there. Himself and Anna never slept in the front room after they were married, but in the warmer (if smaller) room at the back of the farmhouse. They made five good children there before they were finished. And they were happy.

Oliver MacGowan was 80 years old last Tuesday. He told Anna, who is six years younger, that he felt better that morning than he had felt for two years. He was up at nine o'clock in the morning, helping his son Andy in the byre with the cows, their jaws champing solemnly in a row, all plumped out with good feeding and the coming calves of spring. He had two boiled eggs for his breakfast, where Andy had only one, with strong tea, and they listened companionably at the table to the radio news before Andy went out to the land with the tractor, and Oliver brought Anna her tea and toast to bed.

It's a hardy enough day out, he told her, hardy but bright and dry. Happy birthday, she said and gave him a kiss on the left side of his face. They always got on well together, the pair of them. She said that the three of them would go out that evening, down to the hotel, for their dinner and few drinks, that Andy had it booked since Monday morning, and Oliver MacGowan smiled at that. He was ever a man that liked to go out for the evening. He brought out the empty cup and plate from her when she was finished, and told her to rest herself for another hour or so before getting up. There was nothing for her to do anyway, he said.

After he washed the delf and put them on the draining board, Oliver MacGowan suddenly, strangely, got an urge to go outside even though it was so cold. He put on his heavy crombie overcoat, and pulled his cap hard down on his head, and went to the door. When he opened it, the bright square of the morning, and the sharp wind rushed into the kitchen. As always, when the east wind blew, a couple of yellow oak leaves rushed past his strong boots, and fled into the corner opposite, whispering there for seconds like live things. Oliver MacGowan cursed the chill of the east wind as he struggled slightly to close the kitchen door behind him. Then he stood on the doorstep with his hands in his overcoat pockets, a very hardy little man for his years, his shoulders bunched up a little, his blue eyes squinting.

He saw the strong bulk of his son in blue overalls carrying a bale of hay over to the huddled bullocks in the top field. He reminded himself to tell Andy to put Vaseline on his hands before night to keep the hacks from breaking open redly in the wind and weather. He saw the flights of white seagulls fighting the big force of the east wind towards the greener fields and woods miles inland. He heard the incoming tide on the bleached beach at Annagh, grinding the rounded rocks together in the pit of its belly, smoothing and smalling them and rattling them in its salted palm the way it always did. Oliver MacGowan thought that every morning some rock that was huge at one time was entirely smoothed away and ground down into the finest of drifting sand. Standing there, he decided that he needed to close his eyes, just for a second, and to take one deep breath of the cold, cold wind…

An Unusual Friendship Shocks A Parish

In strange twilight years when erring priests used to be silenced in Ireland, there came a big raw-boned priest to the cottage in Cloonboney. An old woman called Armitage willed the cottage to the local parish priest before she died. The diocese later used it as an abode, temporary or permanent, for its Silenced priests. God love them all it was perfect for them.

> **It was nearly always drink, in those days, that led to the priests being silenced. The drink or the housekeeper.**

It was at the end of the last lane in the diocese, the lake behind, the puce mountains before it and the pub within eight miles. It was nearly always drink, in those days, that led to the priests being silenced. The drink or the housekeeper. And those that ran off with the housekeeper, I suppose, kept running and so never came to Cloonboney, so the cottage was for those who had been silenced by alcohol. In my father's lifetime, he told me that the cottage was rarely empty.

I remember only one Silenced under the fatly thatched roof. He was the big rawboned one by the name of Dillon. Hard times then, a hard-featured Church and a hard group of people. The old ones felt that the Silenced had let them down.

"Dillon was out at the crack of dawn yesterday planting seeds in the back garden," they would say. "A great hand with the spade - he should have stuck to it."

He had the garden around the cottage blazing with flowers and plants in my time. I supposed the Silenced were all soilsons and naturally turned to the earth in their silence.

> **I remember, at 12, being horrified that a priest, even a Silenced, would appear in our shop in ordinary working clothes. And with a Protestant child sitting on his shoulders.**

He would come to our shop once a week for his spartan groceries. He would pay with brand new bills from an old wallet. He smoked a crooked pipe. He had piercing sad blue eyes in a heavy head crowned with pepper and salt hair and he was the biggest customer we had, maybe six foot three or so. He had no callers, except priests in big cars now and then, and never went to Mass on Sunday.

Another rarity came to Cloonboney when Dillon had been there about two years. It was a poor Protestant family from England. There was a man called Hookes, his wife called Heather, whose grandfather had been from the parish originally, and an invalid child called Ruth, who was about six and suffered from chronic asthma. Hookes was also invalid from working in the coal mines, his lungs were gone and the family had moved back from some English city to Cloonboney of clean air to spare.

Heather Hookes had inherited the small slated house about 300 yards away from Dillon's place. She was a typist. She got work in a solicitor's office in town and the husband looked after the child at home. Heather was gone all day, from the morning bus to the evening bus. She was a bubbly little woman in her early 40s with a strange accent. The husband was a quiet man and always short of breath and pale. Ruth was only a wee slip of a thing, curly hair and brown eyes and so fragile she looked like she would break if she was touched. And the family did not know how to live, at all at all, in a society where the church dictated to you where you shopped, who you became friendly with, what you did.

Heather Hookes used to shop in our shop instead of the Protestant shop. Hookes himself was the only one in the house who went to the Protestant Church, and then only an odd Sunday. And he never joined the Orange Order. Ruth did not go to school at all. One way of saying it was that she was learning her lessons at home, another way of saying it, in those years, was that she was not going to live too long.

I don't know how Dillon became friendly with this strange family. Some said that he brought them down some spuds from his own garden on the evening they moved in. What I do know is that they became very friendly. I

was standing behind the counter one summer Saturday morning, six months later, when Dillon came into the shop with the child Ruth sitting on his shoulders. Her small hands were tangled in his iron hair and her sandaled legs, either side of his big head, were as limp and white as straws, and the soles of the sandals were clean, so she had walked no step of the mile from home. Her small cheeks were flushed with excitement and she was wearing a yellow dress. It was very clean. The two of them were laughing as he stooped down to come into the shop. I never heard Dillon laughing before.

"Myself and my pilot will have ice cream wafers," said the Silenced. I had to cut the ice creams from the block with a knife, I remember it well, and when I was doing it he bought her two red hair slides from the card beside the front window. And a quarter of licorice also. I remember, at 12, being horrified that a priest, even a Silenced, would appear in our shop in ordinary working clothes. And with a Protestant child sitting on his shoulders.

But they came and they left, both laughing. And they often came again, the two of them, she on his shoulders, all that long ago summer.

It was the scandal of the parish, the friendship between the Silenced and the Protestants. And you never see him out nowadays, said the old people, without the child above on his shoulders, like as if he was her father. It was not the way things were done in our parish. Neither the Protestants nor the Catholics were happy about it.

Cathal and myself were out hunting rabbits one Saturday morning in late August when we came upon Dillon and the child away in the high mountains. He was leaning against a gate, looking over the country, and she, as always, was on his shoulders. She had her two elbows on the top of his head and her hands under her chin, as comfortable as could be, and she was wearing a daisy chain. It so happens that a rabbit appeared out of the woods near them, and Spot caught the rabbit almost at Dillon's feet, or we would not have gone near them at all. Quick as lightning Dillon reached down, kicked our Spot, and picked up the young rabbit before Spot could finish it off.

The child went very white in the face but she didn't cry. She reached down one hand and touched the rabbit ears as it scrunched up against Dillon's chest below her. Rabbits were worth a half crown each to us in those days. We had killed three already and gutted them, and this fourth one meant ten shillings for our morning's hunt. We didn't know what to do.

"Lads," said Dillon, "will ye let this one go?"

I would have said yes, just to get away, but like a shot Cathal said, "Maybe you'd like to buy it?"

"How much is it worth, this wee thing?" he asked.

"A half-crown," we told him.

He took two half-crowns from his pocket and gave them to us without a word. "Hold back the dogs," he said.

He handed the rabbit to the child on his shoulders and got down on his hunkers. "Let it away," he said.

The child dropped the rabbit and it ran. The child clapped her hands. The two of them were laughing when we ran away too. But we marked the spot where the rabbit went and came back when they were gone. A rabbit stays in shock for a good while. Spot had it out and killed in five minutes.

Hughie Dolan always claimed that those with asthma were likely to die in our Octobers when the mists rolled heavily and coldly and chokingly from the lough. The child was sickened and died in the middle of that October. The Silenced spent nearly all his time with the Protestant child. The father was sick too, from his chest, and scarcely able to mind her but still, the old people said, it was not Dillon's place to be there.

When she died, worse still, the Silenced, in ordinary clothes, went to the Protestant church, right inside its curved doors. That night he went down to the pub, sat in the corner and got stone drunk.

Joey rang the parish priest late in the night, the Silenced still sitting there, and the parish priest and the curate came down in their black car around midnight, and brought him away. "I never saw him before but at a distance from me and always with the child on his shoulders," said Joey afterwards.

He was gone from the cottage that day. He never came back. None of the other Silenced were sent to the cottage after that. Its roof fell in after three winters, the dead straw of the thatch as limp as the feeble legs of the child that wore a daisy chain.

A Fenian's Dying Wish

John Hugh Gallagher was a Republican. His father was a Republican. His grandfather before that. Their blood was dyed green and greener still in their mother's wombs. The Gallaghers of Clonfeigh could no more resist being diehard Republicans, all their days, all their hard, hard lives, than Willie Weir the postman down the road could avoid being a black Orangeman. Or Hubert Greer, blacker still.

They all lived, in their times and seasons, in a small village I know well on the Tyrone side of the Border with brown Donegal. In parishes like this the genetic cargo is delivered as unerringly to the doorstep as Willie Weir delivered the letters from his bicycle. You get your letter and you open it and you live with the message. John Hugh Gallagher was even born during the Easter Week and many the birthday he spent in the barracks afterwards for being caught selling Easter Lilies, the little paper flowers of Republicanism.

It was his local lot to sell them, like his father before him. Given the family tree it would even have amazed the Weirs and the Greers and the Armstrongs if he had not. John Hugh Gallagher inherited the battered green mantle of his breed just as surely as he inherited, in time, the home farm.

It was a poor enough mountainy place, running down to the lough as quick as it could despite the best efforts of thick thorn hedges to stop it. A

> **John Hugh Gallagher might have been a priest if he had not been born Republican.**

boundary fence on the east side with rough barkless paling posts, carried its burden of rusty barbed wire all the way down each post shouldering its redrust barbs as manly as the Gallaghers and the Weirs did. Straight as a die down to the shore it went, the fence, and then it marched into the water itself, to stop cattle straying through the shallows, and staggered on out into the cold water to die, resolute to the end. A parable there maybe.

John Hugh Gallagher might have been a priest if he had not been born Republican. He was a kindly man in all his bones, good to his own, good to neighbors. He had a gentle cast of face, with weak eyes behind spectacles, and was slightly built. He was never married except to the mist ghost that is Ireland, and he minded his mother, after his father died and his younger brother was killed in Armagh in an ambush, minded her as good as a trained nurse when he was at home. The same hand that was commanded to do darker things for Ireland, held the spoon that fed the small little old lady in the last years. And soothed her forehead when she was senile.

In between, though, John Hugh Gallagher did his suffering, his slow dying for Mother Ireland. He was a young man in the Fifties IRA campaign. He was on the run for a time until he was caught, kicked, cuffed, interned, jailed. The man with him was killed. John Hugh Gallagher said afterwards that a B Special gave him a kick in the side when he was getting out of the drain, hands up, and the pain never afterwards went away. But he still had to carry his barbed wire. He was in the North when his mother died, and they did not let him out for the funeral. He was in jail when his brother was killed, sitting in the cell in Belfast when his brother was buried. And when they let him out, his term served, ghost white and prematurely aged, they knew, and he knew, and the Greers and Weirs knew, and all the valleyed world, that nothing at all was changed.

John Hugh Gallagher spent most of his life, in the end, in the compounds of Republican prisoners both North and South. I think he was probably ill-equipped for the cross he had to carry. If he wasn't being "lifted" by the RUC, he was being arrested by the Gardai. He had an unfortunate knack of being in the wrong place at the wrong time as far as Mother Ireland was concerned. He spent years in Crumlin Road, years in Portlaoise and Dublin. He was even caught one time in Scotland, doing whatever he was doing, and was jailed there. In the end they must have got tired locking him up and letting him out again.

John Hugh Gallagher got wispy and old and sick before his time, too many wet ditches, dugouts, damp cells. The last time they let him out, from Portlaoise this time, he looked like a ghost. Or even, would you believe, like some strange kind of saint. I think that was about three years ago and already you could look at him… I saw him once… and suspect that he had cancer. He did have cancer, of the stomach. Young Cecil Greer told his father of seeing Gallagher at the gate of his house, leaning on a stick, and he looked like a dead man. Hubert Greer, with what sounded almost like a note of respect, said that the bastard took a lot of killing.

John Hugh Gallagher, down all his jail years, would have made many Republican comrades, men a lot younger and harder sometimes than himself. Towards the end, despite the risks, they would sometimes call to see him by night. The house would not have been watched as closely, in his dying months, as when he was young and active and maybe dangerous. It was to some of these visitors a month before he died, that John Hugh Gallagher said he would like to go on one last mission. He was hardly able to walk at this time. He named a certain RUC Barracks in Tyrone where he had been especially badly beaten once, and stripped naked too, and said he owed them a hot night. If only he was fit, he said, he would have a go at them. His skin was green-tinged at this time, instead of pallored yellow, and he was cancerous and he was almost gone.

The younger and harder men that he had been in jail with came and went in the night. And this is true. And some poeple would see all of this as a cancerous thing, blackly and bitterly corrosive, mindless misguided thuggery. And somebody like myself could scarcely effectively argue otherwise. But what happened did happen, and not long ago either. That red van with a mattress in the back of it pulled up to John Hugh Gallagher's backdoor in the mystery of a border night and his window was tapped by masked men.

There were three of them. They got the excited dying old Republican out of his bed. They dressed him. They half carried him out to the back of the van. They laid him on the mattress. They jolted out of the laneway and on to the main road. There was a high risk involved. There was a long drive then along the back roads and the side roads of terrorism. When they got to a certain place they stopped the van. They got the old man out of the back, staggering on his dying legs. They literally carried him to the top of a hill. There was a machine gun mounted there, between two rocks, jute sacks behind it. Down below was the big building with lights burning in one ground floor window. There you are, Gallagher, said one of the men, there's your police station. And here's your gun.

John Hugh Gallagher did whatever you do with a machine gun pointed at a police station when you are what he was. He fired at least three long bursts at it. The lights went out in the building and there were five or six thrusts of fire in return. John Hugh Gallagher fired back and, probably remembering all his beatings, fired and fired and fired until the men said they would have to run. The carried him back to the van at a trot, laid him back on the mattress in the back, and drove off at high speed. It was hours before they got the old man back home. They put him back in his bed. They patted his shoulder and ran.

John Hugh Gallagher died inside the month. He never got out of the bed again. He never knew that the younger and harder men had taken him, not to a police station in Tyrone, but to a safe quiet valley across the Border in Donegal. What he thought was a barracks had in fact been a deserted old mill house. It had all been arranged to the last detail by somebody, somewhere. They gave him a Republican funeral as well, the coffin draped with the Tricolor. On its way out to the chapel the hearse skirted the boundary fence. The old posts, resolute to the last, each shouldered their burden of savage barbed wire and marched out into the cold waters of the lough until they died.

A Letter To My Father

ello Sandy,

Last night, on the edge of my sleeping, I thought of you for the first time in a while. How are you? Where are you? Did they get you out of your purgatory yet after nearly 20 years? Or are you still there?

Is there peace between Orange and Green in heaven?

I'd rather think of you as being in heaven if that's all right. It's easier to think of your father being in heaven than in any class of deprivation or pain at all.

At the same time, pragmatically, I know well, Sandy, that you were not the class of man that a heaven with any kind of standards would have accepted on the first morning. No way. Your eyes - and I can only remember you as an aging man - were as much the eyes of a rogue who was a little saintly as of a saint who was more than a little roguish. I heard a few stories at your wake, too, from men who were boys and youths with you, which, in time and reason would have had a purgatorial element in them.

Anyway, Sandy, thought of you the other night in the context of this peace process up in the North. That was how you came into my mind. And I know, if you have ascended to your higher places, (which I believe in too, incidentally!) you automatically know more about what is happening, and what is going to happen, than we mortals can know down here.

But what I really wonder, Sandy, is how is Bob Armstrong, the Orangeman who lived next door to you for most of your life? Who was your neighbor, your customer, in the little shop, your best friend - almost - and, in a way, your enemy also since the sectarian divide was far deeper between ye than the alderwood hedge that separated his farmhouse from our garden. How is Bob?

> **When he had finished cutting our young Catholic heads he would comb the quiffs straight across and say, "Now, young fellow, you look grand and Protestant looking!"**

Are ye still friends? Are ye still neighbors? Are ye still divided? Do ye still talk about anything but politics? Do ye still converse about the weather in heaven - or the other place - do ye still talk about boxing and football and the strange turnings and twistings of the natural history of this earth ye have left behind and far below?

Did Bob Armstrong, Unionist and Orangeman, friend and enemy, good neighbor and family barber, did Bob go to hell to roast forever in flames (as another neighbor claimed would happen to him) or did he even have to spend less time in purgatory than you? Or did he go straight to heaven? That's a rhetorical question, I know well that he did not. But are ye still connected socially in the way ye always were? Is there peace between Orange and Green in heaven?

Sandy, drifting towards the ultimate clarity of sleep the other night, it occurred to me how close Bob and yourself were in many ways. And how impossibly far apart. When you went to Dublin for the gold injections for the arthritis in the early '50s, it was Bob who brought you there in his car and helped you up the stairs, between the injections, in the cheap bed-and-breakfast house in Talbot Street where ye shared a room.

And, from talking to you later as a reporter, I know that week ye went together to see a John Wayne film and ye went most evenings to drink three or four whiskeys together in Wynn's Hotel. And ye never once talked about politics.

And you were amazed, for you told me yourself, that when you went down on your arthritic knees at night to say your prayers beside your narrow little bed, that Bob Armstrong, too, went down on his Protestant knees, and prayed to the same God.

And, looking back on it, we minded his farm on the Twelfth of July even though he looked at us differently all through July when the parade season started, and the Orangelust took part of him over. And we would see him at night, quite often, dressed in his B Special black uniform, and carrying his heavy black rifle to patrol the countryside, Sandy, and question you sternly if you were coming home late on your bicycle. Name? Where are you going? Where are you coming from? Your reason for being out at this time?

And the next day, in the evening, he might come down to the shop to buy the exactly measured minority of his groceries over your counter as if nothing had happened. Or to borrow the paper (except in July for July was different), or maybe you would bring up a black-haired cub like I was then to have his hair cut, a deft, short cut, and the two of you would talk about matterless local things under his mantelpiece crowned proudly by the two tea caddies of Queen Elizabeth and Prince Philip, Duke of Edinburgh, very close, very far away at the same time, walking a narrow verbal pathway adroitly between the untold acreage of No Man's Land.

Very sad, looking back at it. A pair of men who never really addressed their differences. When he had finished cutting our young Catholic heads he would comb the quiffs straight across and say, "Now, young fellow, you look grand and Protestant looking!" That was about as far as it went.

On the second day of Christmas you went pheasant shooting together with your two single-barreled guns for as long as you were fit in your legs. And I was so delighted, Sandy, that even though he was the B Special with the rifle, you were the best shot. And when his pheasant often dipped below the shot, yours usually fell.

I remember once, though, both shots struck together at close range, the cock pheasant breaking up almost from your four feet. The bird was virtually blown to pieces, and the two of you were embarrassed about that. "Gentlemen, leave the creature alone," ye said, with one voice, "leave him alone." And we left the tattered feathers lying there, in their gore, on the edge of Cutler's spud garden.

All the fanfare was sounded for the peace process. I don't think myself anything has been solved at all. But maybe yourself and Bob Armstrong, away high above it all now, sitting together, maybe ye know better than I do.

But do you know what I think, Sandy? I think that if the two of you are together, then ye are talking about nice, safe things. Even in heaven. The weather, maybe, the cost of cattle, how much things have changed.

I wonder what kind of a day will it be tomorrow, Bob? Ach, Sandy, sure it should be fair enough?

A skiff of rain here and there, maybe, Bob?

Aye, Sandy.

Aye, indeed. Good luck for now, my father, and give my regards to Bob Armstrong. Tell him I was asking after him.

Reminiscences Of An Easter Rising Vet

he house commands a mighty view of Dublin city, its millions of roofs, the writhings of the fattened Liffey descending down from the mountains into the black eyes of its own bridges.

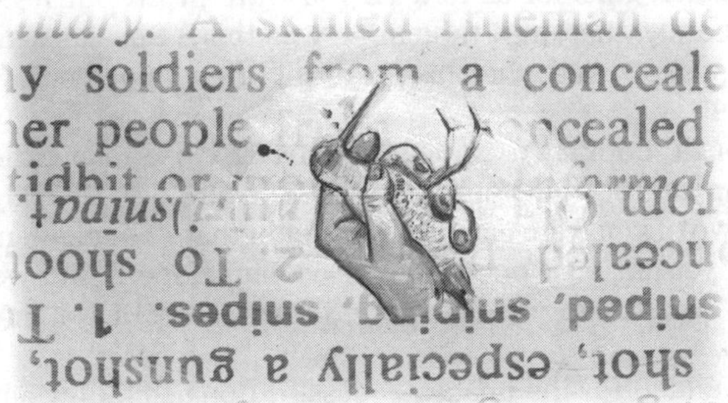

The old man loves the view from his bedroom, especially in the early spring, and it is amazing that his sight is still as good as ever it was, but then, back when he was 16, he had the sharpest eyes amongst the GPO garrison that, above all other groups of Irishmen, best represented the spirit of the Easter Rising that created an Ireland.

He does not tell stories about that himself, and never did, but there are factual reports, from others, that he was the best sniper in the General Post Office and that two or three of the soldiers' bodies up near O'Connell Bridge were victims of his accuracy.

He is 97 now. He is almost translucent against the white pillows and sheets and bedding in the room overlooking the city. His mind is still sharp most of the time. His eyes are like shiny black triangles, glinting away under frosted eyebrows. He has pictures of Pearse and Connolly and Jesus Christ in the room with him, and a yellowing photograph of a long departed wife and young children, all of them pensioners themselves, some dead.

His hands have become white and almost feminine with the passage of the years. They lie on the coverlet on his lap but they don't seem to belong to him anymore.

They say he is the last man living that fought in the GPO in Easter Week 1916.

They are not certain about that, but almost so. There is a Sutcliffe who might be alive somewhere in England because he was only a teenager, too, when he fought. There was another lad called Byrne who drew an IRA pension of only a few pounds weekly until a few years ago, but then, though there was no report of a death, the pension just was not collected anymore. The only veteran's pension that the government is now paying for Dublin survivors of the Rising is being paid to the man in the bed overlooking the Liffey, falling into the darkly inscrutable eyes of its own bridges.

He's a humorous old man.

"Jesus Christ don't mention my name whatever you do, and don't say I'm the last survivor outa the GPO. Sure, there was only a few hundred of us there when the fighting was being done but, for the 50th celebrations back in 1966, there were thousands of lads collecting pensions and wearing medals and all of them claimed they were in the GPO in '16. There's probably a few score of them still collecting and I wouldn't want to do them outa the few bob.

"The one thing that makes me laugh now is the number of lads, down the years, who claimed they carried dispatches for the boys in Easter Week. Jesus, if all of them who claimed they were dispatch carriers were dispatch carriers then we would have had no time to fight. We'd have all been writing letters all the time just to keep them in action.

"And, if a quarter of the lads who claimed they were 'out' for the Easter Week thing in Dublin, well afterwards now, had been 'out,' then by Jesus, we should have won the bloody fight because, according to those figures, we must have been one of the biggest frigging armies in the world. The British shouldn't have had a chance against us. Jesus Christ Almighty, we would have buried them, under the weight of all them dispatches!"

He was hale and hearty and able until the late '80s. He says, his black triangles glinting with will, that he'd be on his own two legs still, well fit to go, only for the fact that his knees broke down from attending all the old IRA funerals in the '70s. All the marching and saluting and guards of honor and that class of work, he ways wryly, went very hard on the old bones. You might go out to the funeral saying that you'd take it easy, but once things got going you'd find yourself trying to march and salute and stand to attention like a young fella.

"It was the old IRA that got me in the end, burying them in all classes of dirty weather, wind and water. The lads who survived always seemed to pick a bad winter day to die and to be buried. As sure as the weather would turn dirty of a week I'd know I'd be putting on the old overcoat and hat and going out into the thick of it to bury somebody. Christ, but they have a lot to answer for."

He always read the Irish Press, and kept well in touch with the growth and development of the state he fought for. He stayed Republican all his life and will have no word said against the Provisional IRA. He went into O'Connell Street on a regular basis for years, sometimes showing visiting American relations where the actions took place.

Then in latter years it became too dangerous for him to go into O'Connell Street. There were too many dangerous thugs around, morning, noon and night, who would rob the eyes out of your head, who would mug an old man in his 80s for the price of some tablet or substance that would send them into moonland for an hour or two. What was worse, to his still sharp eyes, was that the young people did not resemble Dubliners of his experience.

"I saw men kissing other men once, outside the GPO, lads with rings in their noses and in their navels. I've seen drunk girls, 15 or 16, cursing worse than the English soldiers ever cursed, eff this and eff that. I saw young pups fighting in the gutter for a bottle of beer. You'd be in more jeopardy in O'Connell Street now, I'd say, of an ordinary Saturday night than during some of the time in Easter Week itself."

He won't talk about what he did or he did not do in Easter Week. But he will say that he was a dead shot. One time, in Meath, when he was in his 40s, he was out fowling. He had a double-barreled shot gun. They were in a rough bog with short heather, full of darting zigzagging snipe that would always break up together from right under the nose of the gundog. Three times that day he killed a snipe with each barrel, which is one of the hardest shooting things of all to do, even once.

"I held one of the snipes up outa the heather. It was still warm, limpish, with a little drop of blood coming out of its beak. The blood went on to my hand. Its wee eyes were still bright. I said that day that I would never shoot anything again and I never did again. I left it back down in the heather."

He stays quiet in his bed for a good while after this, as another skein of Liffey falls down into the shadows and bright lights of the city. Sometimes, after talking brightly and lucidly like this for a while, his carers say, he slips a bit.

"Over 200 yards," he says then, out of nowhere, "over 200 yards if it was an inch. The poor bastard's bastard!" He says no more than that. He falls asleep under the inanimation of his own two hands, lying on their own on the coverlet in the small house overlooking the city of Dublin, where he saw men kissing, not long ago, outside the GPO, and young girls effing and blinding, thugs fighting in the gutter over a bottle of beer.

And as he falls asleep the Eastertide sun falls down like a golden orb towards a million smoky chimneys. And I can only think somehow of a jack snipe, just dead, a single bead of blood on the point of its beak, eyes still as bright as if it were alive.

A Killer With Secret Regrets

In Doolin I met him only a few days ago. It was the evening time in this little fishing village of all the tourists of all the world. The first striggle-straggle of visitors that come into this country from now onwards always is thickened by the time it reaches Doolin. So there are always people here from everywhere. They come from home and they come from abroad.

He was an avenger for people who had already been killed by Loyalist terrorists. The strange thing about him was that he was not IRA.

He comes from both. I saw him sitting in the shadows of one of the pubs that is now world famous. I recognized him immediately.

Last time I saw him was in London. He was then the man he is now even though it is 10 years later. The first time I saw him was in Belfast just after the Troubles started. Then he was a boy. And he was already a killer of men.

I need not go into the details - maybe I am afraid - but he was a killer.

He was an avenger for people who had already been killed by Loyalist terrorists. The strange thing about him was that he was not IRA. His background was a hastily-formed community association to protect an exposed Catholic enclave. He was a committee member of that. At the time of his involvement they had one aged pistol and two shotguns. Nothing else.

Members of their community were being killed or driven out of their homes almost every night. He was the one they gave the pistol to. He was the one who had already killed men by the time I met him. He wore jeans and a leather jacket over a green t-shirt and he was sitting in a semidetached house drinking tea.

You would not notice him in a group of any six or seven other young men on the Nationalist side in that era. Just another Joe Soap. But he was the one they gave the pistol to. And he was the one who used it. And later he was the one who got a rifle (a Garand?) which was a sniper's rifle and he killed with that too. And I know that through my trade.

And he was never, as far as I could ever discover, a member of any organization at all. He was a kind of maverick vengeance from a quiet street, non-aligned and lethal.

He had then a tight cap of short fair hair and a long face. The hair has grown white since. But he still looks the same. Last time I met him in London he was out of the North for many years, working as a chef in the kind of restaurant where speed is more important than anything else.

I talked to him, in the beginning in Belfast, later in London, in a desire to understand what drove him to do the things he did. I did not know exactly what he had done in Belfast in those days. Only several people I trusted told me he had killed men, that he was a sort of avenging shadow, that he owed allegiance to no organization at all.

Basically, both times, he told me nothing at all. He just talked about fishing. He was a fisherman, a coarse fisherman, who loved nothing better than spinning for pike and perch on quiet rivers and lakes in Co. Antrim. There was no greater sport anywhere, he said, than angling.

As I say, I recognized him immediately in Doolin, sitting alone behind his drink. He has aged in the past decade but not a lot. He still looks anonymous. He still looks solitary. I approached him and he had forgotten me.

I reminded him of locations and mutual friends. Eventually he made the connection. It was only after that I realized he had been tense enough at the first contact. I offered him a drink but he insisted on buying me one. He had a lot of cash in his pocket, a great roll of it.

It was when he was removing a 10 pound note from the outside skin of his wad that I noticed the index finger of his right hand was missing. That would have been his trigger finger. When he was a killer.

We talked. He gave me no details at all about his life in England. He gave me no details about how he came to be in Doolin, alone, drinking. He asked me a lot of questions about myself. We talked, would you believe, about the Beatles and Marianne Faithfull, the ex-lover of Jagger of the Rolling Stones.

She had the best voice he ever heard, he said, especially when she was singing Someday I'll Get Over You. I asked him if he still went fishing, just to keep him talking. No, he said, he had not fished for years.

There are times in this business of mine when you chance an extra question or two in the hope that "closed" people will open up. I chanced

one. I said to him I noticed he had lost one finger off his right hand since I saw him last.

He held it up, without reluctance, to show me the maiming. The finger, it was clear from the scar, had been hacked off in the crudest of fashions.

He did not look at it at all when he held it up for me to see.

There was a silence for a minute and then he said that he was sitting drinking alone in a flat in Islington one winter's night when a madman attacked his hand with a bread knife with a serrated edge. The madman had no mercy at all on him, he said, even when he was screaming and crying out loud with the pain of it. The way the madman saw it was that this finger - he did not say it was the trigger finger directly - had done a lot of bad things.

He did not specify which bad things but I think we both understood he was talking about pressing triggers. And killing people. Unsaid things are sometimes starker than statements.

He said the madman with the bread knife sawed away at the finger until it was done. It took a long time to do it, especially the bone, but the madman broke the bone with his fist and then severed the rest of the finger and threw it into the fire. And then he held up the mangled hand again for me to see. I asked him, there in Doolin, who the madman was. There are questions you just have to ask.

He said the madman was himself.

We had this conversation for about 20 minutes in one of the Doolin pubs where all the world seems to be of craic, of music, of singing and dancing.

Where the world and his mother come to play. And there we were - the three of us - in the middle of it all.

A Prediction From A Sly Country Sleuth

Larry O'Donnell came back down the hills from checking the cattle and walked into the kitchen. Betty was making brown bread at the table, her arms working busily. Larry threw one quick, sharp look at her. There were no flour smudges at her temples. That meant his wife was in good form.

When she was irritable on Mondays she always brushed the hair back with sharp reflex movements. No smudges meant good form. Larry O'Donnell is not a man that misses much. He decided to put her in even better form with a juicy morsel of news.

"Sometime inside the next fortnight," says Larry, "the door here will open and Katie Sloane will come in bursting with news. She'll have the tea and she'll smoke two of your cigarettes the way she always does, and then she'll tell you that Margaret and Austin are going to get married soon; that the question has been popped at last."

"How do you know that? Were you talking to Johnny out on the land? Who told you? Are you certain?" Betty was all excited at the news. The steady line between the two neighbors' children had been going on for only seven or eight months. A very short time in this parish. Both families were of the careful class that did not rush into anything.

"How do you know?" she asked Larry again.

"I was talking to no man or no woman and I heard nothing at all," said Larry O'Donnell. "But I know, all right."

Betty took a long, hard look at him to see if he was joking, and then decided he was not. She knew Larry, and from long experience reckoned he was as infallible as the Pope on such matters.

"But how do you know?"

Larry hesitated and was going to attempt to tell her how he knew, but then decided it would be too difficult. He just shrugged and looked out over his cup of tea and thought about it himself. It was, he thought, a question of keeping your two eyes open all the time. It was just a matter of noticing things.

Young Mags Sloane and Austin Queenan were going out two nights weekly. Tuesdays and Sundays, for three months of the past eight. They were both steady, industrious, decent, honest, Catholic young people. Mags worked in a legal office in town and was a member of the Legion of Mary. Austin helped his father on the farm and also owned a JCB digger with which he did contract work. Both were 26 years old. Both, thought Larry lightly, would still have their Confirmation money.

Careful was the word. They would not lightly rush into anything. Coming home from their dates, since the first month, Austin always pulled into Carson's Cutting in his neat little red Ford for what, thought Larry, would have been a restrained bit of a court. Then he would drive the last 300 yards to Sloane's to leave Mags home. Often, being a light sleeper, Larry would hear Austin passing their roadside bedroom window, always between 1:30 and 2:00 in the morning.

Every morning Larry had to go through the gate at Carson's Cutting to go up and see the cattle. This was where the couple parked. For months now, on Monday and Wednesday mornings, Larry had noticed the small, careful debris of their developing love.

Always, atop the wall, under the hawthorn, there would be a cardboard snackbox from the town chipper. They just bought one between them, the cheap one, with three drumsticks. The three drumsticks, picked very clean, would be neatly lying in the bottom of the box. Larry normally tipped the box into the field so that his dog, Major, could have a treat.

Also there on the ground beside the wheel ruts would be the core of an apple, eaten neatly all around and, on Austin's side of the car, the tipped butts of two low tar cigarettes.

A month ago, glittering in the dewy grass, there had been something else. It had been a strip of 35 mm negatives of the kind that slip easily out of their folder when you are looking at the snaps. Larry squinted through them at the sun. They all showed Mags, smiling, sitting on the bright yellow front of Austin's digger. Clearly, therefore, he had brought her home to meet his people. A significant step.

> **He put all the two and twos together and decided, yes, he was right. When you took all the factors into consideration he had to be right. There was not much room for doubt.**

Larry O'Donnell is not a man that misses much. He replaced the negatives exactly where he found them.

Sitting at the kitchen table, finishing his tea, Larry thought about what he had seen at the Cutting two hours earlier on his way up to the land. He put all the two and twos together and decided, yes, he was right. When you took all the factors into consideration he had to be right. There was not much room for doubt.

On the previous night the town below had been on fete, at the climax of the parish carnival. Larry and Betty had been down themselves, dancing and carousing with the best of them, and had in fact seen Mags and Austin in the Blow Inn. Larry remembered that Mags had been drinking a glass of Harp and Austin was sitting behind a pint of Guinness. The young couple would have been at the dance in the hall afterwards when Larry and Betty were already back home. It had been a fine midsummer night with a huge moon in a clear sky, though there had been just a slight skift of a shower just as Larry and Betty arrived home around midnight. It only lasted about five minutes, barely wetting the ground.

This morning, at the Cutting, things had not been the same as usual. Major the dog had noticed it even before Larry. By the time Larry got to the gate Major was already sinking his jaws into the snackbox. It was lying on the ground instead of being atop the wall, and Larry instantly saw that one of the drumsticks had not been eaten at all and there were uneaten chips, also, on the grass. Larry squatted down on his hunkers to take a closer look at the ground. There was only one cigarette butt on Austin's side. It had been flung out of the car after only a puff or two, not carefully smoked to the end as usual.

On the other side, a large red apple lay on the green grass. Larry picked it up. Only one bite had been snatched from it. With just one bite Larry could see the neat, small teethmarks of Mags Sloane as clear a day with his sharp eyes. She had just taken one bite, hastily, and then flung the apple out the car window.

Still hunkering down, Larry hefted the big apple in his hand and smelt the wild woodbine from the loose yellow flowers coiled around the hawthorn bushes. It was still strong in the morning but last night, he thought, after the shower of warm rain, the aroma must have been as sweet as forbidden fruit. And, he thought, the moon would have been hanging over Carson's Cutting like a golden lantern. And, because of the bar extension for the carnival, the music from the Blow Inn would have come drifting up from below, magically soft.

The whole atmosphere, thought Larry, would be enough to make even a Queenan man forget about the earning potential of his yellow digger. Enough even to make a Sloane woman forget about the Legion of Mary.

"The moon and wild woodbine," said Larry cryptically to Betty as he rinsed his teacup under the tap. "And a red apple."

There was a quick, excited kind of tap on the kitchen door, and Katie Sloane came in. She was wearing a green cardigan and her high heels, Larry noticed, and that meant she was bursting with news…

Guns Don't Kill People, People Kill People

he radio sounded almost like a gatling gun because it was a Northerner who was talking about the peace process. He had that kind of voice.

> **He spent the most of his youth in prisons on both sides of the border. His name is well-known to uniformed men on both sides of the border. It is even well-known to the media.**

When he said the word "decommissioning" with the "g" sound missing at the end, the word ricocheted around the small sitting room in the Donegal borderlands so sharply that the long man sitting beside the small coal fire almost jerked upright in his chair. It was raining slightly outside, skittish rain that tapped the window every now and again without a pattern. Tiny concussions.

The man was - and is - aged about 40, give or take a year, but he looks a lot older than that. There are two deep lines, almost like slashes running straight down either side of his face from almost directly underneath his eyes. The eyes are liquidy brown so that when he looks at you - and I have often noticed this - you can never be certain of the expression inside of them. It could be benign or the other, but the eyes hide the realities.

He has strong eyebrows and a bony square jaw, clean shaven, and since he came out of the last of his jail sentences in the Republic two years ago, his lips have always looked dry and blueish, as from stomach trouble. You see him constantly moistening them with his tongue. The body is the kind of body that has survived hard times but is softening now.

When the news report was over about the blockage of the peace process caused by the lack of progress in decommissioning, the man switched the radio sharply off. He then stood in the silence of the room for a long time

looking out the window. The view he had - and this morning too - is of flat fields running down to a river flowing slowly and flatly.

On the other bank the fields gather themselves together inside heavy hedges like fat sheep and reluctantly begin to climb a sloping rise of land which is about 15 miles from that invisible border. Behind that again, but very far away, is the blued high ground of Derry.

The man looked out the window for several minutes. He had the repose of a man used to looking out of windows for long periods of time.

That is the case. He spent the most of his youth in prisons on both sides of the border. His name is well-known to uniformed men on both sides of the border. It is even well-known to the media.

He has a nickname which he does not like at all. Anyone who has ever used it to his face has had occasion to wonder exactly what kind of expression is inside those brown eyes which look at you very directly but tell you little.

The man has long sideburns. The last inch of them is now pure white, the rest still dark.

The long man began to laugh to himself at the window. Somewhere in the middle the laugh turned into that kind of chesty cough which afflicts smokers. His body shook with the combined effects of the chuckling and the coughing until it was obvious that it was hurting.

He stood up and folded his arms across his ribs until the coughing stopped. Then he took three or four deep breaths until he was fully recovered.

He went into the kitchen off the sitting room. You could hear him rooting about in one of the presses underneath the sink. He took out three planks from the floor of the press and then took out a black plastic refuse sack which was heavy. He carried the package back into the room and left it down between his black shoes. He took the two handguns then out of the plastic sack. He balled up the sack until it was very small and compressed and shoved it into the fire with the end of the power.

At first the plastic sizzled and compressed itself even further. Then it burst into flames that were so bright for four or five minutes even, that they actually added brightness to the little room.

I am no expert on handguns, but one of them looked like what I imagine a luger should look like. The other was exactly like the kind of revolver I often looked at with awe on the waist of an RUC man. I think they are Smith & Wesson's. Very English and artisan in design. It was closest to his right foot. Both looked in perfect condition.

The Smith & Wesson was loaded because you could see the tips of the bullets. I don't know about the other one but it somehow looked loaded.

That was the way the long man was when another man came to visit him by pre-arrangement. We need not concern ourselves about the other man. He does not matter.

The two sat opposite each other in the cheapest of easy chairs and drank from a bottle of whiskey the visitor brought with him. Once a cat came from underneath a couch under the window and just sniffed at the luger before going back under the couch again. She moved silently on her velvet feet.

The long man, after the two had talked for a while about everything under the sun, including, strangely, the mating habits of stoats, eventually touched the revolver near his right foot and said, starkly, that this one had killed two men for certain, maybe three or four, because there had been a time when it had been fired into the bulk of a mob. He did not go into details. None were asked for. The luger-type gun, he said, had a long history before he knew anything about it. Given the places it had been, including Belfast, it had certainly spilt blood.

He stayed quiet then for a long time, in the manner of celled men who are used to that.

Then the long man said that the guns at his feet were not decommissioned, not by a long chalk. Not decommissioned at all.

And the two men looked at the guns then, for maybe a full minute by the click, as if the guns were alive in some strange way.

Looking at the problem, looking at one of the causes of the problem, at one of the attempted solutions to the problem, at one of the roots of the problem, looking at the chambered bullets that can take lives, lying exactly where bullets lay which had taken lives, looking at muzzles as expressionless, in real terms, as the liquid brown eyes of the long man sitting above them. The cat made the slightest of noises under the couch. The fire made small mysterious noises of its own. The visitor made no sound at all.

The long man said, finally, again touching the guns with his shoes as he spoke, that they were certainly not decommissioned.

"But I am," he said. "I am. I have just decommissioned myself. Does that not mean anything at all?"

The visitor couldn't answer that question. He just sat there quietly wondering if anyone could.

The Queen That Got Away

I know I wrote ye a dark story about bees and beekeepers a few weeks ago, but I heard this bee story yesterday from my friend T.J. McGuinness from the deli next door to the radio station and I can't wait to retell it.

You see, there's this lovely man over in East Clare - let's call him Ger - and he's mad into bees. He has an orchard and heather over to the east of him and he has about 15 hives of the finest honey in Ireland. The joy and pride of his life. He wins prizes with his honey at all the shows and his bees are the pride and joy of his life.

It seems, however, that every now and again a beekeeper needs to bring in a fresh queen bee, from another breed entirely, in order to keep his hives buzzing. Ger has been doing this for years inside that region, quite happily and successfully, but recently he heard of a beekeeper in the North who had a magnificent breed of bee altogether and who would be willing to sell him a queen bee of the highest possible breeding. But Ger would have to travel to collect.

Now Ger is a man who does not travel widely. Trips to Croke Park when Clare are playing have been the longest trips undertaken to date. Trips to Ennis once a month are not taken lightly; journeys to beekeepers' seminars throughout the Republic are major expeditions. A trip across the border to

They had come, he said, from hell and were devotees of Old Redsocks in Rome, adherents to Popery and witchcraft and the worshipped idols. Were it not for the fact that there was the bond of bees between them he would not allow them anywhere near his door.

a distinct outside Portadown, for Ger, would be the same as heading off to New York or Hong Kong.

Ger discussed the matter with his good wife Susan and, after that, over his usual two quiet and serene whiskeys in the pub, with his perennial friend whom we will call P.J. It was the aftermath of the Omagh tragedy and Ger, a gentle man, did not fancy being stopped and having guns pointed at him by the British Army or anybody else. Beekeepers are a gentle species.

They eventually decided that a queen bee of the thoroughbred type bred by a famous Benedictine monk was worth risking it all for. The next morning they tanked up the Toyota, fastened their seatbelts, and headed North in some trepidation.

And this was justified. They were stopped and searched three times by heavily armed units of the British Army on the roads between the border and Portadown. At the second checkpoint they were closely questioned altogether and had to stop under the muzzles of machine guns for 20 minutes while their story was checked out and the old Toyota's registration number was processed by the British Army computer.

It was two exhausted and unsettled men who eventually found their way to the Portadown beekeeper's farmhouse on the far side of Portadown. This meant, of course, they had to drive through one of the most Unionist towns in the North, under a thousand Union Jacks, close to the Garvaghy Road and Drumcree, past Union Jacked curbstones.

Worse still, the beekeeper who eventually opened his front door to them was a follower of the hard-line Ian Paisley and announced this at the first opportunity. He harangued them fiercely and quoted entire chunks of the Bible at their amazed white faces before he did business with them at all.

They had come, he said, from hell and were devotees of Old Redsocks in Rome, adherents to Popery and witchcraft and the worshipped idols. Were

it not for the fact that there was the bond of bees between them he would not allow them anywhere near his door. And so on.

But he became a changed man when they were admiring his hives. Religious differences were forgotten. They talked queen bees. And the only time his Paisleyite side returned was in the matter of paying for the new queen.

It was bad enough for him to be sending his queen to the south, said the Paisleyite, but dreadful she was going to be a-buzzing in the land of de Valera and Parnell and O'Connell.

Oh, he knew his history, all right, and his money too, for he charged Ger £115 for the bee. Ger would never had paid it except he had suffered so much to get as far as Portadown. The Paisleyite had a small wit in him. "God save the Queen!" were his parting words.

The queen bee was slightly sedated with a sugar solution (I'm told) and then placed on a bed of cotton wool in a matchbox. This is the manner in which queen bees travel from region to region. In a wool lined matchbox in the trouser pocket. The heat of a human thigh is somehow equivalent to that of a hive. 'Tis traditional.

The lads were stopped twice before getting back over the border. Bad enough, but not so bad as the first time. They crossed the border with the height of joy and sailed back home down the green belly of God's country. They reached Feakle and went into the pub and started off on whiskey and did not stop as they normally did after two. No, 'twas four and five and six. And more. Until they were flying.

And Ger went for his pocket for the matches when he was smoking and he took out the wrong box and opened it when he was talking about the woeful hard day they had and Josie Considine, that bloody eejit, had his cap off his head like a hot, a quick wristy slap down on the table accompanied by the words "bloody bees, I hate them!" And that was the end of it all…

The Cat Who Died For Ireland

averty phoned me this morning to a crystal-clear line from Brookborough in County Fermanagh. His voice was sad but proud. "Cormac," he said, "it is my duty to inform you that Magonigle was shot dead this morning, on active service, by the British army. He died for Ireland. Give him a good obituary."

It was the last report on the most successful terrorist operation ever run in Ireland, jointly launched five years ago by Haverty and myself and fearlessly spearheaded by Magonigle, on a solo mission for the last three years. It was myself, somewhat fearfully, who smuggled Magonigle across the Border from Connemara to Brookborough just this month in 1983.

I drove and Magonigle slept in the back seat, totally relaxed all the way. He came out of the most Republican house in Connacht, and that's saying something, a house that has bled for Ireland in every generation since the time of Brian Boru. My hands were clammy and my brow beaded with cold sweat as we drove through Brookborough, the very heartland of Orangeism and Unionism.

He came out of the most Republican house in Connacht, and that's saying something, a house that has bled for Ireland in every generation since the time of Brian Boru.

But Magonigle, true to his breeding, never batted an eyelid. As we drove past the tightly guarded home of Lord Brookborough - "I would not have a Catholic worker or anything Catholic or Republican about the house" - I shivered, I admit,

> **Haverty reported this morning that Magonigle delayed just a second too long on the top of the stone wall on his way back from another successful mission. It was a corporal from Liverpool that got him. Doubtless he will be promoted to General.**

but Magonigle silent in the back seat, embarking on a most hazardous terrorist mission, never moved even one of his magnificent muscles.

He was only a kitten then, of course, only about five months old, and didn't really know what lay ahead of him. He didn't know the work that Mother Ireland would be asking him to do.

Haverty, whose small cottage is just outside the great stone walls of the Brookborough estate, was delighted with Magonigle when I made the delivery. He studied the coal black kitten with huge green eyes and the wild rebel head in a state of excitement.

"Christ above," says Haverty, "he's perfect for the job." He gave Magonigle a feed of lamb's liver and goat's milk. There was something stronger for me. And then, as the Connemara tom cat slumbered peacefully before the fire, he outlined the details of his operation to me. It was planned in every detail. It was a perfect operation.

The situation, you see, was that the present Lady Brookborough had brought to the great House, the seat of Unionism and privilege where no Catholic or Republican blood were allowed, she had brought to this house an exclusive breed of Orange cats who were first cousins to the cats of the Queen of England.

These she-cats, according to Haverty, were half Siamese, huge and fluffy in shape. Orange or marmalade in hue and very aristocratic. Most of them were the champions of upper-crust English cat shows and all of them, according to Haverty again, were virgin cats whose state was protected by British soldiers day and night - as they protected the Brookborough family.

The intention was to eventually breed these she-cats with a London tom belonging to the Queen herself. The stud fee, said Haverty, would keep himself and myself in brandy for three years. "But sure, maybe," says he, winking toward the Republican tom cat stretched before the fire, "maybe we might be able to save them all that expense. I'll put him into training tomorrow."

I returned home to Galway and received regular reports from Haverty thereafter. For the first seven months Magonigle was fed to the eyeballs on pork liver and Haverty trained him to avoid the British army on night-time expeditions. He taught him all the tricks relating to action in the field. Magonigle made excellent progress and first went into action on a frosty September night.

I remembered it well. I stayed up half the night for the progress report. Haverty phoned at six in the morning. He was jubilant. "Operation successful in every detail." An Orange she-cat with a pedigree a mile long called Lady Samantha of Westminster, despite being protected by a full platoon of British soldiers, had just met her maidenly waterloo.

"She won't need to travel to London to discover what life is all about. Lady Brookborough is in hysterics. Magonigle is now sleeping, uninjured, and grinning from ear to ear." That was Haverty's report.

Subsequently, despite all the risks, Magonigle gave his all for Mother Ireland. He was in action every night. I had weekly reports of his successful operations. He came under fire on five occasions but escaped without a scratch. He was like chain lighting.

Meanwhile Princess Dina of Surrey, Lady Sarah of Westchester, Lady Lucinda Albion of Chester and six other Orange she-cats in the Big House - all apparently with the greatest of pleasure - developed interesting conditions just like Lady Samantha of Westminster. The London tom cat received no stud fees at all and the security forces around the estate were fiercely criticized by an angry Lady Brookborough.

It had to come to an end sometime, of course. Haverty reported this morning that Magonigle delayed just a second too long on the top of the stone wall on his way back from another successful mission. It was a corporal from Liverpool that got him. Doubtless he will be promoted to General. Still, it was too late.

All the young cats rising up around Lord Brookborough's heels today are as black as coal. They have wide rebel heads on them. And they have those huge green eyes that seem to blaze with ancient fires every time the word Unionism is even mentioned.

That's the legacy of the gallant Magonigle. One of Ireland's greatest heroes. And this is his obituary.

Not All Knights Have Shining Armor

Margaret Cummings was a very pretty girl, probably the prettiest girl in town. She worked in a solicitor's office, looking absolutely luscious with her cherry lips and lustrous black hair behind a large typewriter. She had her lunch in Gino's Café in Middle Street in the town. I was working in the town at the time and I remember it was a pleasure and a torment both to see the beauty of her heading towards her roast beef and two veg and glass of whitest milk, the little finger elegantly crooked as she healthily devoured all that was on the plate. Alas at the time I was only 18 and Margaret Cummings was 24 and the prettiest girl in town and away out of my league on every score that ever hit a scoreboard. So I can be objective enough about the story of Margaret Cummings.

Being the prettiest girl in town at that time, in the '60s, also involved another ground on which I did not qualify. It was Margaret's perogative, by dint of her position, only to have dates with boyfriends who owned cars or who had cars available to them. Accordingly, since she was a lively young lady with an active social life, it is a fact that Margaret was going out with a Vauxhall Cresta

> **Yet still there was no apparent favorite going on the basis of the cars stopped outside the flat at all hours of the morning. One was as regular as another. Or as irregular.**

with mighty silvery fins, with a Ford Cortina, with a Morris Oxford and with a red Volkswagen Beetle. On another scale it could be said that Margaret was going out, on a more or less equal basis, with the Munster and Leinster Bank, with a JCB digger and with the Neighing Horses or one-fifth thereof, and with Ballinatoolan National School. This is because the aforementioned vehicles were owned by a bank clerk whose name I forget, by Malone the digger contractor, by Paulsie Simons, the guitarist with the local rock band, and by Martin Ignatius McCormack, recently appointed primary teacher at the school.

Now it is fair to say that in the town, and certainly amongst its unmarried male population, there was keen interest in who was doing best in the Cummings Stakes. It is equally fair to say that Margaret, who lived in a flat with two other girls in Townsend Street, was, for a long time, totally evenhanded in her tradings and socializing with the lads. There was no pattern at all to her social life, as revealed by the cars calling to the door of the flat. It was as likely to be the Morris Oxford as it was the Cresta. Sometimes one saw the Cortina and sometimes the red Volkswagen. You were as likely to see one as the other.

Our smart money was on Malone the digger. He was the oldest of the lads involved in the chase by maybe two years, aged about 29 and he had the advantage of having been abroad, both in the States and in England. Furthermore, he was a pleasant and relatively handsome young man, big and brawny and smiling. He also owned his own huge yellow digger which was constantly employed, either doing drainage work for local farmers on the outskirts of the town or gouging out foundations for the rapidly emerging new bungalows of Ireland of the '60s. One of the bungalows, in the most telling factor of all, was his own, a sturdy and comfortable house close to the edge of the forest.

His nearest challenger, we reckoned, was the bank clerk whose name escapes me now. He was from Dublin, tall and fair-haired. He played golf in the local golf club, wore cravats, drove with dash and panache, and looked like the kind of boyo that had a way with women.

The outside bets would have been Paulsie Simone and McCormack.

Paulsie, though by far the most handsome of the lot of them, like a younger Celtic clone of Elvis Presley, lived in a council row of terraced houses and had no other income apart from the Neighing Horses. They were a rising band who looked as if they would never quite make it. Though they had a considerable local following. McCormack was the real outsider because he was a meek slight lad, with heavy-lensed glasses, a deferential air about him, fairly prominent ears and a mother, with whom he lived, who was the kind of battleaxe that would have felled Cromwell.

Now the bank clerk went first. He was transferred to Cork, a long distance away even by Cresta at high speed. There was a major party at the gold club when he was leaving and Margaret was there on his arm but the Cresta only appeared in town twice thereafter, on both occasions for formal bank functions like their annual dinner dances. Margaret was his partner at these, naturally, and beautiful she looked too in green silk on one occasion.

But that was the end of him. And that left three.

The smart money then transferred itself to Malone, who at this stage had added a conservatory to the front of his bungalow. Also rose bushes that were crawling up his bachelor walls.

Yet still there was no apparent favorite going on the basis of the cars stopped outside the flat at all hours of the morning. One was as regular as another. Or as irregular. You might see that Malone was in action two nights on the trot. Then he might be out of sight for a fortnight and it would be Paulsie Simon that would be in command. Paulsie's band was on television one time and Margaret actually took the day off to travel up to Dublin with the rising band. They sounded well too.

But then there was a County Council election and did it not happen that Malone ran for Fine Gael. It was a bad stroke as far as his love life was concerned. He was elected to the Council all right but the Cummings clan were always Fianna Fail, Margaret as much as the rest of them, and, from the day that he took his seat on the County Council, Malone's car was no longer seen even once outside Margaret's flat. We did not know if the two things were connected or not, the politics and the passion, but those are the facts anyway.

So we have two down and two to go and it is the summertime, carnival season for showbands like the Neighing Horses and holidays for the schoolteacher, and there were months at a time when Paulsie Simone was on the road and not in a position to call-a-courting in a battered old Morris Oxford. Except now and again. And McCormack went to England to work for the summer and boost his teacher's pay and he was only there sometimes as well. There were lads tried that summer to add their cars and persuasions to those already at Margaret's doorstep but there was nothing doing.

> **And a schoolteacher still has high status in the countryside and its small towns.**

Then, in a story which was big news locally but created neer a stir elsewhere, and certainly not in Tin Pan Alley, came the breakup of the Neighing Horses. It happened, we were told graphically, on the main road outside Mullingar at about two o'clock one autumn morning after an engagement. The lads hammered the bejeses out of each other, Paulsie's guitar being broken in two halves and the drum being stepped upon and a lad called Comer who played the saxophone being left with such a split lip that his saxophone never sounded the same again. And, whether or not it was coincidental, that was the end of the Morris Oxford and the next thing the school was open again and the red Volkswagon was squatting on Margaret's doorstep most evenings and that was that. The invitations went out and there were to be 100 guests at the wedding.

Small towns are very small and have good ears. Somehow it came to be known that, all things being equal, Paulsie would have been the man for Margaret except for the fact that he was no longer riding proudly up Tin Pan Alley. And a schoolteacher still has high status in the countryside and its small towns. And Margaret, from farming stock, always had her head sitting firmly on her shoulders. So that was that.

The invitations went out. They were dignified and golden around the edges. It would be the wedding of the season. I got one of them myself because I played football along with McCormack and, having no brothers or friends worth taking about, the poor divil invited the whole football team.

Now the band that Margaret and Ignatius booked to play at the wedding reception in the hotel was a well-known outfit from two towns away called the Knights of the Road. Many's the time I heard them provide the music for weddings before and after. They were good, they knew their business, and they always played the mix of waltzes and foxtrots and quicksteps that were popular at the time, along with the odd Irish dance like the *Seige of Ennis* and the novelty things like a Paul Jones. Yes, the Knights knew how to get the crowd going.

The reception meal was excellent and when the cake was cut and the photos taken the floor was speedily cleared and the Knights moved in. And who was there in the middle of them, tuxed and dickie-bowed, but the bold Paulsie Simone. We now know that Paulsie paid £20, a small fortune at the

time, to the vocalist to allow to stand in for the day. It's a regular thing with bands, how was the original vocalist to know the hidden agenda of passion and intrigue?

The dancing started and, true to tradition, the bride and groom led the dancers. McCormack had scarcely a foot to put under him though Margaret had always been a featherlight dancer. And there throughout the whole affair, presiding over it all a dark specter, dark and handsome, was the bold Paulsie. He had always been a good crooner but that day he sang his heart out. I remember one song in particular. Are you lonesome tonight? / Do you miss me tonight? / Are you sorry we drifted apart? / Does your memory stray to that for summer day / When you kissed me and called me sweetheart?

He sang it just like Elvis, only, on the day, probably better, this Knight without his Neighing Horses. The atmosphere, I'm bound to say, was electric. Them that didn't know the score, the guests from outside the town, even crowded up around the stage to hear this great vocalist. They stopped dancing. But I watched the bride like a hawk and you could see every word was going straight to her heart. And Ignatius still knew nothing.

And, later on, Paulsie sang a Jim Reeves song called *Adios Amigo*, ironically the love song of a man on horseback, and I reckon that was the one that did the damage. I'll ride to Rio, sang Paulsie, where my life I will spend. Adios Amigo. Adios my dear friend.

Mighty stuff. And he followed it up with another hit of the time, something about helping him make it through the night and I reckon that was that.

All right, I was a guest at the wedding on my day off but a reporter is still a reporter. I was discreetly responsible for the story that hit the national papers the following day. It was the story of the Going Away that was different because the groom was left behind. It was the story, a good one too, how the bride went to her dressing room in the hotel and donned her Going Away outfit and then disappeared, before everyone in sight, with the musician who was the Knight without a Neighing Horse.

That story helped me buy my first banger of a car. From time to time my banger would pass a battered red Volkswagen heading in the opposite direction, sometimes, it emerged, towards very complicated Catholic marriage tribunals which eventually ruled that a marriage which had been unhorsed by a singing horseless Knight before its wedding night was not, in the end, a marriage at all.

By then, in Manchester, Paulsie and Margaret had two children, an Irish showband doing quite well, and a Vauxhall Cresta which, apart from the yellow British plates, looked exactly like that of the bank clerk whose name escapes me now.

The Fall Of A Living Legend

here was a hard core to Dowd's team of encyclopedia salesmen. They were all women. There was Mrs. Loftus. There was Junie Conroy. There was Patricia Mortimer. The others came and went. Often they came a lot faster than they went. It was a rare salesperson that lasted more than six months. Dowd often wondered how it was that the women were so much better at it than the men.

Dowd now prided himself on his ability to recognize a recruit's probable lasting power on the job the minute he saw him or her.

Patricia Mortimer was probably his best. She could sell a set of books in 20 minutes flat, and the others were not too far behind. The men that answered the small ads he placed in the papers often looked perfect for the job when they responded first. But, invariably, they could never match Mortimer.

Lately, as the recession deepened, the recruits were so poor that some of them quit on their first day. They just phoned in and said they couldn't take anymore. One guy had just disappeared with the sample set. Dowd now prided himself on his ability to recognize a recruit's probable lasting power on the job the minute he saw him or her.

He was sitting in the hotel room on the Monday morning waiting for the recruits. As always, in a new target town, his regular team members were out servicing the people who had returned coupons from the advertising campaign earlier. The recruits would be simply doorstepping, chancing their luck. It was all commission work so they earned if they sold. And if

they didn't sell, they didn't earn. As always, too, Dowd was reading the sports pages and sipping coffee as he waited for the troops to come up the stairs. They always came.

He was reading the report of Cork's relatively easy win over Kerry in the football championship when an almost apologetic knock came on the door. He called "come in please" without even raising his head because he had always been admiring of Larry Tomkins' play and the report endorsed his view. When he looked up, the big man was standing directly in front of the table, his arms straight down by his sides, and Dowd's first thought was - this one won't last till the end of the week. A no-no for sure.

"Sit down," he said.

The big man was about 52, 53 over six feet tall, wearing a dark grey suit, white shirt, blue tie. He had a full head of silvery hair over a ruddy, solemn face. The hands dangling by his side were huge and soft, their backs freckled. The man had very gentle blue eyes and heavy black eyebrows.

"Jesus,"said Dowd again, "sit down." He actually jumped up from his own chair, rattling the coffee cup in its saucer and pulled a chair over from the side of the room.

"Would you like a cup of coffee?"

"Yes please," said the big man, not surprised at all. He lowered himself slowly into the chair, one knee crackling as he did so.

When he was fully seated, he left his two big hands on his lap, one on top of the other, and said nothing while Dowd got on the house telephone and asked for coffee. When it arrived, as it did quickly, he sipped it slowly, cradling the saucer in his left hand and continuing to gaze at Dowd without speaking.

Dowd was quite excited. He forgot all about the job of recruiting men and women to see books of knowledge to people who normally didn't want them. He forgot about his sample cases behind him, the literature on the wall, the brochures on the table, the business in hand. He was back under Croke Park's giant echoing roof for the first time, a boy of 10, watching a mighty giant of a dark-haired man playing Gaelic football at its very best. Flying like an eagle.

"I saw you," he said, "at your best. I saw you the day you made history. I have a scrapbook at home all about you, even; I show it to my sons. I never thought I'd see you in the flesh."

"You saw me at my best," the big man smiled faintly. "Now you are seeing me at my worst as well. Have you any jobs for living legends that need a few bob?"

Dowd was jolted back to reality. "I thought," he said," that you were a farmer; that you wouldn't be into this line of business." His accompanying gesture encompassed the temporary world of paper and posters.

"That," said the man, "was a good while ago. A very long time ago."

Dowd, looking at him with eyes that were unfocused, remembered a particular fetch he had seen the big man make in his prime. The ball had been sailing away over the heads of the quartet of midfielders, the big fellow amongst them, when suddenly, in mid-air, he had seemed to elongate his body in some marvelous elastic fashion. He had stretched one arm upwards, with its great taloned brown hand, and the ball had seemed to adhere to it. Purists still talked about that fetch; maybe the greatest ever seen in a championship game.

Dowd looked at the hand. It was holding the coffee cup. It was white, not brown, and the little finger was, grotesquely, even cocked a little like that of an old lady.

"Do you know," asked Dowd, "that you are even in our encyclopedia?"

"No," said the big man.

"In the section for Gaelic football," said Dowd. The big man was remembered for his historic scoring feats, still unsurpassed in a championship year.

"There is even a photograph of you."

He opened the book on the table. He found the front page. There was a bright color photograph of the young eagle in flight.

The big man only glanced at it. He finished his coffee and left the cup and saucer carefully back on the table. When he talked his choice was as soft as that of a very slight man.

That year, he said, had been his ruination. When they brought the Sam McGuire Cup back home they had a party which lasted two months. Everybody wanted to shake his hand, to clap him on the back, to buy him a drink. They flew him out to the States, to New York, every second Sunday to play over there and the parties were even more hectic.

"I got a taste for the drink. I did not know that the party had to stop somewhere."

They were knocked out early in the championship in the next two years, he reminded Dowd. They would have got through, at least one of those years, if he had been able to play reasonably well. He was not. The drink had him by the throat.

"Have you a job, son, for a living legend?"

Dowd had a (commission only) job for a living legend. He briefed the big man as best he could. He gave him his sample case and the literature. He picked a good middle class area to send him to.

"You are well known, famous," he said to the legend. "Use it for all you are worth. Come back to me this evening after seven, up here to this room, and we'll have a drink and a chat."

His professionalism surfaced again as he watched the big figure walking out the door. It came on a full tide of regret. He thought that the big man would scarcely last out the week. Even selling an encyclopedia with a picture of himself inside.

Pretty Maids All In A Row

Almost every Friday evening, heading back to Dublin after a weekend on the road selling toiletries and shampoos, Christy Meehan arranges his evening so that he arrives into any of the Midland towns just before the factories in the industrial estates close down for the weekend. It is easy to find the industrial estates because they are all located on the edge of the towns, their gates disgorging their workers into working-class streets which all bear the names of saints. Christy Meehan's grandfather, back in the old times, was a deerstalker for the old Lord De Bermingham. He was so good at it, the old man, so knowing, so immovably patient and lethal, that the old Lord used bring him over to the Scottish Highlands for the big shoots over there. When his grandson locates the industrial estates he parks his car in a position where he can watch the gates and then he just sits there waiting. He told me this himself.

The overwhelming majority of the workers in the Irish industrial estates are female, certainly the overwhelming majority of those

> **Christy Meehan told me that the pretty girls never look back, pretty girls don't do that sort of thing, not even when he starts up the engine within seconds and gets back into the car.**

who pedestrianate through the estate gates on Friday evenings when the weekend beckons bright are female and young, nylon overalled, many of them, bound tightly together into laughing joking groups by the new pay packets in their purses and by the unity of the upcoming night out. Christy Meehan grandson of the deerstalker, told me that he scarcely looks at the laughing groups at all, no matter how pretty and vivacious the picture.

He told me that almost every Friday, outside almost every factory estate gate, a pretty girl comes out on her own. He told me that you can see directly that this isolation from the groups is by personal choice. You can see immediately that this girl is a little different from the others. It is, he said, as if she is making a deliberate statement of this appearing on her own. Almost always she is a little older than the frequently teenage groups that have already passed his sight line. Usually she is not wearing the overall uniform of the factory and frequently she is wearing high heels. Very often she has a large shoulder-bag rather than a small purse. Always she is walking with brisk purpose rather than slowly and, incredibly often, said Christy, she has her hair in a ponytail which swings from side to side when she strides down the street towards home.

The instant he sees her, when she is still a hundred yards away, Christy Meehan gets out of his car, leaving the driving door open and a cassette of James Last playing quietly. He then opens the bonnet and, by the time the footsteps have reached the trunk of the car, Christy has his oily hands already entangled in a cleaning rag, his tie slightly awry, and a rueful expression on his face. Christy Meehan has a very ordinary face, more choirboyish than anything else.

As the pretty girl reaches the bonnet Christy Meehan emerges from behind it, flustered and looking foolish, James Last still playing just about audibly, and then says "Oh Shit!" just like that - it never changes - and then claps one oily hand to his mouth - that never changes either - so that his cheek is soiled slightly - and then says, "Oh, I'm sorry Madam" in some confusion and with the same voice that he uses to sell toiletries and

shampoos in the supermarkets and stores of Munster. And Christy Meehan told me that he reckons that it is the use of the word "Madam" and the oilmark on his cheek, which almost every Friday stops the pretty girl in her tracks and with a smile on her face. He also contrives it that, although not obviously, he is actually blocking her path. He's no threat anyway, a slightly built young man in a suit and collar and tie with a dirtied face and a car in trouble.

And then, almost every Friday, Christy Meehan says to the pretty girl that the car is misbehaving and would she, by any chance, know of a good garage nearby in case he cannot get it going himself in a minute of two. And James Last plays in the background and he looks rueful and a bit ridiculous and a bit out of his depth and the pretty girl, almost every Friday, knows where the nearest garage is, or the nearest backstreet mechanic, and is very helpful. Even slightly interested. Sometimes, Christy Meehan told me, he can see them, almost stopping themselves from reaching out and straightening his tie. And almost invariably, the pretty girl tells Christy Meehan that he has got oil on his face.

And he smiles the smile that sells toiletries and cosmetics and says thanks very much Madam and says sorry for troubling you and for using bad language. And then he moves back courteously and unblocks the pavement and says he hopes he can start the car himself. And the pretty girl smiles again and says, almost every Friday, that she hopes he can, with James Last still playing softly, and then Christy plunges under the bonnet again, with the rueful smile and resigned shoulder language, and the footsteps click away down the street. Christy Meehan told me that the pretty girls never look back, pretty girls don't do that sort of thing, not even when he starts up the engine within seconds and gets back into the car.

Almost every Friday, in the evening streets dusking with the velveteen if the upcoming night, he is able to discreetly shadow the pretty girl to her home. It is never too far away and, sometimes, if it is very close and he sees her fishing for her key he will actually drive past and sound the horn at her, waving and shouting a thanks Madam as he goes past with the window down. His cheek still oilstained. And the pretty girl will wave back and smile good-bye quickly. Sometimes, he told me, he can even sense a little regret in the quick wave. Not always, but sometimes.

Christy Meehan drives down to the nearest hotel them cleans himself up and has a leisurely dinner. It is the only hotel dinner he has all week. The rest of the time is bed and breakfast and cafes and soup and sandwiches. But Fridays are different. Usually Christy Meehan has a fish dinner with a glass of the house white wine. He takes his time over his dinner, savoring it all. Sometimes, after dinner, he will go into the hotel bar and have just a slow glass of beer, keeping an eye on his watch. He's not a drinker. By 9:45 p.m. in the evening, never any later than that, almost every Friday, inside the next forty-five minutes, she emerges from home and it is immediately obvious that she is heading out for the evening. Incredibly often she is still alone and, equally incredibly often, the ponytail has been dispensed with so that her hair hangs down both sides of her head. Christy Meehan told me he usually knows exactly where she is going. Most of the Midland towns have just two nightclubs and the pretty girls who walk alone through streets named after Irish saints always head for the most upmarket of the two. He follows her there, at a discreet distance, and enters the nightclub about five minutes after her.

When the grandson of the famed deerstalker gets inside the nightclub, almost every Friday evening, the first thing he does is to shove his tie slightly awry and arm himself with a pint glass of beer. And he finds the pretty girl in a matter of minutes and, no matter what company she is in, but he told me she is usually alone, a little remote, a little wistful even, he comes walking up directly to her and smiles his rueful smile, that he sells toiletries and shampoos with, and says fancy meeting you here, the only person in town that I know even slightly.

Almost every Friday it works.

Perfectly.

Penance Was Never This Fun

top at the mouth of the valley nowadays, more than 25 years later, and it will bring a quirky kind of smile to your face when you know the beginning of the story that has resulted in what your eyes are seeing.

> **Shyness, especially in relation to the opposite sex, killed a lot of valleys in the west in the last 40 or 50 years. This valley of simple people was accursed with shyness, inhibitions, ancient useless old prides and factions.**

You are seeing the kind of west Ireland valley that Walt Disney would create if he were filming here now. There are still thatched cottages, even though they are now for the visiting fishermen. There is the proud little church with its aged blue bell standing in a separate belfry. There is a strong settlement of new farmhouses and bungalows, and the most sharp-eyed amongst ye will notice that there are healthy clotheslines fluttering behind the majority of them.

By healthy I mean big men's trousers, the frilly things of young wives, the brighter, smaller splotches of children's clothes.

Every dog in the valley has his tail in the air, as if proud of the place, the chimney smoke squiggles happily into the eddied air that hangs over such valleys and, best of all, there are skeins of children forming and reforming in the schoolyard if you happen to be viewing the place during breaktime.

Look closer still and you will see that many of the children are redheads, and have a gangling length to them, and that brings us back to the beginning of the story.

Father Aenghus Dermody, who now lies benignly beneath the freshest of the Celtic Crosses in the shadow of that stubby belfry, would have seen a totally different valley when he arrived to take over the parish that quarter-century ago. The school was almost empty, the houses that were occupied were squatting grimly against the land. There is a fine line between a parish which is progressing and one which is stagnating, and the valley had crossed that line maybe five years before.

Father Dermody had come from the mission fields and he knew the signs. I never knew him but he has been described to me as a burly big man "with the head of a cattle jobber on him." He suffered from malaria from time to time, a reminder of the missions, but otherwise was full of energy. And he was very wise indeed.

I've often said it before and now again. Shyness, especially in relation to the opposite sex, killed a lot of valleys in the west in the last 40 or 50 years. This valley of simple people was accursed with shyness, inhibitions, ancient useless old prides and factions.

The most of those grim houses when the new priest came were occupied by bachelors who needed to get married quickly or they would get married never. In the other houses were spinsters, "the ones that minded the parents," whose plight was even worse. They had to wait to be asked.

The most of the men in the valley were and are called Gallagher. The redheaded Gallaghers of this place are known far and wide, even beyond the county, for their bashfulness, for their big feet, and for their capacity for pints. One of them at that time, known as The Hog Gallagher, could drink up to 25 pints on a Sunday and frequently did.

Against this social problem, subtly at first, then ever more boldly, the wise old Father Dermody deployed the fundamental element of the Blessed Sacrament of Penance! The penance itself!

Ye all know - or most of ye - that when you go to confession and tell your sins then penance follows. Traditionally, then and now, the penance takes the form of Our Fathers and Hail Marys, silently uttered in dark benches.

But Father Dermody's form of penance in this valley was totally different. Very different indeed!

The very first evidence of this came a month after his arrival. Until then the chapel had been divided into the men's side and the women's side. On this dramatic Sunday, totally against ritual and tradition, and with his ears and face flaming, one Seamus Gallagher came into the chapel in his big boots, hesitated, and then blunthundered right up to the front of the church and into the bench of the Mallon sisters on the women's side.

People thought he was drunk! He was not. It later emerged, and is now in the folklore, that poor Seamus (lucky Seamus) was the first victim of a Dermody penance had been to hear his Mass sitting in her bench for four consecutive Sundays.

By the end of the month the lugs of Seamus were no longer so red at Mass. By the end of two months, however it happened, himself and Ita Mallon shyly at first, but then with obvious delight, were "walking out together." They were married the following year and there is no knowing how many children they sent to that school afterwards.

The Dermody penances which followed were largely of the same kind, they were not penances at all. One that is remembered forever came on the Sunday when the saucy Susan Hines sat in the Hosey bench on what was the men's side still - though not for long after - right next to Tommy Hosey. This revealed to all and sundry that what was sauce for the gander was also sauce for the geese!

Tommy and Susie were married not long afterwards of course. And by then going to Mass in the valley of a Sunday had become very interesting indeed! There were three or four new Dermody penances clearly in operation every Sunday.

And there were more marriages in the first four years of Father's pastorship than in the previous 20 years. That's a fact. Look at the parish register if you don't believe me.

The Dermody penances were far more effective than that though, as a positive parochial instrument. One Friday afternoon, for example, without a word, the two meanest me in the parish - no names here - arrived at a widow's house with spades and shovels. They set her garden of spuds, cleared all her drains, repaired all her gates and fences and, though there was agony in their eyes, refused all payment.

And what happened to the Hog Gallagher was classic. One morning awful early he was seen out on the mountain, all his portered flesh jiggling, and he was clad in a tracksuit and running uphill! That went on for a full month. Everyone thought he would die stone dead and profits at The Inn dropped sharply because he was abed very early in the evening.

But running is addictive, as we all well know, and long after the Dermody penance had expired the Hog Gallagher was still running, lean, now as a whippet, and clearly doing it for the fun of it. Inside two years he won a marathon, and inside three, never having touched a drop of the hard stuff for 18 months, he was one of the best distance runners the country had ever produced.

I could go on forever. It is not necessary. I think the point is made. Look down on the valley today and you see a landscape where the judicious application of the great Sacrament of Penance has revived the usage of those other sacraments whose usage would have eased altogether long ago otherwise. I refer specifically to baptism, confirmation, Eucharist and, of course, matrimony!

About the Author

Cormac MacConnell

Born and raised in County Fermanagh in Northern Ireland, Cormac MacConnell lived for many years in Galway, working as a journalist and writer with the Irish Press Group and other organizations. MacConnell is a well-known columnist, in both Ireland and the United States. Drawing on his experiences and intimate knowledge of the unique people and traditions of the West of Ireland, MacConnell's popular weekly columns in the *Irish Voice* and *Irish Emigrant* have garnered him a loyal following of readers. He has also written a novel about Gaelic football called *Final Moments*. MacConnell and his wife Annette, affectionately known as "The Dutch Nation", currently live in County Clare where he is a news editor and on-air presenter with Clare FM Radio Station.

About the Publisher

The GreenBranch Company L.L.C.

The GreenBranch Co. L.L.C. was formed from a passion for Irish history and culture and a belief that there are many others like us out there - people who may or may not descend from Irish ancestry but who have been captivated by the fascinating history of Ireland and its people, or perhaps by the spellbinding work of Ireland's many writers and musicians. Our mission is to create high-quality and enlightening products that celebrate the unique history and culture of Ireland and Irish people around the globe. To learn more about our latest products, including a unique line of posters, please visit us on the web at www.thegreenbranch.com or call toll-free, 1-888-547-4154.